Seeing Through
the Spell
of Transference

a novel by

Michael Lyons

Vol. 4 of the Sextet
My Years of Apprenticeship at Love

HiT MoteL Press

Library of Congress Cataloging in publication Data

Lyons, Michael
        Seeing Through the Spell of Transference
Vol.4 of the Sextet *My Years of Apprenticeship at Love*
I. Title

ISBN: 0965584240
            978-0965584241

Published by HiT MoteL Press

Designed by Michael Lyons

to John O'Keefe
elan vital of the playground

A man is born of two women, they say.
His mother and his wife.

Seeing Through the Spell of Transference

Table of Contents

Berkeley Doldrums

It was right after Walker started psychotherapy that he met Cora Rosenov. You know how it is in that first blush of therapy: new feelings leading to a hope-filled new you. You are in a good place — open. So when he met Cora at a Tea Dance Social in the lobby of the Shattuck hotel, he was upbeat. It was around Halloween and though people were not in costume, some of the women were in vampy, slinky, jazz-era get-up. Walker had managed to score a suit somewhere.

At 37, Walker was living in Berkeley. He felt at home there. He passed for a graduate student. He looked younger, because of his long hair. And though he was wearing a sport coat, he didn't exactly look comfortable in it; not his usual blue jeans and long sleeve faire. The suite was from the Good Will. You could buy a nice old blue serge suit for a few dollars more than a pair of pants. Reagan was president, and for the unemployed, the trickle down had dried up. Now though, the suit improved his sense of belonging in the hotel lobby.

Walker felt at home walking the UC Berkeley campus. In his bohemian years knocking around the warehouse on Blake street, he had been skinny. Getting settled into his own apt on Dwight Way, he had not put on any weight. His hair was still curly and his eyes were still as blue as the sky. He had a bohemian appearance that he had to keep up. He was in therapy because he was not getting anywhere in his professional life.

Cora had gone to the dance at the Shattuck Hotel in Berkeley for the live music. She was with her dance class. It was in the bar. She loved to dance. She had on a shiny black dress and was wearing gloves that covered her arms past the elbows. She was wearing nylons with garters under the lacy hem of a sleek silk dress. Cora was sitting by herself at a small circular marble table in the black and white tiled room of the hotel bar which opened to the main ballroom.

The man approached the woman from across the room. From the back he could see the thin straps of her silky black negligee show lean girl muscles. She was playing out her fantasy side: an intelligent mysterious spy sitting by herself at a table.

He got in front of her so she wouldn't be startled by what he felt was his hulking size in this suit.

He caught her eye and waved his hand in greeting.

"Hi I'm Walker Underwood. Jeff at Dome Works wanted us to meet up."

"Oh yes."

She smiled and looked gracious. It was clear she was a little flushed from all the dancing with the members of her class and others.

He pulled a chair over to her table and sat down.

They tried to talk over the band. Walker spoke loudly across the table: "You're a friend of Jeff's? How did you meet?"

"We play on their softball team."

She smiled at him as though she were taking him under consideration.

He couldn't help but appreciate her get-up. She had on a little pill box hat, like a page boy might wear, and this black headpiece held a birdcage veil of black mesh that fell over her forehead so that this vale went across the horizon of her eyes. She was wearing elbow-length black gloves of lacy gauze and they had what were probably exquisitely sensitive velvet finger tips. It was a knock out. She was this exotic Goth operative from the House of Love in a far away gypsy place like Prague or Hungary.

But the first thing you noticed about Cora is her eyes. You had to notice them, the whites of her eyes show not just above the irises but below them too. It made her look so bright and intelligent. She was petite, almost pixie sized like Audrey Hepburn but with these big Joan Crawford eyes. Cora's eyes had that same kind of resolute sadness in them. As well as an avid hunger. Her eyes were wide open, ready to devour the future with judgments about perceptions. And empathy too perhaps. She looked to be in her mid 40s.

They tried some small talk about soft ball, but mostly ended up being quiet in each other's company. She was here with her dance class. She was expected to do a lot of dancing, and she got called up onto the floor by some guy.

Walker waited at the table, and found himself going through the progression of thoughts that qualify or disqualify a person upon first meeting.

She seemed OK.

When she came back, she asked him if he wanted to dance. He followed her onto the hardwood floor of the ballroom. She turned and took his hand and looked up into his face, but did not smile. She was focused on the ritual of the dance. He put his other hand on her waist and gently pulled her to him. He could feel the heat of her body through the filmy satiny fabric; she was hot and flushed from dancing. Walker was surprised at how sinewy her taunt lady muscles felt, through the black film of her shift. Her muscles were delicately rippling under the sheer sheen of slick synthetic nylon sticking to her sweaty skin.

Luckily it was a slow dance and Walker managed, with a basic ball-room 4-square step. He was grateful that she did not seem disappointed at his dancing skill. Feeling her body through this clammy polyester drape, he noticed he was starting to get a tingling down below, a binding against the fly. He remarked to himself: My, that hasn't happened just from dancing with a girl in a long time. Come to think of it, it was dancing with Marynell in the eighth grade. It was an embarrassingly awkward state back then, all chaperoned over by nuns. But now it was nice and suggested he ask her out. It always behooved one to follow up on the pointing vector.

Walker hung out for a while, sitting by himself when she kept getting pulled away to the dance. When he got up to leave, Walker and Cora smiled at each other as she was again pulled into the group of her dance friends. He would get her number from Jeff, the guy who put them together.

He drifted down Shattuck Avenue back to his small apt across from the hospital on Dwight Way. Walker continued to live here because it was cheap and he was still hanging on to being part of the theatre community in the Blake St. Hawkeyes warehouse across the parking lot behind his place. Though this community too, was drifting and dispersing. But this was the Amphictionic theatre and he was bound to it by one of those crazy commitments you make, like a young monk might do. He had taken on the responsibility of seeing that the spirit that dwelled in this temple was kept alive, though it too was afloat and disbanding and going forth.

When she got back to her house Cora thought about Walker, wondered if he would call.

What if they ended up going out? He is definitely younger than me, but not that young.

What did he think of my outfit?

Did he find it hot?

I enjoyed teasing him, crossing and uncrossing my legs. Showing him a little garter.

He's a pretty good dancer. I'll have to give him some lessons if he wants to go with me.

He seems to be put together OK; he can wear a suit and has his own apartment.

At his place Walker thought about her being older. He was experienced with older women from the commune. They need love too.

Presenting Symptom & Preconceptions

Walker had to start seeing a shrink because he had recently got his heart broken around this woman Dahlia, who was very involved in a polyamorous psychotherapy cult in San Francisco. And in those days in Berkeley everybody either was seeing a therapist and/or was a therapist. So one day, feeling particularly desperate and miserable, Walker called the Alameda County Mental Health services.

He couldn't afford the expense of a private practice therapist, so thought he'd take his chances with what the government had to offer. The government was the reason there were no jobs, and like unemployment benefits, they had allocated some money for shrinks to keep the populace from spiraling into financial despair and further subversion and going into shadow projection seeking revenge on the rich for the way they exploit others to further their wealth and power.

The initial intake interview was with a senior male staff person. This robust and sanguine mental health professional looked the picture of privileged white male wholesomeness. The assessment was of a positive prognosis and Walker's case was assigned to a graduate student at the clinic. Her name was Anna Zane.

When they met for their first interview Anna Zane was this gorgeous young Jewish woman whose hair curled all around her intelligent face. She had this goofy empathetic smile which Walker could see was endearingly supposed to play down how very intelligent and accomplished she was. This woman was a real beauty and he told himself, "Even if she doesn't help me, it would be worth the money just to spend the hour looking at her."

You entered the therapist's office through a padded

double door. This gave a sense of ensured privacy. You closed the outer door by pulling it to you, and then when you closed the padded inner door, it made a ka-woosh sound — forcing out the air between the two doors, thus creating a hermetic seal, like the lid on a pressure cooker.

He turns and looks at the lovely Anna Zane. She is looking at him with those big eyes behind big thick glasses in a grey frame. He felt in her gaze a curiosity and interest, and some fear too. After being in therapy for a while he began to feel like he was a foreign specimen impaled on a stick pin under glass.

He got into a transference on their second date. She observed it and was slightly taken aback remarking, "I hadn't thought it would happen this quickly." Walker could not hide his boyish delight combined with hope upon entering her dominion for a session. He was like a smitten lover at seeing her. Or a child seeing his mother, but who now must transfer the captivation of love reducing you to a previous stage, to being possessed of the higher goal of self-understanding.

Instead, for the first several months he kept trying to seduce his therapist and she kept rejecting it.

Therapist: So what's going on with you. What came to mind just then.
Patient: I thought about you as a little girl.
Therapist: About me as a little girl?
Patient: I just wondered what you were like.
Did you have braids. You probably sat in the chair and looked at people with big eyes.
(They both laughed.)
Same size eyes on a little girl.
Therapist: Does it feel like I am a kid looking at you?
Patient: Some, yeah.

Therapist: Why does that come to mind now.

Patient: It feels like you are there, like you are always there, for me. It feels pretty nice.

Where did you go to college?

Therapist: What are your thoughts about that?

Patient: Uhh, I'm just curious. I wanted to know where you went to college.

Therapist: What comes to mind.

Patient: Nothing. . . So what is the orientation of your therapy.

Therapist: You are curious about a lot of things. What I was like as a little girl, where I went to college, an academic definition of my therapy orientation.

Patient: Yeah.

Therapist: I think there's more to it than just curious.

That it is such a common pattern, at certain times for you to wonder about things that pertain to me.

I wonder too how it relates to what we talked about Tuesday.

Walker is a little embarrassed that he has actually said, "I'd have to get a lobotomy to be able to stay on these jobs," in the last session.

He had tried to tease her with, "Would you prescribe a lobotomy?"

But therapists take everything literally.

"No," she said. "But if you quit your job you'll be back eating at the soup kitchen."

"But I don't care," he said.

"At least I know I would have time to create."

What he did not say was this: If I have to go a few days without creating, I tend to just start wandering around like some kind of bovine alien entity shuffling along through the labyrinth, hardly even recognizing the objects obstructing my way; not knowing what they are for.

Because he knew this is not something you say to a girlfriend, if you could keep one.

Aren't we a pair he thought. Here is a hippie, committed to the beatnik life of creativity and poverty. And she is a young uptown, upwardly-mobile Jewish princess doctoral candidate psychotherapist. He reads Bukowski and she reads the Psychoanalytic Quarterly. She was a couple of years younger than him, a normie, and he thought probably naive.

Because of his experience in talking therapy in the commune, Walker could give the appearance of being forthcoming in his feelings. The experience had given him a skewed and intense baptism-by-fire introduction to psychoanalysis and tantric Buddhism. And somewhere in between losing the girl in the psychobabble of the cult, and his commitment to his artist / monk hippie path toward self-awareness, he had misplaced his ego.

In order to participate in the commune, in order to be part of the experiment of constant, around-the-clock, 24-7 group therapy and plural marriage — all living together under one roof in a huge, one-room penthouse loft in San Francisco — you definitely got your ego ground down. Apparently therapy was supposed to be painful.

So in addition to reeling from loss of this beauty Dahlia that he was totally in love with, he was confused about the way forward — to fulfillment, and happiness. He told himself: I am not a lost soul away from this group. The whole experience (again a therapist getting into sex with the women in transference with him) had made him suspicious of psychotherapy. He wanted to experience real psycho-analysis.

The idea of seeing a therapist had become normal after

being involved with the House. Their whole lives revolved around constant therapy. The commune was a group of group marriages. The people in the small group marriage slept with each other, man and woman; and woman and woman; and man and man; changing each night, in every possible binary (and sometimes nonbinary!) combination in linear rotation. They were a tantric sangha. The men and women were to use sex as a sacrament to get one in touch with the deity within. They were servants at the body-temple of ecstatic being. These sleeping arrangement brought up much jealousy and possessiveness at the daily small group meetings. There, one was committed to exploring these powerful defenses of the ego. This being real with each other, allowed them to live their life in a certain sense liberated from the external sign that one was supposed to always present to others. Lovely-dovey romanticism was met with sarcastic derision. Of necessity they had to become as connoisseurs of the therapeutic interaction and talk. It was like a chess game for them. In fact that was part of Walker's motivation: He wanted to learn the language of shrink-speak so he could talk back to those assholes and wrest this girl away from them.

He was trying not to be bitter; he was down: Here I am with this fabulous education, I used to be a college teacher. Yet I am once again unemployed and without resources. I wasn't going anywhere with my life. I needed to change my ways. I have to do something. I don't want to end up miserable and broke and alone. Surely this was not my fate.

They smile at each other: the analyst Anna Zane, and the analysand Walker Underwood. He hated how she referred to him as a "patient", while he preferred "analysand".

For a long time he kept insisting: "I don't really have a great problem except that of self understanding."

Therapist: Let us use our time in here as an attempt to be
more present in the here and now.

Walker wanted to help her get her practicum done so she could get her degree.

And who knows, maybe here in this office with the light behind her and the book shelves all around, he hoped this will help him undergo the kind of metamorphosis he needed to undergo.

He thought: I am looking for myself, someone I once was, who got lost along the way. Perhaps here I can be more truly myself, not the one living out the American dream or aspiring to it; not the bohemian struggling artist slacker hipster; not the dutiful son.

He thinks about how Ms. Zane never backs down. No matter how much he tried to question her, about a fact of her life. We are two people who have come together to fulfill our dreams and create our whole selves. A train coming out of the fireplace mantel. This is your life.

Ms. Zane wrote in a report to her supervisor about Walker in which she said:

> I reminded him that since he is currently in analysis, that there is an unwritten admonition to not start new serious relationships, because in therapy one can be in a vulnerable state of transference while studying your psychological defense mechanisms.

The Lady of Hiddenbrook Lane

Cora Rosenov had a house in a very nice part of north Berkeley. Walker hoofed it across town on Milvia Street over to her house from his studio in a much partitioned Victorian on Dwight Way. She had invited him over for dinner. She said she would bake a fish. He was bringing a bottle of white wine. He walked down Milvia, all the way to Cedar, then down into her neighborhood. Now here was the more gentile, idyllic Berkeley of curving lanes, meandering on the contours of hills. These houses were all kinds: English Tudor, next to Spanish Adobe, next to Tyrolean Chalet. It was bucolic, natural, with fairy-tale settings such as gardens, streams, stone cottages, and yuppie hobbits of the shire.

The houses were set at different depths into the lot and were all surrounded by bushes and plants and little gardens. They had redwood fences and decks upon which there were wisteria vines climbing trellises, and arbors of roses and lemon trees adding to the sweet Berkeley potpourri. It was like a medieval encampment with strong smell of oak wood fire coming out of the chimneys. It was a different side of Berkeley than what he was used to.

Cora's house was smaller than her neighbors. Upon entering your see this giant baby grand piano lacquer black on thick legs taking up a corner all surrounded by open shelves with sheathes of sheet music. She gave him the penny tour. There was extensive back decking that went up in steps outside the French doors off the kitchen. She had a separate little studio out back. This studio room was piled high with wood from the renovations jobs. She had lived there a few years. She bought the property after her parents left her some money. The Rosenovs were Jewish immigrants from Russia.

In her parlor Walker looked at her books. He found an extensive collection of math books. This lead to a huge surprise as to who her brother turned out to be. She had stored his math books at her house, and they were on display all around the shelf of wainscoting around the top of the walls. Seeing these math books it was like old home week. "Wow," he remarked as he kept running across these many books: in advanced algebra and disquisitions on numbers, some of which he had studied out of. Paul Halmos on Vector Spaces. And there were even some of the Springer-Verlang books with their bright canary yellow covers, published on newsprint from meticulously typewritten and hand lettered facsimile.

"My brother is a mathematician," she explained. "He teaches at U.S.F."

"I have studied with some of these books."

"He lives in North Beach."

Then in dawned Walker that he had seen her brother before! Of course. He remembered having seen what had to be her brother — they had the same stunningly sensitive eyes — over in North Beach. There in famous old Vesuvio's tavern, filled with Tiffany glass and laminated posters of historic bohemian San Francisco, this large man was sitting at a table, holding forth to what appeared to be a bunch of advanced students. Walker didn't know what subject the man at a table full of bright faces was excited about. But this man was quite animated above the hubbub of the room. Walker noticed the face on this happy man was luminous in his bright eyes. Walker tried to remember the scene: there was a long bar with a mirrored bar-back and tiers of bottles. The landmark bar is across Kerouac alley from City Lights. Walker was shocked when he remembered and connected the dots: no one else on earth could have had the same eyes as

Cora, other than her brother.

Walker felt a slight shudder of recognition as synchron-icity sent an electric fate-wraith undulating through the parallel dimensions containing this room.

"I think I saw him in Vesuvio's once," he said.

"Maybe you did. He hangs out there a lot, together with his students."

Walker wondered what it meant, that he had noticed and indeed thought about meeting, this intelligent man in North Beach and here he was a few months later randomly in his sister's house. That kind of thing doesn't happen very often. It might just be a coincidental metaphor, or it might be something deeper. But something had flipped over from being stochastic to being propitious.

Walker mentioned it to her casually, and she showed him a picture of her brother and it WAS indeed the man he had noticed in a random bar on a random day in North Beach. This changes the moment into an occasion. Clearly she had the same robust intelligent eyes. Walker did not remark on the coincidence further because he was aware that his hippie tendencies to broaden consciousness, fun though it was, did not serve him well in straight company. And Ms. C was straight company. (In his mind he had begun referring to her as Ms. C in a kind of formal deference; she was certainly not a Miss.) Though, she did mention that she had gotten herself swept up in the Mario Salvo Free Speech activity in Berkeley. She got arrested, got probation, had to pay a fine. Walker had just started Catholic Academy for Boys in San Antonio at the time.

Cora Rosenov. She had been born in New York, and somehow the family got out here. They had some money. Though her brother was a renter in N. Beach, a bohemian math teacher. He was quite a bit older than her, nearly 17 years older. So he was more like a father figure for her.

In the conversation Ms. C mentioned that she had been in a long term relationship with a physicist, and she had enjoyed spending time with this man and her brother. As she said this Walker noticed a brief expression of sadness furrow her brow. It moved underneath the stoic composure of her visage. She seemed sad that she was no longer with him. It hurt to miss him.

But he and she were hanging out. An I and you perhaps becoming a we.

She had this old-time stove. It was a work of art. It had claw foot legs. It was two color, mostly white baked enamel with the trim around the edges a light muted green, outlining the oven doors and drawers. The burners and top were black wrought iron. She had a special pan for baking the fish. Ah these Russians know what they are doing when it comes to fish.

They drank wine. Before, during and after dinner. He did not offer smoke, she seemed too straight.

It came out they were both, at the moment, on unemployment. That was another thing that would get them together — helping each other find a job. She had been operating a large day care at a big corporation but somehow that had been eliminated. Walker too had very little profes-sional experience on his resume: he had been an instructor and electronics lab tech in trade schools and junior colleges. Lately though, he was once again employed in the trade of his youth: doing knock around construction and landscaping. He thought of it as noble — romantic even: an artist from the working class who did his art for love and spirit and supported himself by physical work.

In the House he had encountered older women in group before, had even slept with them. They were people too. And people were supposed to try and be close.

So then he used one of the things he had learned in the commune. Just to lie down and go for some feelings, trying to be close. She was bowled over by the straightforwardness of that. So they got back down onto her bed. In the bedroom just off the hall off the dining room. It was in the back of the house, beside the kitchen.

There they were in her bed.

She was having trouble relaxing and was skittish.

"We don't need to get into anything," he said. "Just relax and be together."

And Walker just put his arms around her and held her. It was a long empathic hug. He thought to see if he could get their breathing relaxed. This was a kind of meditation they did together in the House, and it often led to sex.

He was cool with going slow. People get really strange if you try to induce them to do things they haven't yet thought up themselves.

Walker kissed Ms. C. He had learned how to kiss from a book, *Stranger in a Strange Land*. There Michael Valentine who had grown up on Mars, a world with little water, talked about how to put your whole focus into the being of the other when you got into a kiss. It was a shock for women, and it had the effect of making him lucky in love. And it could at times be somewhat ruinous too.

And one thing led to another, and they started kissing then rubbing bodies through clothes, then touching genitals through clothes, then touching genitals through under clothes, a man and a woman slowly exposing themselves to each other. It had been a long time for both of them. It was awkward, humbling, fumbling and trying to be light and joyous about it. He knew that she was so straight, and it had been a number of years since she had gotten together with a man, that she would be safe from disease. So he didn't bring up the subject. It's kind of unromantic. Nor did she. Though they did have talks on this later. Straight people did not pay much attention to AIDES. They thought they were immune to this gay cancer that also infected intravenous drug users; or if you were Haitian. The apocalyptic scourge of deadly venereal disease had not yet impacted straight white people who eschewed risky behavior. As always he wore a condom. That night they had good, straight, orthodox, Christian, condom-protected, hopeful sex. It was old school, trusting, naïve and one might even dare to say, comforting, caring, loving.

Love is reading signs.

Later Cora thought about what had happened. She was bemused. I have always dated men that were my age or older, what if for once in my life I let loose and dated a younger man. It could have its down side if he started to meet my friends. What if we started going together. My friends are older and they have been through marriages and own real estate. His friends are probably still in the party phase, still hanging out in clubs and getting drunk. Not my cup of tea anymore.

Walker thought about it too. What if we started seeing each other. It had been nice to commiserate around unemployment.

Walker liked that she didn't have a TV. Neither did he.

Maybe they could be in a relationship without so many distractions and barriers to getting close. Fear of feelings marshals the defenses. Rationalizations. She's not pretty enough. He's not professional.

Figurative Abstraction, Crystal Ball, Maxwell's Daemon

Baywolf

Walker was trying to act cool after getting into sex with Cora the night before. No doubt we will have to talk about it in therapy. Her eyes were large, dark, and when she fluttered her lashes at you, it made you think of the delicate buffeting of a young bird.

The ceilings in Walker's studio apt were so tall in this old Victorian, that he sometimes felt like he could watch himself from the outside like he was some watcher floating on the ceiling. Here was Walker Underwood pacing back and forth in his little Berkeley apartment on Dwight Way across from the hospital. We see a tall slender man, 37, with long, light brown hair to the collar. He had the John Lennon glasses, that made him look seriously metaphysical.

The old house was painted like those Victorian ladies should be. Broad stairs up to a grand porch. From there through a front door you entered a vestibule that had two doors: one to each of the two front apartments. The left door was his small studio, you entered and there was a big dormer window that faced out onto the street, and to the right a short hall that led past a small bathroom to an equally small kitchen in the back. On a great big desk in front of the dormer window he had an Underwood typewriter. His bed was a mattress on the floor. He had a down mummy bag.

On the desk scattered here and there were the typed pages of a book he was working on, about the commune he had lived in in San Francisco. It was a tantric Buddhist commune that was a group marriage and the experience had seriously confronted his received notions of consensus reality, not to mention his persona / ego and he was trying to make some sense of it.

He had a little carved wooden bowl with weed all

watched over by an intricate, thumb-sized figure of a Kachina doll in authentic regalia.

He rolled up a smoke. It was good being on unemployment. The world was changing, it looked like a lot might soon to be going on with computers.

He had been doing landscaping work and it was good to be more physical. He was glad to get out of teaching. There was often knock-around carpentry work with a crew of friends in San Francisco. There was a lot of good stuff happening, especially the feeling of getting higher and higher.

He recognized something of himself in Cora: his tendency to be overanxious to please, to placate, to be nice. He supposed it was from being the eldest of 4 children and always having to be the responsible one. The one who let the younger ones go ahead, and not be competitive with them.

Walker Underwood strolled the streets of Berkeley past the barricades and round-abouts up to Telegraph avenue and back down to Shattuck a couple of times a day. To look things up in the many bookstores or go to the library. He usually wore blue jeans and white shirt.

During the years of his time in Berkeley, he worked on his writing, and usually wandered up to Telegraph avenue towards evening to get a macchiato at Café Med, which was frequented by lots of long hairs. Walker didn't interact with them. Usually he wrote in his notebook at the marble tables. Then he went across the street to Moe's books or a few doors down to Shakespeare or Half Price Books.

His forehead was becoming pinched in consternation. He was on some huge time consuming quest. Occasionally he would eat at the quarter meal in the basement of the Presby-terian church near People's Park. Although he tried not too — there were mostly loud obnoxious stupid street people now, you hardly ever ran into an old philosopher or artist.

Not like you used to.

In his little studio apt on Dwight Way, near the hospital and the warehouse he had a huge metal desk, all gunmetal gray and governmental. On the desk he had a few of the books he was reading about Jung. Jung's ponderous book *On the Psychology of the Transference* with all its verbose history of alchemy. The amazing Jung. He sure went out of his way to be recherche´. It was a look across the ages to understand the transference being a kind of container to boil the soul and distill it through transformation into being the true bird of flight for the psyche that it was. Walker had the Hillman book *The Myth of Analysis*. Jung's books on synchronicity and flying saucers.

A book about the relationship with Pauli. And The Portable Jung. A couple of popular books. He liked reading and writing from memory and stringing this together into a theory by mixing it with his own stuff and other thinkers. RD Laing. And G. Spencer Brown *The Laws of Form*, Tarot, the books of Berne on Transactional Analysis and Games and Life scripts. Books of Gestalt and American Indians. Walker was way too much in his head as everyone said. He had snatches of poetry everywhere.

Jung saw the first world war coming in a vision. He lived through the second world war and the cold war. He saw that the world was on a cataclysmic course because of its denial of the archetypal aspect of human psychology. And yet Hitler was obsessed with archetypes, too. As is advertising. So much so that it is denaturing and one tries to escape the saturation bombing by media by denial in the form of desensitization. The thing that hippies fear most and abhor is "loss of soul," which is the greatest disaster that can befall any human being. Shadows from the unconscious move men about as puppets.

Walker was working on a piece called Baywolf. About

his friend. Though some might say he is writing about this artist friend who he whished he had the courage to be like.

It was based on his friend Peter Wolf, a transplant from Germany. He had been in Dresden as a child, when the terrible saturation bombing by the Allies turned that old world city into a slaughterhouse by fire storm.

Walker wants to feel what it is like to be this free action painter artist boho. Walker wrote monologues in his character Baywolf's voice.

Art and Electronics

I sleep in my van, listen on the Sony to all the radio stations in the world at night. I like to go to sleep listening to the concerts on the BBC or some German station playing Brahms or Mozart.

I've got a good down sleeping bag from Army surplus downtown Oakland. It has been in the war, but it is excellent, light and warm. I call it my dream machine. I just get stretched out in the back of my van with the window open pointing to the sea, and I pull this fine old army down bag up over me, and travel up into my mind and dream.

I don't want to have to apologize for trying to live more equally in the here and now by living more remotely in the oneromancy of dreams. I dream about art. I try to be in an art dream. I live for art. And I have done less straight work and made less money than any white man who has ever lived. There's got to be something more than working your head off and furnishing your apartment and dressing for success. A man has to go on vision quests sometimes. It can't he all trapped and trying to be a tool of business.

I'm going to tell you about my search for the Spirit. I am also going to give you flashbacks so you will understand my troubles with existence. That's what I'm trying to do, capture all existence in an artwork.

Freewheeling

Like when I'm out riding my 10 speed thru Berkeley. Cruising on my bike. It's an extension of me. We are one. The bike goes up through my spine and I extend down through it and out to the feeling wheels. We move as one thing.

Perfect balance. Freewheeling Down Telegraph Avenue.

I'm 43 and free. You may think it undignified for a man my age. I'm the last of the Bohemians. I was an artist in Germany before I came over here. I was a Beatnik in San Francisco, and hippie in Berkeley, and recently, in my 40s many punks count me among their associates.

Now I'm living out of my van around the Bay Area. I do a little rough work: carpentry, landscaping, tile and stone work, painting. I occasionally sell one of my paintings. I deal in cash. It's nice to get cash, the government doesn't have a hand in it. I'm an unknown, a non-entity and I like it.

I get off work and I'm tired. Need to take a shower somewhere. But first I must drink my after work latté. The city is my living room. But sometimes I get the feeling that there is no place to be?

Walker viewed these stories as ways he could talk about himself in the persona of his artist friend. Storytelling develops admiration, shared vision, deep understanding as it becomes a kind of intimacy among friends.

Walker did have a van, and occasionally he would meet up with Peter Wolf and they would drink and smoke pot and ride bikes and sleep outside by a park or some driveway where they ended up parking for the night. Walker had his apt to go back to, Peter lived in his van.

Here's one that Walker wrote that is more Walker than Peter.

Lucy

We were all amazed by the discovery of the protohumanoid Lucy, with her upright stance. I could just see her little child self brandishing some tool in the ancient savannah of Africa.

They had a free museum night at the museum in Golden Gate Park. I went to see the tankas. These were truly the finest paintings on earth. True pictures of Gods. I am a student of the iconography of art and see a similarity between Eastern and Western art. The key that connected them I thought was the idea of the beatific. Beatitudes. Beat Attitudes. I was interested in the Beats and the beatific vision. I knew that when I was in a beatific state, it happens occasionally, for a few minutes after sex sometimes, I can see auras of color around the lady I am with.

Now there are lots of auras and colors in Tibetan tanka paintings , and they have a iconography relating to the chakras in the body. Where do these kinds of things occur in Western Art. No where, except in the halos of the saints. And sure the saints area kind of Bodhisatvva. And we all have the same physiology.

What I finally came up with was that in the beatific state, we are seeing signals that come up into the cortex from the deep spinal, autonomic self. That can happen after the cortex has relaxed its guard.

You don't get much of that in the Western religious art. You get Freudian Madonna pictures, big breasted Italian women feeding little golden hair chubby Jesuses.

The tankas were OK. But what really knocked me out was the jade carving. They made me run out of the room; I started weeping, they were so beautiful.

I saw them, these intricate carvings in stone, so meticulous. They actually followed whole scenes and valleys hallucinated into the stone. There I was, standing with the free crowd in front of the jade carvings in a big world class museum, and I was watching a carved river flow down into a stone horizon, and I wept, to think of the dedication and mastery of the hand behind that, and had to run from the room, a ridiculous imposter, a dilettante, a fool. I could hear delicate little intricate Aeolian zither sounds in the stone. I could see the floating world, little junks floating on a great river, trained ducks, with tight rings around their necks diving and retrieving fish.

My God . . . I was standing in front of the work of a cosmic artist. Not the individual artists themselves who made these carvings, unsigned, knowing there work would he transmitted down 3500 years, and would be around as long as there was humanity to care about such things, but the — Zen — the culture — the human nervous system that hallucinates patterns in the stone — that whole delicate sensibility that fostered these artists. I wept.

I came back after gaining my composure, and it happened again with the next carving. The exquisite delicacy of these intricate little immortal worlds was spoke of a sacred covenant of a gift given and used to celebrate the generosity of the giver.

Here is one bit where supposedly the artist is speaking, but it is Walker talking about Dhalia, the girl of the commune, or trying to talk about her.

At the Dahlia Dell

It is perhaps the world's finest crop of dahlias that come into bloom at the hand of Roy Naguchi in Golden Gate park. I dropped in after the big rain that came during the harvest moon. There are 2 flower beds, one over 100 feet long by 20 feet up a hill, terraced. Another oval about 60 feet in diameter

The beds were crowded with full grown dahlias raising their huge round hydra heads shooting out in arcs from each green stock--white dahlias and red ones as big as a basketball. Dahlias of deep regal purple, looked like chakras unfolding, in every bright known hue and shade.

Like flying herdsmen riding high among them, soared huge monarch butterflies, circling and landing to gently sup the nectar of dahlias. And then upon closer inspection there were the bumblebees. They relish their work. Get right down to business, are unperturbed by me. I like to watch them violate the flowers. How could 2 creatures be so different and so alike as the butterfly and the bumble bee. The butterfly is all lightness and grace, floating gently aloft, while the bumble bee is a preposterous, bent over, hulking, hirsute assault vehicle.

Through the 36,000 compound eyes, what they see.

The deep infrared nature of the flowers. I look at the flowers kind of funny. Let my eyes relax and notice the field of tied motion, released in the breeze. The strange preternatural sheen, the ultraviolet shadows on the edge of the frieze of flowers.

The horrendous and ungainly bees career around reaching deep into nectar dells, rooting, occasionally slipping and grabbing on violently with another of its independent suspension arms when the flower heads would nod, or take a long slow pole vaulting bow in the breeze. Then he easily leaps into space and touches down on another world.

The flowers are female, nurturing, rooted, stable. The butterflies and especially the bumblebees are male, and though they seemed to spend a good portion of their lives (a few minutes) with the same flower, they are another kind of being destined to be always moving.

Roy was walking through the garden in his old straw slouch hat. No matter how much you praised him, or related the ooohhhs and aaahhhs and gasps of delight of the tourists to him, he always grumped around saying it looked horrible, that the rain had done him in, beaten up his garden — that he didn't think he would be doing it again next year. Maybe that's just Japanese style.

He let me help him one day. He talked about his oldest daughter going to Yale or Harvard or one of them places, and about how they were going to name a certain hybrid after him. That was the kind of respect and admiration he heard.

BAYWOLF in the phantasmagoria of his van. He lays in bed knocking off drawings and occasionally poems, that are scattered all over the van floor.

The eye is in the palm of the hand
/ moving in quick gesture making a quick sketch / of the position and distance that form and / dimension take of things by the reflection of / waves of light / and the eyes are swathed in facial muscle / held in the palm of the head //
and it is only because there is an I to see / that the eyes are placed in the time / that the trajectory takes for the waves / to go out and return at the speed of light / for to see is to have reflection / through the I which opens the eyes.

On the desk in Walker's studio were typed pages of his novelette Baywolf. It was about the chaotic landscape of an action painter writ large to be the chaotic storm throwing ability of a renegade rimpoche student of black magic who was some kind of cross between Milarepa and Tesla.

The story got into a feedback loop with dreams and fantasy as they do. Like him and Peter Wolf we were out in the forest in the hills on top of the bay at Berkeley. When they'd ride bikes out to the old Nike missile sights.

This scenario was the terrain of the familiar in the dream. It would go from transparent to opaque to fuzzy. Things just sort of dissolve. Baywolf was bringing a huge storm up into existence and the wind was blowing and the garden furniture was flying through the air and the trees were shaking and being uprooted and the utility poles teetered and toppled, and a big church bell danged and dinged it's last in the dark.

He and Baywolf the action painter running around in the wind up in the hills of Berkeley were made privy to the minds of Tesla and Milarepa.

Just as the action painter is able to create these fantastic landscapes of figurative abstraction with paint, the dreamer's mind is able to throw storms against the trees in the canyons above the city.

Teslans. They were a network or community of physicists, buddhists, atmospheric scientists, lucid dreamers, engineers, naturalists / geologists, medical intuitives who sought in various ways to promote the use of free energy from the spheres, atmo, tropo, bio, geo, no, hydro- spheres.

Just as Tesla was influenced in his thinking by the Indian swami Vivekananda (JD Salinger was influenced by him too) so the Teslans believed space was filled with a luminiferous

ether. Tesla, like Leibniz thought this subtle energy was
kinetic; and he was enlightened to find the words akasha and
prana were names the Vedanta used for it.

Tesla and Milarepa were running around in waving fields of
tall grass on the hills outside of the Lawrence Berkeley Lab
where the first cloud chamber was. Conjuring up storms. Tesla
looking like this little Charlie Chaplin man, high, spiffy turn of
the century starched collar, high cheekbones, Serbo-Croatian
beauty. And Milarepa was dressed like a pilgrim in first 1050
Tibet. Milarepa is carrying a thick manuscript under his arm. It
has wooden covers, and it is written in this long fluid ancient
Sanskrit script I don't understand.

Then they are in the van and watching the weather on
the news. They are sitting around the little table in the van
watching this portable battery powered TV.

On the screen the weatherman is about one and a half inches
tall, and he is pointing to a curved earth map on the screen
with a pointer but it becomes like a wand.

And this funny little weatherman — he has one ear bigger
than the other and turned out like a parabolic dish — is
pointing his wand at the screen and he is able to change the
weather with his wand, but Baywolf KNEW, in the dream it
was Tesla controlling the pointer like a vector or a ray, coming
out of a parabolic dish on the roof of the weather station and
it was being directed up to the Nova machine, the Strategic
Defense Initiative, "star wars" platform and it was directing
those space weapons to fire their particle beams into the
pellucid brane layer covering the atmosphere, and they were
burning holes in the tropopause causing low pressure areas to
form and untoward circulations to ensue causing storms and
tornadoes to occur.

And next we see Baywolf working on a painting. He is
creating a huge painting from big arm swing action strokes
like Jackson Pollock.

And as he is pushing measures of color around on the
canvas, he is talking to some bohemians visiting him at the
van. He keeps up a steady patter as he works: "Weather. The

sun drives the atmosphere machine. The wind moves up from the hot fire of the equator to the ice of the poles, twisted by the Coriolis effect — the prevailing westerlies, pushed along by the tunnel effect of the jet stream." And he makes a long dark curve across the space with his pointed brush.

"Just like all that stuff the weatherman talks about on TV. Happens just like the weather man on TV with his pointed stick. Only he could control the weather."

Baywolf says, "Like when there is this incredible pressure like steam in a kettle and it starts getting too great, and it wants to go somewhere, to expand and go somewhere to blow off this excessive energy so it won't reach catastrophic proportions, so it won't be utterly catastrophic when it does blow. It sends up an air mass which runs into some other kind of opposite air mass, like two armies clashing at the front, like when the cold front runs into the warm spell, and it wants to let off some turbulence, it causes moisture to condense and rise and that makes some of the charges separated, and then the clouds start to appear in turmoil and BAM that sends down bolts of lightning and THERE YOU HAVE IT, A THUNDER-STORM.

Like he was Van Gogh or Jackson Pollock describing an action painting, he dances the moves swinging his arms in the shape as he speaks them: "From over the tropical ocean it poured forth its warm and moist air. Then, as it might have blown against a gently-rising range of mountains, it met the slope of the retreating northern air, and spiraling upward, swerved in toward the center. It thrusts it's snout violently under the hem of the warm south front.

"Sudden treacherous wind shift, which dismantled many a good vessel despite . . .

"What?

"Figurative abstraction tried to avoid the line, or enforced a very strong line at the edge of the self."

Outside beyond the bay, a 5 hundred mile line of white caps, the cold front swept forward. Dark thunder clouds towered high above it. Its passage brought the terrors of the tempest —

squalls, drumming rain bursts, hail, thunder and lightning, the fearful wind-shift. Dark thunder clouds towered high above it.

The passage, however was quick as it was violent. In a few minutes the front had rolled on. From the blue north the clouds were breaking, and ever widening patches of blue showed through clear and clean.

The Teslans see the sea of energy in which the earth floats, the torrent of energy from the sun. This solar wind of ions interacts with the earths magnetic fields which funnel the streams to the earth's magnetic poles where they light up as the aurora borealis. They waver and undulate giving off electromagnetic radiation all known hues but mostly in the green color. The undulation reflect surges of activity from the sun, the sun being electromagnetic emits waves that carry power which beat and surge against the earth.

So much happens in the narrow visible spectrum at the center of the sun's range. In heat and color the life on earth in the biosphere grows and evolves. They evolved an atmosphere at the top of which is an ionosphere, it is the ionosphere that causes radio waves to skip like the way a flat rock will bounce over the surface of a pond all around the earth off the underside of the atmosphere. It is called an ionized gas (like you see in fluorescent lights overhead) or it is a plasma.

The Teslans see the clouds of water vapor become charged by induction as they travel parallel to the ionosphere.

The clouds are like capacitors that will discharge in lightning when they become too full of charge from coupling with the ionosphere. There is a cloud discharge about one hundred times a second somewhere on the earth. Now this lightning delivers 2 billion watts in a flash. That's enough to light most of the households here on the earth.

The Mystery

At his next therapy session with Anna Zane, Walker knew it was incumbent upon him to mention new relationships. He somehow wanted to protect his therapist from feeling jealousy over his recent tryst. So he down-played it with: "I might be starting to get together with a new girlfriend."

The action of session starts when he sits down in the old comfy chair across from her. It was like stepping from one world into another. He started to observe himself as if from outside of himself, from above. He is committed to telling what he knows of the truth about himself and what he will allow himself to know, and listening. And listening to ourselves listening.

There is a window under which a spy could eavesdrop but that thought would be paranoid and we needn't entertain it. Ms. Zane, the fine looking babe therapist is sitting looking proper, trying not to be provocative in her chair. They are seated in large comfortable chairs facing each other across the small room.

_____ a long pause

Patient: I don't know what to talk about. . . It feels like we are getting together too often, I just don't have anything to say.

Analyst: We get together too much. . . I would say, what you were saying was fairly on target.

Patient: Well I said it. The Crux of the matter . . .
I kind of would like to write a mystery. Something like Miami Vice. Have a lot of violence in it. Modern fire power, like grenade launchers, attacks against the SWAT team, and stuff like that.

Analyst: Something very aggressive,

Patient: Very scientific, too, very technical and the hero would be just sort of this real . . . kind of everyday guy who just fell into all this incredible stuff, you know and was a survivor. Caught in some kind of Cross fire. Cocaine cowboys and Mafia Indians.

(embarrassed) I'm sort of getting off the subject here. I can't relate to it very well.

Analyst: Indians and stuff?

Patient: Well whatever we were talking about before this

Analyst: Well I think it is a fantasy that reflects whatever's in your mind.

Patient: Fantasy's about. . . machines, technology, powerful machines and aggressive action.

It's not me at all really, I don't usually write like that, just more psychological or. . . I'd like to put my friends in it too, as sort of characters, only you know they would be kind of superhuman. They would be getting in gunfights, maybe even you would get in a gunfight.

Analyst: Even me?

Patient: You'd be up there.

Analyst: How do you mean.

Patient: Well let's see. Maybe you'd run some kind of hideout where people came to hide out and maybe help us break out of jail or something. You'd have some cool house in the country, where we'd come over there and hide out, when they were on our trail. And we would sit around in your kitchen. Linoleum floor, tables, we'd be eating big breakfasts and smoking dope and talking about religion. At Anna Zane's house. Till, till she got real pissed-off and throws us out. Cause we were interfering with

something, something more spiritual, some serious
thing she had going with somebody.

Analyst: Hum, that's quite a dream.

Patient: She'd protect us too, keep a watch, maybe even
shoot a bad guy or something. Kind of a moll.

Analyst: A moll?

Patient: Yea, a gangster's moll.

Analyst: What does that mean, I'm not sure I know.

Patient: Just a real with-it woman, good looking, could drive
a getaway car, very capable, on our side, in my gang.

Analyst: A haven in a cruel world.

Patient: Yea. Maybe even help us figure out the mystery of
who done it. I mean why should we be figuring that
out. I don't know. I mean we're certainly not the
police.

Analyst: You and I are doing that.

Patient: Pardon.

Analyst: You and I are doing that.

Patient: Yeah . . . right.

> It, it would, It would have to start off with the
> discovery of some dead body or some indication of
> that, you know, or just some, something to start it
> off. Start off the reasoning.

Analyst: Something you have not come to terms with there.

Patient: Really, what.

Analyst: I don't think, that is a surprise to you.

Patient: Well we all have to be in some kind of fight against the polluters. We would be some kind of vigilante types who decided to use stronger means to stop the . . . save the earth or something.

Analyst: So all of a sudden this group shifts from gangsters to. . . Ecological Freedom Fighters?

Patient: Yea, have some master detective sort of finding a trail to us, and then sympathizing with us. I don't know. I don't usually work out much plot stuff at all I never felt like I had much imagination for plot.

But I would like to write something.
Lately I have just been writing about a painter who lived in a van. An artist, a real lonely sort of thing.. Solo man thinking about art. With no other people in it. You know, I'd like to have more people in it.

Analyst: You're wanting more people in your life.

Patient: Yeah. . .

I was just having nice thoughts about sitting around in Anna Zane's kitchen, you know, it's kind of a country place.

Analyst: What was the connection between that, and wanting more people in your life?

Patient: I have no idea. None.

Analyst: Well, what's stopping you from perusing that? Like these women you saw this afternoon and you were very attracted to.

Patient: Well they were just there, in class. I mean I'm sort of generally turned on my them, but I don't want to bother them...

Analyst: Bother them?

Patient: Bother "her" . . . them. Or accost them, or us; undergo the risk of rejection, of pushing into their trip. Pushing . . .

Analyst: Bother, accost, push . . .

Patient: Yea

Analyst: Well it's kind of like your story in a way, you start off very aggressive, gangster, it get's watered-down a little bit, well political activists, then not aggressive enough, you know you have strong impulses to be quite active, to pursue these women; you get worried that the attention is going to be too much to them. Your fantasy with me is quite similar, it would be this raucous time, eating, smoking dope and being quite loud, and I kick you out, couldn't take it any more.

Patient: So it's sort of a fear of being real active. . . Pushing, bothering accosting . . . pushing.

I started thinking about always being taller than everybody in school and everything, that I was bigger, and could hurt somebody, or just, I guess afraid of my anger. I feel so angry sometimes. I was afraid of Cora or Darcy seeing that you know. There is just a real meanness. . .
I started getting flashes of being really big and tall, and of having to act dumb somehow, dumb and gentle. You know, somehow for my little brothers and sisters.

Analyst: Why is that?

Patient: Something about competition, about... maybe being afraid of hurting them somehow. I don't remember.

Analyst: Why do you think you are so concerned about hurting them, rather than that they'll admire you for being strong.

Patient: "You're hurting your mother." That phrase always comes to mind. "You're hurting your mother when you do that. My father used to say that to me.

Analyst: Because you're leaving her for someone else?

Patient: I don't know if that's it or not.

Analyst: What about hurting your mother?

I don't know, just doing something bad was hurting your mother.

Analyst: Like what?

Patient: I don't know, just being real willful . . . I don't know what it was I did. Sullen, being real sullen, staying out a lot, I guess I was more of a almost a teenager by then.

I guess those are the two really big ages in a person's life is around what 2,3 and 4 and then teenager, the teenage years. Aren't those are big psychic development years.

I mean is that true?

Analyst: What do you think

Patient: I don't know, I'm asking, I just had that thought myself. Seems like in here . . .

Analyst: Well, I think that's interesting, when you say something to me, that you obviously have opinions about, and you are talking about, and I wonder if the fantasy isn't something like: 'If I get too independent and go out and stay out late, and do things like that, and act like and adolescent boy should be, I might be hurting my mother", just like with me you often times pretend you don't really know the things that you do and say what do you think about that.

Patient: Humm . . .

Analyst: As if you want to make sure, that I'm not going to be threatened by how smart you are, or how many ideas you have. How big you are. Or how you can really put things together by yourself.

Patient: Hummm

Analyst: The relationship with me is like the relationship with you mother. It brings up a fantasy that I couldn't tolerate it if you became independent, that I need to keep you. . . little, and dependent on me for some reason.

Patient: Bad news

Analyst: What bad news.

Patient: That's tough

Well this dependency I am getting on you, Ms. Z.

Analyst: This is bad news?

Patient: Yea

Analyst: What do you mean?

Patient: Well, it is, it is sort like this huge, thing, here that is influencing my life. I'll just try out this idea. Uhh that I am avoiding getting into stuff with women, because I am in therapy with you.

Analyst: Well, you're repeating something here! It's not being in therapy that's stopping you from doing it, but your fantasy about how you couldn't be in therapy and get involved in something . . .

Patient: Why not.

Analyst: I think that what that tells us is that the fantasy when you were younger is that you couldn't keep your mother's love and find a girlfriend. Stay out late and really grow up, and become a man. With a woman. Which is a way of knowing that you're a man. With a woman.

Then again, I think the confirmation of that idea, is, your response to my comment, saying "Uh-oh, this is bad news this therapy, this therapy is stopping me from getting involved." Where does that fantasy come from?

Patient: Well I agree it must reflect some earlier stage, it's not so much the therapy. . .

Analyst: Well, what about that.

Patient: Although I'm not so sure.

Analyst: Oh, you're not so sure!

Patient: I mean sometimes it's like, wow, this is my therapy, this is the only place I'm really relating to anybody in my life. It's big in a lot of ways, I mean I structure my week around it, this all consuming thing I'm into.

Analyst: Why would you make it be that for you?

Patient: Well, uh, I don't know. It's interesting. It's one of the few places I really feel myself during the week. I forget to feel myself during work, or most of the time.

I've always been kind of a loner. Always. It's just my way. You want to preserve that for some reason. I start thinking about how awkward it is just to go up and make small talk to somebody. But this self talking here is really exciting, you know? But I'm always afraid of some look in my eye is going to put them off, or scare them, they're just going to reject me.

Analyst: Some look in your eye?

Patient: Some look in my eye, yea. Like well, the women would know I just wanted to have sex with them, or wanted to get close with them.

Analyst: Wouldn't that be so terrible.
Patient: (laughing at being teased) Yeah.

Analyst: Again the fantasy. I would think that they would
be flattered and enjoy being perused. Not that you
would *injure* them somehow.

Patient: Uh-huh. Yea, somehow. That's it. I have some
kind of guilt over injuring them, getting them to do
something they didn't want to do. It's not really true,
but it may as well be, you know.
_____(long pause)
I feel like you are really staring at me.
Analyst: Why is that. What's you fantasy.
Patient: It looks like you were really thinking about me.
Thinking about what was being said. I had a lot
of fear of you the last time. Remember, I was real
worried about, uh, the privacy of this contract.

You look nice in that blouse. It's a real work shirt.
Kind of like how I see you around that kitchen.

Analyst: So first you see me as scrutinizing you, and then
you feel affectionately again that I'm sort of a haven.

Patient: Uh-huh. What do you make of that?
Analyst: When you were just talking about special relation-
ships being one's where you don't cut them off . . .
Then you went into a kind of dissociation.
Patient: Yea? . . .
Analyst: That they would be someone who would stick with
you in spite of your attempts, to dismantle it.
Patient: I was getting off track a little bit.
Analyst: Maybe it is right on track.

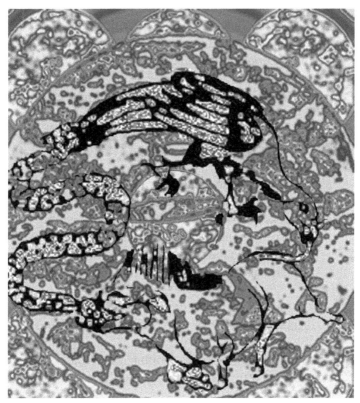

The Great Mandala

showing the snake the pig and the cock

Mandala — Wheel of Samsara

Walker had often pondered over the meaning of the three animals: the pig, the snake, and the cock — chasing each other around, head biting tail of the one in front, at the center of the wheel. Their influence seemed to fan out in pie sectors to generate the mandala.

Then one day it just dawned on him that they represented the three main drives born of evolutionary necessity: aggression, revenge and jealousy. Aggression is an engine of evolution to feed and take life and to reproduce and to get ahead. It is symbolized by the pig. Revenge is necessary because you have to demonstrate to aggressors that there are severe consequences to their aggression. It is symbolized by the snake. Jealousy is a part of the drive to hold and protect your mate. It is symbolized by the cock in the center of the mandala.

It felt good to understand.

Your mandala will find you say Buddhist students of the Self. A mandala will seem to emerge in the periphery of your mind in trying times, when you are forced by circumstances to be shifting there, running in place and getting nowhere; or enduring other destabilizing life transitions. Shivering and shimmering between lacunae gaps and traps.

Walker first got to study the Buddhist thanka paintings closely in the House. They had several of these outsized beautiful wall-hanging Tibetan religious art paintings with their plethora of fierce and terrifying images of wrathful deities and expositions of the workings of the cosmos flowing in all known hues. Walker had been exposed to the idea of mandala much earlier in the 70s through Jung's book on the Flying Saucer as Modern Myth related to the mandala.

The Mandala is a diagram (a kind of icon) of the forces and realms that attract one away from mindfulness in the moment. There are lots of other definitions of mandala, some people use them like a spider's web to attract wealth and good fortune by being more aware of the archetypal or parallel universe forces at work in our world.

Walker had taken part, along with Dahlia and others of their sangha, in the Kalichakra Initiation conducted by Kalu Rimpoche at Fort Mason, San Francisco in 1982. This is a meditation and dedication of intent upon Chenrezig, a lama bodhisattva or saint who came to represent or incarnate the archetypal instinct of compassion. Walker had not known what this initiation was about, but the venerable little monk Kalu Rimpoche who had spent years meditating in a cave looked upon the throng of young white American devotes with great feeling eyes (almost like a baby seal on an ice flow looking up at you). The Kalichakra is the wheel of Time one of the main subjects of mandala. The mandala shows illustrations of both samsara and bodhicitta, ignorance and beatific enthrallment. The wheel one is tied to and is trying to get free of. In dedicating himself Walker had signed on to be an agent of compassion in the world.

The Buddhists call these domains of blind ignorance generated by the animals *samsara*, or hell realms. There was the famous hell realm of the hungry ghosts. It shows white, unnourished, bald figures with long necks. It represents insatiable hunger for possessions. Rimpoche Trongpa points out in psychological reading that this image is about the grasping ego operating out of narcissism, enraptured by the signifier of wealth and power. The basic instinct of preservation has been enlarged by aggression and turned into a greed that can not be satisfied. This is because the operation from the Self has been taken over or shifted away from the

Self to the Ego. Another hell ream is self-destructive anger. Another is the Animal realm concerned with security and comfort, like the way an animal operates on instinct and does not feel any mystery. There is the human realm, with its passion and unending pursuit of sensual pleasure. Walker thought he might be down for that. There was the realm of the jealous gods: this was supposed to be about paranoia and narcissism.

These diagrams were not just representations of spiritual thought. The convocation in a circle of icons, the idols, the panoply of deities, literally spoke to ancient man. Bicameral Mind theory suggests that in the childhood of humanity, in the time of neolithic man the people heard their own thoughts; there ideas were like an inner voice telling them what to do. This is because the left and right hemispheres were not so well sutured through the corpus colossus and the brain shouted the thoughts along a shorter pathway to the audio cortex where they were processed as heard. (It probably sounds like your super-ego mother guilt-voice admonishing you not to mess up.)

With the growth of society the tribals sought to manip-ulate these energies and other entities that arise from man's religious imagination as elements of control. People felt their own self as emanating from a grid of in-and-out energetics which became societal admonitions, mythological beliefs, taboos, kinship experience, the obligations of war and love. These they felt as psychical objects that can move around in their world, or be active in other ways. The gods, the fates. In particular, these thoughts can dip down and get convolved with other moments in memory when the psychical immune systems, the system of defense mechanisms, has repressed them into a black hole called the unconscious, as some of the tanka paintings expressed.

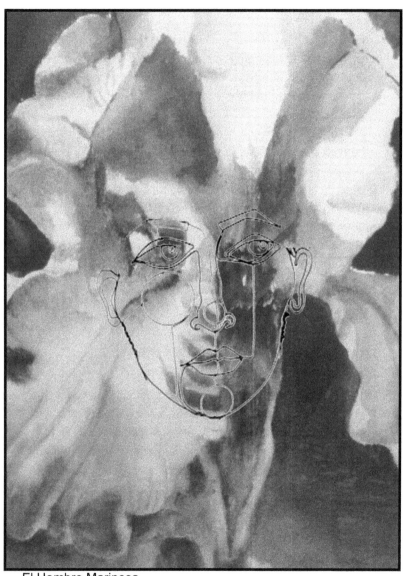

El Hombre Mariposa

At the Dance

Ms. Cora Rosenov carried herself like a dancer. She held herself in a very nice relaxed readiness that would have been called rangy if she were taller. Like a ballerina she was contained but expressive. She was a musician too. In her living room she had a baby grand piano. This shining lacquer-black machine took up almost the whole space. But she had to have it. There were great piles and sheathes of music scores festooning out of draws. She took classes at the Conservatory in San Francisco.

One quickly realized how important dance was to Cora, Ms. C. She had Walker drive them in her car over to the Avenue Ballroom on Taraval Street in the Outside Lands district of San Francisco. It was a bit of a drive from Berkeley, over the Bay bridge, down Fell, past the Haight, down Lincoln skirting the Golden Gate Park, then south on 19th Ave, then by some tricky cloverleaf of no left turn, onto Taraval. Upstairs, pay the small fee and they are in the Avenue Ballroom. West Coast Swing was their thing; though Oz Koosed and his dance teachers did Jitterbug and Hustle and Vienna Waltz and everything else.

The large hardwood floor hall was filled with people all of whom were completely enamored of the dance. Asians dressed up; a lot of white people; couples and some singles; slightly older people. Sometimes they did traditional dances, the Waltz where you whirled and swirled around the room in a long oval of counter clockwise rotation. People were dressed up, and there were colored lights. There was a little half-door snack bar at one end of the room where you could buy water and pop. Also there were little alcoves along the side of the ballroom with the floor to ceiling windows that opened onto small balconies. Here people cold lean out and rest and cool down feeling the breeze off the ocean. The scene was enchanting and there was so much talk! — talk on the side-lines, talk while dancing. It was a wonder the instructor could be heard at all; she did use a wireless mic attached to a transmitter on her belt that connected into the sound system.

The dance-besotted women liked to wear twirly dresses held up on thin straps. This revealed their sleek, elongated girl-muscles. In the dance, the convention against physical touching was suspended, and you could reach out and hold a girl. She was just some little white sister there with her boyfriend, or an Asian, or slightly chubby Filipina, or good-looking older gal from the days when people jitterbugged and did the west coast swing.

At the dance Walker and Ms. Cora became a we, they got into a groove together. It was so sexy, the way she wore polyester that clung to her hot dancer's body; then it lifted off and became unstuck when they went outside on the terrace to get a bit of fog. Out here by the ocean, they worked up a sweat. Even though it was not that ecstatic solo hippie dancing that Walker was more experience with, it was athletic.

She got into a gay and careless groove, she was in her element. She was a danceaholic and her drug of choice is west coast swing! She was in the feline predator pace of the dance and she was wanting him to join her. Beckoning him into her whirling and swirling, circling frame. He wanted to be there for her, make it fun; maybe she was an agent of the goddess. Walker let himself be taken up into that world of colors and motion and heat; it became their world, it lightens their load and grips their souls. Dance is a most powerful aphrodisiac.

At the Avenue Ballroom he was not on the make for any of the other women, he was the escort of Ms. Cora. He tried to keep a low profile, because she was often caught up in a flocking, gaggling troupe of dancers, who moved like quail with grace, in and out of the group. Walker was tall and the little women love to feel themselves in the arms of a big man.

The music lifts the attention and thus lightens their load as it motivates the people to slide and weave, spin and hold on the dance floor. Music and dance is a mellow steroid to enhance endurance. Music and dance are, next to marijuana, money and the mons venus, a most powerful aphrodisiac.

They danced. How they danced. Together. Together. Body on body. Breast on breast. Body on body. Breath on breath.

He held her in his arms, and placed his hand in the middle of her back and guided her across the floor, and she gracefully moved with him. They were face to face, breast to breast. Her body his body breath to breath. Ms. C, and he were in a game. They had made a commitment to be with each other, two moving as one. It was OK for him and it was a real turn on for her. He couldn't keep his hands off her. They were getting in sync, side by side, jointly in the bedroom too. Ms. C was poised and self-possessed. She was a grown woman, and able to take care of herself, though sometimes she could be a little girl too.

When they left it was late. They slipped out into the cool San Francisco ocean air, and headed back along the late-night arc-light streets, shooting back by the park and through down town San Francisco, and across the Bay Bridge back to Berkeley.

- - - - - - - O - - - - - - -

When they got back to her place they couldn't keep their hands off each other. Cora remembered how as soon as we got back to my place Walker was on me. I laughed and gave in. He started taking my clothes off as soon as we got inside the entrance. I let him take my panties off over my heels while he was kneeling on the floor. I had barely managed to close the door. Haha!

He turned me around and was kissing my stomach and pussy under the skirt.

I pushed myself off of him and we maybe had a glass of wine, and got me to kiss him. We sat down on the couch and he was moving in closer and closer leaning into me, then I reached for Walker's dick. I squeezed it in his pants; it was bulging behind the fabric. I petted it. He unzipped his pants and put my hand inside, and I closed my hand around his hot hard throbbing cock. While French kissing him, I pulled on his super hot dick and I took it out of his pants. And I started pumping it.

Walker started fingering me and we were feverishly french kissing.

We went in the bedroom. He held me strong from behind and kissed my neck and shoulders. I took off the shift and the nylons and striped down to my hot naked self and he did too.

I was sitting on the edge of the bed, Walker was standing next to me. I took his dick in my hand and bent way over and kissed it. Walker ran his hands through my hair over and reached his hot hand over my boobs and let his fingers linger tweaking the nipples. It sent a shiver through me. And I took his dick inside my mouth and started sucking it. I gave him a blowjob.

Then…he pushed me back on the bed and started licking and fingering my pussy. I let my mind go blank, exorcised the critic and enjoyed. We had mind blowing sex.

Walker was surprised to discover that Ms. C was one of the hottest, most orgasmic sexual partners he had ever had the honor to work with. And because he was pretty sure it was not going to last into a long term commitment and he wasn't all caught up in love and in spite of all the stress from unemployment, the sex with Cora, the way he was free in the relationship started making him very sure of himself then.

They were moving face to face, jointly, breast to breast. Her body, his body -- breath to breath. Her eyes starting to slip back up into her head, her mind searching for orgasm, inside her totally aroused being. Moaning and breathing heavy in each other's ear. Sympathetic, they glowed. They were not apart but were a part of each other. (: -)

From time to time Ms. C taught Walker a few steps at her place: they rolled up the rug in her living room. And she played these classic rock'n'roll 45s from the 50s on an old portable player. And she made sure they arrived early at the ballroom in time for the class lesson.

Cora thought about what had happened when they got out of the dance the last time. We could not control ourselves. We started off outside the car. On a street in San Francisco. While kissing like lovers, he put his hands on my ass.

When we got into the car we made out some more. He pushed his hand inside my shirt and started feeling and squeezing my boobs and then bent down to give me a wonderful French kiss. He reached under my skirt and I spread my legs and let him drag his fingers over my cunt. The panties were wedged up in my ass and crotch and I didn't care. I felt the cold leather of the Volvo seat all the way back to Berkeley.

House of Tricks

Walker was beginning to realize that his conception of therapy was changing. At first he thought he had to be entertaining — if not deep. He believed psychoanalysis would be some great insight into his life, that it would change his life forever, that he would get on some great path of destiny, and see his life in its converging paths of parallel interests and that he would be able to more easily move creatively in and out of the imaginary and the symbolic and the real. But maybe not.

His therapist, Ms. Z — he thinks of her as a Ms. Z in a distancing move — her face is framed by luxuriant waves of curling girl tresses, and she peers intently from behind very straight-looking glasses.

It is a convention where he tells her everything about himself, and knows nothing about her. He wanted to show his therapist that he is making progress in one of the two things you need to be happy according to Freud: Work and Love. It is necessary to be able to Work and to Love.

Often he felt like his therapist would be judging of him. He held back in order to protect her from his anger and despair. He put himself under the pressure of commitment to be a good analysand, who did homework and studied as he sought to conform to ideals of honesty explored in the verbal / linguistical act of free association. Walker made it a point to never get stoned on therapy days. That's for sure. He wanted to give it the focus it deserves. He wanted to bring his best. If that required wallowing in his own misery unbenumbed by smoking pot, then so be it.

There is good light in the room coming from the industrial steel latticed windows of what was once a school. It was a spellbinding time on old Grove street.

Today he is stuck in those long pseudo-profound silences that so often befell the therapy sessions. In them Walker sometimes has fantasies of what Ms. Z is like in bed: I wonder what she says to her lover / husband. What would I like to have really said to her? I love you. I realize that I buy your time with me. It makes me feel like a trick. I come and I go in your presence on the agreed upon hours. And I am visited by your presence in my mind often during the day. How would SHE work out the current confrontational situation in a thoughtful, feeling way.

I am lifted up, noticing a glow flowing out of the beings I encounter on the street. I love you.

I realize you would just say it is transference. I should learn to recognize it. And yet I also know, you have feelings for me. I can see it in your eyes sometimes. But then perhaps that is just what I look for, that empathetic understanding.

Ms. Z has the most hypnotic way of speaking. Slow and distinct, measured and suggestive, the words spin and drift from her lips and mirage into the space of conversation — crossing dimensions of I and Thou through a kind of hypnotic persuasion. Walker considered that she might have studied neuro-linguistic programming from the hypnotherapy of Milton Erickson. Although he doubted it, he didn't know: she may have. She was a PhD candidate in psychoanalysis. She always refused to divulge her background and kept one in a perpetually powerless guessing zone.

Anna Z did old school psychoanalysis, which means to maximally frustrate so as to enhance transference effects while experiencing defense mechanisms. And damn! It was often unbearable. To Walker this beautiful smart Jewish woman therapist looked almost exactly like a sister of Loni Sanders, the cutest porn star who ever lived. It was sheer torture of the most exquisite sort to be in her presence.

Sometimes the sexual fantasies he perpetrated on her were pornographic. He undressed her with his eyes, he was always in an excited state. He saw her sitting on his lap and them smooching, then further, them naked and her squatting down on his hard cock in a dandy reverse cowgirl screw. Since he paid her for her time he got his revenge by making her play the whore. He would imagine her saying: You spent good money to buy me. Don't hold back. Make me do disgusting, degrading unspeakable things. Fuck me raw.

He tupped her over that plush walnut chair with the upholstered arms, making her stick her naked ass in the air many times in his mind. She would say: Pull my lacy panties down and finger my ass. Make me squeal. You own me. Treat me like the prostitute I am. Pound my ass. Sometimes the fantasies were so strong he couldn't concentrate. Those long profound silences were filled with her vulgarity: I am your whore. I am your slut. The money is just there to keep score, to elevate me above you. Don't hold back. Take what's yours. Don't go easy. Fuck my face. Make me gag. Leave me sore. I'm here live, to please you. In the next hour a new stranger will buy me. I will be his. They will be on time. I can't wait. She must have known it; sexual attraction is part of the transference, though he tried to hide it from her.

At other times he felt in therapy or after walking out of a session: I am rising, rising on the field, floating over the world between heaven and earth. I am rising, rising, on the feeling field rising lifted, turning in monk-like spheres of Buddhist realms amidst the hustle and flow.

One is constantly asking himself a flurry of questions: How do I know if my therapist loves me? How do I get my therapist to love me? What do I do if I think my therapist loves me? Am I supposed to hate the therapist I love?

It did occur to Walker that he was trying to make his

therapist feel jealous that he was starting a new relationship; or that he was trying to make her see that he was lovable.

In these early days of therapy, Walker was still very much imprinted on Dhalia from the commune. He was still friends with several of the sangha members. Many of them were not trying to find there way into relationships but staying the course with someone they had already developed a deep trust and love for.

Issues that kept one from being able to Work and Love were what they were supposed to be working on. For Walker it felt like he was trying to conform to the ideal of what was good. This was the pattern of how he spoke to his therapist as she was right before his eyes shimmering and oscillating back and forth between being his therapist and his girlfriend. A lot of men are like this with women, aren't they? It was something about not objectifying people, especially women. Of trying to relate to the being and not the object the being seemed to represent.

Walker wrote a little poem about Therapy Love.

Therapy Love

Transference and countertransference
in a session behind closed doors
we left the world outside.
We each had a role to play.
Perhaps it was a game we both taught ourselves to believe in
transference and countertransference,
therapy love.
A game with a script.
She wanted to be a famous therapist like her grandfather
I wanted to be this visionary writer like Borges
I did make her smile often.
She listened to my tale of woe.
It was good sharing thoughts with someone who listens
we are helping each other grow.

It's therapy love.
I was hoping to experience more numinosity
and she was trying to get me to hold on to a job.

The speaking cure —
 my soul laid bare and her's clearly there too.
But she was so damn foxy / and so full of moxie.
How could this other who really sees you in your struggle
have feelings for you but not want to snuggle.
It's therapy love.

I got lost in the woods. Had a broken heart too —
where mad passion you can't forget
was tragic, but still hoped for
was alive and moot,
like a love ghost . . . on fire . . . in the rain.
It hurt that your soul mate, would never be with you again.
So therapy love to set a back fire
to know what love and desire are.
She held out a promise of a kind normalcy
something that was foreign to me.

So many times we were silent in each other's gaze.
Some days whole hours would pass with hardly a word.
It felt like a brain stuttering,
trying to find the cube root of the absurd.
Therapy love; it is therapy love.

We had the unconscious
that got formed when we were very very young
in a family that was our lifeline to survival
and yet we were too innocent to know and so easily inspired
to take up heroes and live out script.

We were sworn to look at the wall of defenses
one girds 'round the self,
to go back to the place we started from
before our truth got cloaked in stealth.
We dropped into my shadow,

its therapy love.

They make you fall in love with them; it's their con
they get inside your head and take your parents on.
You have to feel how much you hate the need
for the loved one, how that helps the darkness spread.
At other times there was so much joy in therapy love,
— some get addicted.
She was there to bear fair witness.
She was a worthy opponent, it's therapy love.
Its therapy love.

Walker in therapy had discovered, by god I too have
an unconscious, and he was enthralled by it. Although self
knowledge did not necessarily make him more able to act
on it. He was blindly unable to see that he was projecting
the prior relationship he had with authority, the father and
mother on his therapist at the moment. He would rather not
think about it; in these silences he would disrupt feelings
from his past if need be.

The Hired Hand

Cora and Walker were a help and a consolation to each other during their unemployment. She got him a little labor job for one of her friends. Ms. C had these older friends, all of whom owned houses. Walker ended up doing landscaping work for one of them, Ruth. She had a fabulous Berkeley craftsman house, with all this elaborate wood trim work, carved newel posts and inlaid wainscoting and stained glass windows. And the grounds and gardens were quite large for Berkeley. Walker designed and built strong rose trellises all along the far side of her back yard, to support a wall of roses that climbed 10 feet into the air. It was a giant hedge of roses. He was polite and nice, and grateful for the cash.

Ruth kept looking at him funny. Walker wondered if it was embarrassing for Cora that he did work for her friend. Alas as he suspected, it was more about Ms. C telling tales out of school about their sex life.

Cora was telling Ruth, "Walker knows how to work the machinery of my sexuality. He discovered that I can have an orgasm sometimes just from him playing with my nipples. He really turns me on. We were kissing me passionately while he was squeezing my breasts and pinching my nipples and I came.

He fucked me so brilliantly, so beautifully... I had 2 orgasms that night."

Ruth looked upon her friend with new found respect and said, "I'm so glad you've found someone you like. It's been a long time."

Cora dared not tell her friend about the more risque and, dare one say perhaps even perverted behavior Walker was trying out on her. (Partly she was embarrassed and partly because she felt her friend would be envious of her demon lover. Images flashed across her mind of what she did not say: how he held me . . . put his hands on my body….my breasts, my pussy. . . he lovingly grabbed my hips . . . and touched my clitoris with his tongue . . .it made me so wet… sopping wet in his hands.)

Walker got invited to a dinner at Ruth's house where he was the youngest person there. Ruth served a sumptuous dinner party of nouvelle-Californian cuisine, which was mostly gigantic salads festooned with healthy greens with whole cherry tomatoes. New potatoes and lean fish. The men there were all these rich old teddy bears, with their joie de vivre, talking serious about current events and such. Or team sports. Or real estate. Or stocks. Or golf game. As usual Walker felt it was obvious that he had not learned well how to be in male bonhomie.

Ruth was very pleased that Walker was going out with her best friend. And Cora looked upon herself as changed. She changed a lot in the time she and Walker were together.

Walker did worry about what Ms. C said about what went on in their relationship to her girlfriend. Walker was surprised that Cora was the way she was. He had not expected sinuous moxie. She was this mousy looking older chick. He thought she would be very uptight and not much fun in bed. He was surprised at how hot she turned out to be. She worked out, went to the gym often was very involved with West Coast Swing dancing, and it showed: she was trim. She was stronger than he would have guessed from her slender frame. She felt solid, resilient in his hands, not plush of pulchritude. And that ass: If I dropped a dime on that ass, it would bounce back into my hand.

Walker had decided to make it a project: Since he and Ms. C were out of work with time on our hands, why not spend a whole lot of it fucking each other's brains out. She was a nice middle–class woman who had her own thing together; she had hit a slow patch career-wise. But things were shifting around. Maybe they would both get some benefit out of it.

He talked to her openly about sex. He talked to her about AIDS and herpes. She seemed kind of old school about it, that it didn't concern heterosexuals. And there hadn't been anyone sexual in her life in quite a few years. She had pretty much resigned herself to a life of spinsterhood. She worked with children's day care at some big companies, HP and some big financial institutions. Also a local community day care. She loved children. But circumstances had kept her from marrying and having one. Twice Cora had been in long term relationships with university professors, one a physicist, the other a mathematician. These marriage engagements had broken up and she found herself on her own. Some time after that in fact fairly recently she had bought her house. Her parents had passed away and there had been enough money to buy a house in Berkeley outright.

Walker did get to meet her brother when Cora intro-duced them at her house in Berkeley for dinner just the once, though he lived in San Francisco. Her brother WAS that mathematician Walker had noticed holding forth in bright conversation in a saloon in North Beach called Vesuvios before he had ever met Cora! He had the same intelligent feeling jubilant eyes that his sister had. It felt outstanding to be seen by those eyes. The brother looked upon Walker with suspicion. He was so much older than Cora, he was like a father. They were from a Russian Jewish family, who had fled the old world and moved to America. Cora and her brother were born here. Walker only vaguely understood the Jewish post-holocaust psychology, how it imparts an adaptable character haunted by a trans-generational survivor-guilt some of which is passed to the next generation.

Cora kept herself busy with weekly dance class and piano classes. There had been that long affair with a man who claimed he was going to divorce his wife but he never did and she had to break it off with him. It left her disappointed but she was too romantic and hopeful to be bitter.

She had a lot of Jewish woman friends and went around to their houses for dinners and sociability. The wives wondered about her. Generally she was thought to be a spinster. Though not by her single girl friends. She was a Ms. And she was nobody's fool!

And Damn! Who knew that normal straight women could be so hot? And yet she had this somewhat annoying, imploring way of looking up at him just when he was about to enter her, and they were about to bang like hell saying, "Don't hurt me." Walker was somewhat jolted by that, for he was the most solicitous and careful when he handled girl flesh. Maybe his size was a bit forceful for her. He was much bigger than she was, she was petite. In spite of her often said plea, he found himself thinking sometimes: I am going to tare this scrawny little bitch up, cause she can take it.

He decided that Ms. C liked to portray herself as something of a white slave girl beset by a horny pirate in order not to take responsibility for her own sexual desire. It was a bit odd, because as everyone knows all Jewish women enjoy sex. Still his ears turned red and he knew they were talking about him when he noticed the two confidants Cora and Ruth across the room chatting and gossiping and laughing risqué.

Walker could tell that he and Ms. C needed to get into a whole lot of sex. (Don't we all!) But though he spoke well, he was poor and seemed to be on the outs around ambition. Perhaps she saw him that way. Walker had been in the commune, it was kind of a group marriage and was pretty open about using sex to get to your own feelings. It seemed like a very reasonable approach — one that was more psychological than romantic. Romantic behavior was ridiculed in the House. It was thought to be dependence or other defense to avoid feelings, it took over a person and made them as though acting out parts, like in the movies. One was not truly present. They would get into bed and fuck so well it would burn down the walls of ego. And then maybe it would lead to spending time and getting to know each other intimately, whatever that turned out to be.

It was good to be known by someone who was capable of knowing you in a way that you need to be known. That wasn't too much to ask was it?

Walker began to sense that Ruth smiled at him in a knowing way. And, she was a Jewish therapist who, it came up in conversation, actually knew Walker's Jewish therapist. In Berkeley everybody was in therapy, looking into the mirror and trying to find their soul there. So they understood if you were. They understood how, on a fundamental level, transference operated, and that you were in some kind of spell. And it was OK. You may get something out of it. You were working on yourself, trying to be all that you can be. You were suffering. You had a pet grieve. You are looking in the mirror and trying to see the beauty despite it all — carrying on despite the tragedy of your deeper nature. We are all, in our fashion, coming to terms with life.

Who knew there was this great interlocking sworn-to-secrecy mind cabal among psychotherapists having patients. When he was talking about therapy, Ruth asked, "Who is your therapist?"

He told her, "Anna Zane."

"Yes, I know her."

Walker tried to be innocent and nonchalant when he asked, "Is she married? You know these therapists, they don't tell you a thing about themselves."

Ruth said, "No she isn't but she is engaged, I think. To a young business man."

Ruth was quick to change the subject for it is an unwritten rule among the shrink cabal: No knowledge out of school. She even actually did say: "I can't tell you any more because it might undermine the transference."

Walker in transference in a session.

Analyst: Well, It is the same kind of thing: Work is a relationship, with people, especially bosses that are like your father figures, and how to hang in with that.
Love and partnering off with women, is sort of trying to be in a similar kind of relationship like work like being around your mother

Patient: How's that?
Analyst: How *is* that.

Patient: I guess I expect a lot; a lot of expectation, but . . .
Analyst: But what exactly was like your mother

Patient: Being really close, physically close to a woman, I mean I'm not saying it is like my mother, but I'm trying to make a parallel, dealing with work is like trying to deal with your father, and with women, it is trying to deal with your mother.
Analyst: Well just the feelings that come up in physical closeness are like the feelings of when you were a little baby, I mean getting into sex makes you feel like that sometimes.

Analyst: It takes you right back there.

Patient: And then we were talking about being more manly, being like the men at work, being more manly trying to be around women, in just an equal way, instead of being like a boy or child, or trying to be in some special relationship

Analyst: What did you mean by special relationship
Patient: I don't know, that's a word that you used once about our relationship.
I mean special, like you want to be special for someone, you want them to keep on relating to you, no matter what, no matter how you test them.
I have to sever my relationship with her, uh, get to make it right.
Analyst: Sever the relationship?
When you were just talking about special relationships being one's where you don't cut them off...
Patient: Yeah.
Analyst: That they would be someone who would stick with you in spite of your attempts, to dismantle it . . .
.Patient: I was getting off track a little bit ? . . .
Analyst: Maybe it is right on track. . . Opposite.

Patient: The opposite?
Analyst: Yea and then your next thought was of severing a relationship.
Those things are connected in your mind.

Report
Here is some of Anna Zane's treatment plan as presented to her supervisory authority as part of her PhD candidacy in clinical psychology about the analysis she was conducting with her patient Walker Underwood.

Although Walker Underwood reports marijuana use, and affinity to the slacker life style, it behooves us to use therapy to explore the underlying causes of his self medicating behavior rather than the chemical nature of his addiction. The addiction is a symptom of lack of coping skills as well as difficulty engaging their environment,

Walker Underwood is a 37 year old Caucasian male who is currently seeking counseling in the Grove St. clinic. His presenting symptoms were recent break up in love life and unstable work history. WU does have a high level of education.

Mr. Underwood claims that he uses cannabis "to overthrow the tyranny of the super-ego critic" and that makes it possible for him to engage in his all-consuming passion for creative writing.

Mr. Underwood may have developed a negative self-view as a child because of his lack of intimate connection with others around him. Mr. Underwood may also be afraid of the level of intimacy that is required from any non-superficial relationships, because his parents did not model intimacy for him. However, he masks these fears with being a people pleaser and a light hearted joker.

Addicts often are ill equipped to deal with strong emotions, leaving them pre-disposed to drug abuse, and at even greater risk for relapse.

Freudian psychoanalytic theory associates addiction with the oral stage, the first need-gratifying stage of development.

Opiates were said to produce a state reminiscent of a blissful closeness and union with the mother, which resulted in avoidance of separation anxieties aroused by the adolescent dependency crisis. Addiction theories all tell us that drug and alcohol abuse act as a defensive strategy that bridges the gap between a person's functional and defective ego, allowing them to cope.

At another soiree at her place, Ruth did feel it incumbent upon herself to point out Anna Zane's betrothed. Seeing this handsome Neanderthal relieved Walker from feeling like he had to seduce Ms. Z. For now he knew there was no hope of it.

Therapy is a journey into your mind. Your mind not your ego knows what is best for it and wants to divulge this truth to you. The therapist is a guide you have hired to go along on this journey who presumably knows the way.

You have to fight a spell with a spell. The therapist is weaving a spell. The analysand is trusting, and becomes more sophisticated and grows. The analysand is also manipulative, the two are working their way into a difficult alliance. The analyst seduces and controls the analysand. Walker wouldn't admit it, but he might have taken his frustration in the analysis with Ms. Z out on a surrogate Ms. C. Freud did say somewhere that being in analysis brings out the worst in people. Anyway it is not so much "taking it out on," though sometimes the sex did approach the fevered fervor of a Hungarian grudge-fuck, it is a man and a woman trying to get to a more liberated physical way of being with each other. Trust, and dominance; trust and submission. It's an age old story. Boys and girls make much fun for each other.

The therapist has to invite and encourage with a kind of professional warmth. She has to tread the fine line between appearing as a friend and confident, while at the same time be a fair witness in the service of the truth. Anna Zane had these reasons for her performance. First, she had to win him over to therapy, it was a kind of religious conversion and luckily there are little manifestations of the power in the beginning — just the act of someone paying attention to you and listening to what you were saying was beneficial. Second, she needed to have and keep clients in order to get experience to get her PhD. Third, she knew she had to set up the transference. Last she was genuinely interested in Walker as another human allowing you into their world in a most intimate way. And it was this countertransference that would give her the insights to his mythological utterance but yet which had to be watched with suspicion lest it be exploited, seduced or otherwise compromised in pursuing the possibility of them coming to understand the true nature of mind. Being in therapy is like having a dog or a child it is a commitment where you are bound to spend time with this other. And make good use of the time to study yourself and the obstructions to intimacy.

Ms. C felt like Walker didn't always take her seriously.

She was telling her friend and confidant Ruth: "My boyfriend constantly teases me and psychologically argues me out of my stance. The other night when we left your party he coerced me into giving him a blow job in the front seat of the car. He just pulls over to the curb and pushes my head down into his crotch.

"I think my boyfriend is trying to turn me into a slut."

Wordstar

Ms. C had just finished taking a word-processing class at Vista College in Berkeley and she got Walker started in word-processing too.

The word-processing class allowed him to type up his novel on a word processor and he could see the value of being able to work on the mechanics of writing without having to commit it to paper as a typewriter does. This was huge, and in fact word processing was the killer application that made the personal computer at first. Like many all over the country, Walker's first introduction to personal computers was studying Wordstar.

His stint typing up his novel at the city college campus on Milvia St, lasted a few months; he made sure to keep failing the final so he could take the class again, just to get the lab time on one of the school computers. But there wasn't a lot of time to appreciate his new novel because learning word processing gave him a new skill which catapulted him from the $15 / hr. construction job down to the $10 -$12 / hour office temp jobs. The whole country was moving from productive useful blue collar jobs to meaningless discon-nected data mining information processing. Somehow our school system had sold us on the idea that white collar was better. At least as far back as high school that had been the message. Vista College provided basic services primarily for the benefit of the downtown office world. These trade schools were practical and related to the community that way. It was good for enrollment. It looked like most people worked in offices now. He got pretty good at Wordstar. Typed up the whole book on the green screen. Printed it out in the fan-fold perforated paper of the high density dot matrix printer in its sound proof booth.

The novel was a roman à clef about the tantric Buddhist sex commune that had recently imploded. The story is true, only the names have been changed, to protect the innocent. Walker had it typed up on his old mechanical Underwood. And was retyping it into the Wordstar program and saving it onto a floppy disk. They had the program in the C:\ drive and one saved his files onto a big DOS floppy in the A:\ drive to take home.

When it was done he said to himself: OK. Now I am a novelist. Walker considered himself a part of the San Francisco beatnik school. He had been totally enthralled by Kerouac since high school. Walker loved how Kerouac wrote from the right brain in jazz riffs. It was touching how Jack loved his friends and saw through their human frailties to their archetypal core and tried to hold them closer to himself through his writing and for them all to go over into immortality with him. Everyone should have such a friend.

Walker didn't want to write in some genre, western or thriller or fantasy or spy; didn't want to have a bunch of violence, no head bash, no car chase. If you want that stuff you can go to the movies or watch TV. For Walker the hero is someone trying to create truth and beauty in poor conditions of urban oppression and meanness. For Walker, the ideal of writing was the letter. When he wrote he thought of it as a letter to a friend: somebody he loved, somebody he trusted to be able to say things to, important, intimate things. And this imaginary correspondent was somebody he wanted to let know him. Someone who he wanted to make laugh. The epistolary novel is bottom-up; it is a weaving of a great many improvisations that have to be related to other improvisations, like creating your own jigsaw puzzle pieces without knowing what the grand scene looked like.

Like Borges and Sartre, Walker was interested in a literature of knowledge. Yet he had grown up in the modern world with its mythology of science. So he wanted a kind of abstract science fiction in which the characters were probes into information. And under the influence of Jung, he wanted a writing as active imagination, writing as recollection, writing as spiritual practice. The writer was an experimental artists performing the phenomenological experiments on himself. He was an avatar of a semiotic space drifting into the magnetic resonance imaging of signs coming from the real world and the world given to him in dreams created by the Self. He was a conduit out of a tunnel into the psyche, out to be integrated into the story of his tribe in their time. These were his idealistic intentions anyway. Though Walker wondered if there might have been a shadow aspect to the whole novel operation — some kind of getting even with the commune for how they influenced the girl to reject him. At the same time Walker had so much respect for the bravery of intention of the commune that he wanted to write its history in such a way that one could use the book as a blueprint to construct a Sangha to work together on the utopian dream. He thought of the book on the scale of *Ulysses*. Where Joyce had created a simulacrum of fin de siècle Dublin, he would in *Dolores Park* document the flowering of 60s idealism in San Francisco.

So yes Walker was exploiting his real life for the sake of his art. That is the beatnik way or way of the psychological novelist. Walker often heard himself say: People really need more real intimacy in their lives. I want an art that was a spiritual practice, like thanka painting. If it got known. . . it would be nice — you could eat for example. And not have to live the life of a breatharian bricoleur in ceaseless poverty. But fame wasn't what his quest was about. It was service, to the ancient feeling psychology of man. Trying to let it find him in our time.

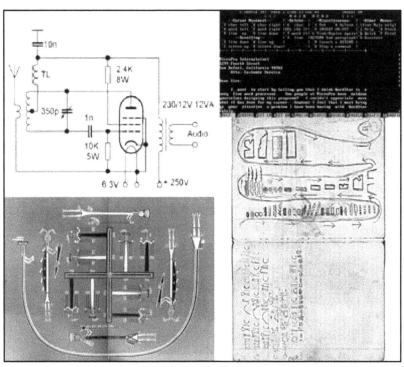

Myth Radio, Notebook Thrall, Wordstar

Walker tried to talk about his writing in therapy but knew a lot of Freudian type therapists thought this behavior was being too involved with thinking and avoiding feelings.

"There is a muse behind my desire to communicate by writing," he said, "probably my anima."

He waited to see if she would react to this concept he had started to use from Jung. She looked puzzled.

"You know," he continued, "I have to say that it was my mother who got me into in poetry. I remember being quite taken with words. They were kind of magical. They were pictures and sounds together. In 3rd grade where you were supposed to use the words of the spelling list in sentences, I used to make these giant sentences concatenating all the words into one sentence. And then enjoy the strange statement proposition it made."

Ms. Z appeared to be listening.

"I think she was what they would call bipolar. She loved playing piano and drawing and verbal play (slang). She had a sharp wit. Though she only went to high school, and did believe in resurrection, and did not believe in Darwin. She could get really wound-up hysterical at times.

He did not mention the time he saved her from drowning and how she panicked.

"The only opinion my father had of poetry was that 'it is for queers' and that was his final judgement on the matter. I never saw him open a book."

Walker WAS worried that he was breaking a confidence in writing about the group therapy session of the commune. He was betraying not only the confidence of friends but also the fundamental premise of therapy: That what is said in group therapy is not repeated outside the group.

But he persuaded himself it would be terrible not to. It was a privilege to fall into this great experience with therapy

and Buddhism and an honor to receive it. He felt he HAD
to share it. He had to write about it to make sense of it. He
was going to protect his friends, he was going to honor their
intentions, if not their actual actions. This is not going to
have any horribly poignant constructions because though
they are true in life, they are fakey in fiction. Actually the
death of the head guru was that horribly poignant. It was the
first experience of someone he knew dying and he was still
trying to understand it.

Walker missed having anyone to bring these misgiving
about his art to. He had never gotten any good understanding
about it from anyone in life, except his friends at the Blake
St. Hawkeye theatre. And they might be shining him on
too. He understood that therapists see it as intellectualizing
feelings. So it just wouldn't do to try to involve this shrink in
his aesthetic struggles.

He also knew that therapists are trained to see more, to
read more the signs of what goes on inside their struggling
selves, for we all struggle with the same thing. Though long
term you were supposed to find your way back to the child
within. You can use the integrating of past experiences; see
how your ego learned to split-off (repress, defend against)
painful experiences. You can see your own mythology and
find your way past whatever shapes your complexes have
constellated into. To find your way out of this labyrinth into
the creative. The study of psychology was a good way to get
in touch with parts of himself that are being (re)-presented,
discussed, understood, analyzed in the current free association time of the session. The past was able to come more
to the fore. This would be gestalting the past and perhaps
reframing it. No doubt he projected these attitudes: I was a
frustrated writer. And: My therapist, as other women, has this
pre-disposition toward therapy that is more Freudian with
new terms.

Walker asked himself: How did I get inspired to be going down the path of creativity. Isn't everyone? Was there some inception I gave myself? A commitment to the muse.

It started when he was too young to realize that such a covenant took control of your life. Still, it is how he wanted to conduct his life. Though it made it iffy for him in the work world. He had to be available like a surfer waiting for the call from the involution ocean. It was hard to look at it: Wow these are some of the memes or inceptions vying for control of my life.

Walker did let Ms. C read the manuscript, because he wanted her to know him and what he was trying to do. She thought the sex fiends in the commune were horrendous. Or so she said.

The Wordstar class had given Ms. C a new skill and she was soon working as a typist for some personnel department. At tea with Ruth. She was talking to her friend:

"This unemployment is really worrisome. Ever since I got downsized from the day care it has been slow finding another job. I'm glad to get this.

"Thank god I have my own house, and a lot of activities. Dance class. Working out at the Gym. Baseball, but I need to find a real job.

"Walker has been kind to me during this time. He gives me validation and praise, he doesn't think I'm completely worthless. I don't want to lose all of that.

"I have friends, but no lover. You know I've been engaged a couple of times but it got broke off. My parents are gone.

"I am looking for some kind of deeper relationship with him, maybe it is too much to ask. But even if he is just using me for sex it's far better than what I had to deal with, no job and on my own."

Poets Essayists and Novelists

Walker was talking to his therapist Ms. Z in session.

Patient: (Sigh.)
> It is just a crummy job and I can't get anything else. And they were going to cut my phone off today because I didn't pay my bill in time. And I got really angry.
> I sent off to PEN International (Poets Essayists and Novelists) to try and borrow a little money to pay my phone bill. And I wrote them this 12 page plot outline. Kind of, I don't know, all a very un-businesslike letter. Telling them how I had to type this beast up on WordStar at my adult education computer class which I continue to fail so I could continue to use WordStar to do word processing on my book. And now I was ready to unleash this intense beauty on the world. It was funny, a sob story to see if . . . to see if I could get money out of them. It is this Writer's Guild.

Patient: (Laughs.)
> I don't know who they are. It was sort of fun doing it though. . . you know. I was imagining some secretary getting this huge letter and a bunch of writing in the mail and didn't know who it was from. And they had to look at it through their own curiosity. But anyway I've been feeling just kind of high and low. All this being out of work. . .

The Kelly Girl

The agency came and recruited Walker right out of word processing class. He passed a typing test to get the job.

At the Kelly Girl agency all around the meeting room little pink post-its had been stuck to walls with suggestions and saccharine wisdom about spirit. He was attending some kind of indoctrination on how to be a Kelly Girl. There were pictures and magazines of color-coordinated dresses and blouses. One was supposed to look professional.

The assignment was to a mega commercial real estate firm headquartered in downtown Oakland. It was in a high rise overlooking Jack London square. Now Walker too joined the hoards of workers on BART to get there. The heavyweight real estate cartel owned a lot of downtown Oakland as well as much of California — every where you looked. He was somewhat amazed to get $11 /hour to spend all day in their office, occasionally typing a few pages of this or that. It was quite different from tromping around in boots, swinging hammers and sawing boards on a construction site. He was in the temp pool of the corporation. In Walker's situation —here was this older white guy when they were used to docile young women — Walker sensed that he was part of fulfilling some requirement to demonstrate equal opportunity of the sexes. If they had not hired some men, then they might have gotten a sexual law suit or something, he didn't know; politics was not one of his interests. He was an alien in an strange land.

His being male did confuse a number of the Grubb accountants. They had difficulty asking him things and probably saved them for the "regular girl" when she got back. Consternation drove home the importance of sexist social relations in the corporation.

The gig wasn't bad. He had a great view from the thirty-seventh floor of their tower on Market street in downtown Oakland.

And he could look all the way down Broadway and back to Berkeley. It wasn't that long ago when he drove a cab through Oakland back in the era of hot pants. He used to stop at Soul Brothers kitchen on Broadway. It was like a concrete bunker in there. The lady behind the 2-inch thick transparent plexiglass bullet-proof wall dispensed the awesome barbecue to die for through a pull-down slide-out drawer. Someone asked them, "What's this big wall for?" And the plus sized sister in missionary-white said "It's to keep them out there and us in here."

I am getting a slice of their sweet potato pie.

Walker found that most of the Temps were like him in that though they worked in an office, they self-identified as dancers, photographers, artists, etc.

He began working on a story about his painter friend Peter Wolf. He did not yet think to bring in a floppy and do his own work on the side; besides it was a Wang, though it must have run Wordstar.

Walker said to himself: God I feel like a lowly grub doing this job. If you live your life like I do, never taking a job unless you absolutely have to — we used to say that we lived underground like the Cong — then you might end up at the age of 37 working as a male Kelly girl.

But at least is was something; the construction jobs weren't happening. And the indignity of this kind of work would only be for a short while because he was a temp. That's what made it doable. A few bucks to keep body and soul together; pay the rent; put in enough time to get on unemployment. That would be his work pattern for the next many years.

Mandala — Defense Mechanisms

Walker wanted to know himself underneath the defense mechanism behaviors or the complexes — how they have a hold on your personality.

Books he was reading say the primitive defense mechanism from early immaturity — denial, somatization, hysteria, hypochondriasis —which he saw a lot of in his mother she could go pretty hysterical, and she was an inveterate hypochondriac generating symptoms in the body where no physical cause is discerned — with shoe boxes full of pills. And she was very narcissistic at the end, it was all about her.

If something bad happens to you, you use the defense mechanisms available to you. In fact they are a kind of sign that reveals a lot about your personality.

If you are a narcissist say, and you are constantly trying to appear as the greatest, constantly having to prove that you are the best, insisting you always come out top dog in every situation, winner of every contest, indeed every encounter gets turned into a chance to demonstrate your superiority, then you are probably operating from revenge from having been in a subservient position.

These defense strategies bespeak a soul so beaten down it was painful to think about it. And he felt sorry for contributing to it. He set about becoming aware of these defense mechanisms so he could avoid ending up like that. And make sure he didn't let it happen to himself. Walker felt that learning this stuff from his own experience would help him become a kind of psychologist or liberating agent, or artist, one that has learned to observe in this space of ideas and unconscious forces.

And that narcissistic hungry ghost projection out onto the world of the rage you feel for having been slighted drives you into accumulating way more than is necessary for survival so as to set up ramparts and buffers to insure that you are in a higher status or position. That narcissistic drive becomes your main mode of dealing with the world. Projection is out of hate for having been in that suppliant position. Hate uses the energy of revenge which is a primary evolutionary archetypal way of being. It is symbolized by the snake in the old mandala.

It takes a lot of practice to become aware of your defense mechanisms because they are unconscious, automatic and autonomic. This "intuitive" or predisposed way of action is second nature. The cells are first.

For example suppose your mother (or wife) comes home in a bad mood and yells at you about the house is a mess. If you say the house isn't messy and you don't know what she is talking about, you are in Denial. However if you blame it on someone else, you are in Projection.

Or if you say she should relax and not worry about the mess; or you just ignore her and go on with what you were doing, then you are in Dissociation.

He started writing little versicles to help remember the defenses.

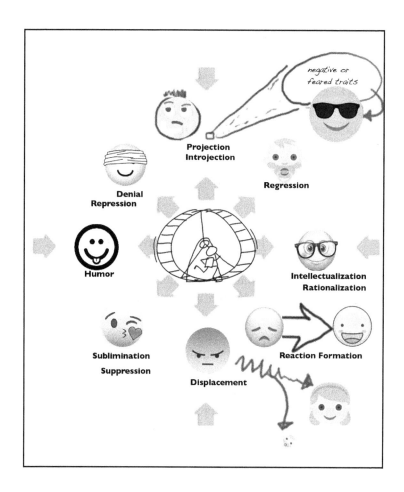

Some Defense Mechanisms on the Samsara Hamster Wheel

If you think it is your fault
and they are a god, and you are just salt
then it is Reaction Formation.

if you bitch out friend and stranger
to avoid the fear and danger
then it is Displacement.

if you scape goat someone
just for "fun" because they are "un"
and different from you
then it is Projection.

if you avoid because afraid
of the anxiety and anger you feel
then you are Avoidant

You have to catch yourself in the act of Projection or
Denial or Dissociation. How do you do that?

You have to get your own internal Inquisitor going. This
pang or wraith of self consciousness is not quite accusatory
until it switches and then it is. Essentially it is your guardian
trying to bear fair witness and help you find the truth.

In the throws of denial you might notice a voice inside
yourself repeating phrases over and over. It is the samsara
hamster on the wheel, admonishing actions to take. This
defense mechanism hamster is an allegorical creature
dwelling deep in the self-delusional mind; it is particularly common among criminals. They can explain away
anything. "And then the gun just went off." "Well he left the
drawer full of money unlocked." From birth, the Rational-

ization hamster enters a symbiotic relationship with its host, whereby insane cravings to do something with bad outcomes gets him to spin its wheel really fast. From nothing the magical samsara hamster wheel can spin long stories of neat rationalizations for the mistaken efforts.

To get off the wheel, to get off the drama triangle you have to step off and observe your thoughts. Mindfulness is paying attention to your thoughts like you would to a dream.

These moments of lucid freedom will flourish for you.

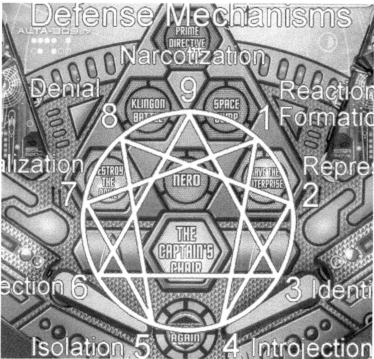

Defense Mechanism Pin Ball

Walker for a while there, was afflicted with Beginning Psychology Student Syndrome, where it starts to seem like you have all the defenses mechanisms in service of all the personality disorders you are learning about. He felt like his hamsters had been turned out onto the playing field of a pin ball machine bouncing around among the red rubber buggy bumpers of defense mechanisms.

If the Doc says you're gonna die
and you say no way I'm too spry,
or that the doc must be nuts
Your are in denial.

But if the Doc says you're end of tenure is nye
and you say its God's fault
why would he do this to me
You are in Projection

now if the doc says you're on your way out
and you only have so long to live
and you start designing the awesome coffin
you would be in Dissociation
or Reaction Formation.

But if you are sad and get back to normal
and decide not to waste you last while depress
then you are Suppressed.

if the doc said your number had been pressed
and instead of being depressed
you got into extending your feelings
into an intuition entrained into art and thought
your would be in Sublimation.

The Concrete Man

At the Hot Tub

Walker took Ms. C to a hot tub. It was a classical California experience; she had never been to one. The spa was in a nice light-green tiled building on San Pablo Ave at Solano in El Cerrito. You paid to the young healthy folks working the front desk, and then you were given towels and a key to the tub room. You entered through your assigned change room with benches and clothes hooks. This opened out to a private outside hot tub, surrounded by stone walks and wood benches. It was nice. There was a tree, and the sky above the wall and then a roof. There were showers.

Going to a hot tub was going to a private place of secret pleasure. Good clean innocent fun soaking in a hot bath. With the one you love. A steamy, warm, bubbling hot tub. As hot as you can stand it for as long as you can stand it. There are few things better in life. Until the hour you paid for is up. They let you know, a bell they ring from the front desk will sound in your change room.

Walker and Ms. C both felt exposed when they got naked in daylight; and tried to be sophisticated about it. But it was too hot. It started in the little dressing room before they even went out into the showers before they got into the hot tub. She has her foot up on the bench and is rolling stockings down her angled leg. Her bum just above the hem of her mini skirt. Walker had coerced her into wearing it.

She looked when he pulled off his underwear, standing there before her and letting her see what she had not gotten a good look at in the light of day before. His body was white and lean, hairy and bony and had its own distinct smell. She had felt the weight of it — delicious, hard flesh pressed against her own body, it was impressed on her now. As was hers on him.

They got into the tub, slowly. They were trying to act cool but her . . . but their . . . pulse was racing; not with fear, but with arousal.

In the swirling hot water he reached for her to pull her to him. They could be weightless like astronauts. She knew she was teasing Walker by making a play at pulling away and being shy and making him reach for her. Walker grabbed her around the waist and pulled her onto his lap.

He grabs one ankle and places her foot on his thigh, then does the same with the other foot. Then he cups her buttocks in his hands and pulls her in tight. She can feel his hard cock between her legs. Her legs fall all open to him. He gently runs his fingertips along the length of her pouting pussy lips. She gasps and inhales volubly. He gently spreads her lips. Ms. C moans softly, deep in her throat and pushes back against his stomach, "Mmmm, yesss." she murmurs.

With both hands he holds her tighter to him. His fingers touch the entrance to her cunt then moves further down to lightly drub on her anus, causing her to wriggle and convulse in his arms. He drubs it on her clenched anal pucker. Then moves his fingers back to her heated, swollen labia for a few more seconds, enjoying her sighs and wriggles.

Then after a few more seconds of teasing to heighten her anticipation, he pulls back her pussy lips and gently rubs up and down the length of her little clit. Then insinuates a finger between her pussy lips, and is surprised at a stream of slickness coating his fingers up to the knuckle below the water. He slides it out over the top of her clitoris. He does this back and forth. He reaches further and further up her and then out of the tight embrace of her cunt. "Yess!" She hisses.

Back and forth, his hands shuttle between her legs, swapping fingers with each gentle thrust into her body, Alternately teasing her clit and her ass hole. "Oh Yess! God yesss!" she moans in a husky groan.

She reached down and gently enclosed the head of his penis with four fingers of her hand and drew upward. He shuddered and moaned.

Cora and Walker were completely melting, their body temperature was hotter than the water. They poured out sweat. It feels so good to be weightless, he could lift her and slide her up and down on his cock if he wanted to.

When he hauled himself out and was sitting on the edge of the tub with just his legs in the water she came over to him, got between his legs and kissed the head of his hard cock sticking up at her.

She let her gaze fall freely along his body as she stood their squeezing tightly on his erect penis looking him in the eyes feeling her power over him.

She took Walker's cock into her mouth. It was large and very hard. She was letting herself feel it with her mouth and tongue and throat as he had said. And it felt incredible! It was much fun and she really liked to do it. And he liked it when she sucked his cock. And he knew she liked doing it! She was good at it. She was a natural. She was oral, she loved chocolates. Sucking cock for her was like a cigarette habit, she had to have his dick in her mouth often. Yes, he thought, I'm down with that.

She sucked his cock, with her eyes looking up into his as he had asked her to. Make eye contact. Then they changed places and he licked her pussy. There was a lot of slow purposive passion, real affection, evident delight.

While still hot and naked in the dressing room as they were standing, about to get dressed, he lifted her right leg and put it on the bench and from behind held her tight to him around hips and slipped his cock up into her wet pussy. They pressed their bodied together strongly, trying to push into, and draw up the essence of, the other. So that they could be for a while one body, one point of connection, one heart.

Cora and Walker were completely melting and they couldn't dry off. He told her not to wear panties under her skirt when they were getting dressed to leave. Outside they were sweating when the went out into the light. They couldn't wait to get back to her bed and continue. She enveloped his cock in her wet snatchel.

After the passion in the hot tub, Walker found himself thinking about her a lot. He remembered and relived in detail the moments of hot sex they got into. Almost as if it were happening to someone else. For once in his life, he felt really empowered in sex. It *was* possible to get a more spiritual abstract distance sometimes,

Getting into sex invites one to be taken over by the archetype of love; or dominance and submission which is it physical representation. It was like indeed the two of them were avatars of the self, representing the male female generative grinding of opposites.

He had to admire her, this lonely woman making her way in the world without anyone, opening herself to him sexually, and he thought for her it was sometimes motivated by love. For him it was motivated by a kind of spiritual quest, a kind of Buddhist bonhomie of compassion.

Walker endeavored to teach Cora how they made love in the House.

"First and foremost be present with someone who is helping you get to your feelings. Don't be somewhere else in fantasy like some image from a magazine. Let your heart hook-up in eye contact and be more present."

He was always trying to get her to be more present;

because often he sensed that she would go off, and be in some kind of fantasy, like: "it's a woman's duty to satisfy her man, regardless of how I feel about it." It was like that because then women didn't have to run the risk of initiating sex. He wanted her to take responsibility for her own pleasure. Moreover wanted her to get really excited and turned on and feel her own power and desire.

Above all the idea in tantric sex is that one convinces oneself that they are in pursuit of some high spiritual motive accessible through the doorway of sex. The cunt is the doorway to the soul. This liberates the (repressed catholic) mind from feeling like they are just in pursuit of getting off.

And this sexual work really worked out well for her, for both of them. She turned out to be amazingly hot. Walker was shocked, she was multi-orgasmic squirting hot. It made him feel like a stud, or a slave master, or a whore monger. He had never felt more in-command. No it was not so much in command as it was that he had come into his own body — at last! Or at least a more relaxed and purposive owning of what was going on in sex.

For example once he dared to say to her: "I am going to use you vigorously, my dear."

And he tried not to blush, and she tried not to blush, for he had never said anything like that, (and much worse) to a woman before.

Vida

Cora got a job working at Vida, a big biotech company in Emeryville. She could drive her Volvo to work. It was a huge campus.

As Walker's grubbing Kelly Girl gig was short, and he was between jobs again, he would sometimes go to see her during her lunch break. She told him about how the scientists had started giving free lecture presentations on biochemistry and molecular biology during the lunch hour. Walker and Cora started going, it was in a big theatre, and there were some pretty spectacular visual aides on the screen. Walker enjoyed sitting with her, in the amphitheater of bioscience. She had friendships with other women workers there and he could see they were pleased she had a beau.

One day after the lecture, which had run late and most everyone had returned to their jobs, Cora and Walker were among the last to leave. As they were walking down a hall, and after doing a quick look around and not seeing anybody, Walker opened a hall door that led into a janitor's closet. He had worked as a janitor before, and this was a nice big closet with lights and a table, and it was unoccupied. He figured it was safe to assume the cleaners were at lunch.

Ms. C was somewhat surprised at this whirlwind play-assault.

In the closet she said, "What the hell! It's too dangerous."

They were getting to be much better at sex, and had practiced the Quickie a couple of times, once when Walker pulled over in the car and had her give him a blow job in the front seat. Another time in an elevator at the Claremont Hotel. There he did think to scrutinize the ceiling and all around to check if there was a camera in the elevator and he didn't see a lens. But maybe they are immortalized on some security tape somewhere, him molesting and grinding on her, her rubbing his cock.

He said "Don't worry, darling, lets enjoy." He locked the door to the closet from the inside.

They started kissing passionately.....very hungrily. Walker was squeezing her boobs while French kissing her and he started slipping his hand up under her blouse and fondling her boobs.

She said: "Be careful not to mess up my starched blouse."

He opened her blouse. He reached around and unhooked her bra to free her boobs and started feeling her tits. She was careful not to undress too much, incase they had to make themselves comportable in a hurry. And she reached and pulled his zipper down and he slide his boxer shorts down and she reached for his super hot and hard dick and grabbed it tight. Squeezing and pumping it.

With her other hand she hiked up her skirt from the back and he pulled down her panties a little, enough to get his fingers in her quim and he started fingering her hole. That made her hornier and she pulled on his engorged hot hard dick vigorously, using it to pull his whole person into her. He pulled away and took off her panties, not all the way off, just down around her ankles above her dress shoes with the sensible heels. This, ankles hobbled in panties, was a look Walker really liked. And then he had her bend over on the table and he fucked her from behind. They were standing. He was too tall so he dragged over a nearby box of Drano cans and had her step-up and stand on that. She was bending over on the table and he had his rigid engorged dick inside her pussy, and he drove it in and out very slowly, shoving it up into her and slowly drawing in back out. They were stuck together like two dogs in a lock-up hump. So graceful to move together like that.

She loved it. She was smiling. She came and a trickle of juice ran down her bare legs. He wasn't wearing a condom and after few minutes of this stopped; he didn't want to come inside her. He took a rough brown paper towel from the nearby dispenser to wipe off the back of her leg. Then he slid her panties back up. Then he had to bend way over to force his boner back into his trousers; he tried to stand up straight slowly without breaking it off. The couple tried to arrange themselves as though nothing had happened. Then they slipped out of the closet one at a time. She went first, back to her office. And he headed out of the building back to his old Buick in the lot.

A week or so later, Cora put in a good word for him and got him hired for a little word processing job at Vida, working in the temp pool. And they didn't do the deed at work again after that. They had too much at stake. In the hall if they passed, it was fun to be in this actorly place, so polite like they hardly knew each other. Now they were only comrade coworkers in the information economy.

But Ms. C told a different story when talking to her friend Ruth.

"Walker is much bigger than me, and though he'd never threatened me or be physically abusive, he did mention that I often say to him, 'Don't hurt me.'"

"He is so strong," she said.

Cora felt really held in his arms.

"I feel like he might believe he's my last hope, since I'm older. And I do own my own house. He's really tall. And neither of us were working. We kind of supported each other.

"He encourages me in the exploration of my sexuality.

"The other day he dragged me into a closet at work and he fucked me standing up on a paint can after he forced me to suck his cock. I felt like puking from the stress of the fear that I would be caught and lose my job. He doesn't care, he ruffles my hair like a child, kisses me or tells me he loves me."

"I think my boyfriend is trying to turn me into a slut."

"It seems like when I try to talk to him about some of these things he always manages to distract me."

Cora asked her friend, "Do some of your clients talk about the same thing I'm talking about?"

Ruth found herself thinking, I'd be OK with that. If I had a boy friend.

Walker didn't realize that she would get herself so involved with him; her mind got a little bit fogged up by the sex. He would later characterize their time together as: We got into a desperate draw close then run away behavior; that certainly was what it felt like to me most of the time.

He wondered about why she often said, "Don't hurt me."

Cora said to Ruth, "My friends and coworkers were happy for me, they were glad I was with somebody. It has been a long time."

Ms. C admired him and since she wanted her friends to like him and him to like them, she cut back on the complaining to her girlfriend.

She thought to herself though, He knows how to touch

me and hold out the promise of love. Is it a kind of bribe?

Cora blushed as she thought about when he fingers me in the butt. He tells me, "Don't think of it as anal sex, but more exploring the Muladhara or root chakra so as to free aspects of my psyche centered down there. Shame and being dirty."

I just think of it as a way of making him happy.

She mentioned to Ruth, "We have been together a while. And get close then something happens and he runs away and we break up for a while. Then we get back together.

He insists that I come to his house sometimes."

She did not mention: When we do go over to his place, then I know well enough that we are going to get into all kinds of oral or when he wants something more, like anal sex, he gets me so hot I loose my mind and let him. He knows when to push me down with my ass in the air and fuck me into a drooling mess.

And even if I'm not really in the mood at that moment I know it's something he really appreciates.

Sometimes when we're over at my place and he's not really in the mood he will still finger bang me 'till I cum, even if it's only just to shut me up.

The Electron Beam Microlithographer

It was natural for Walker to get into Technical Writing. He had worked as an electronics instructor at Heald College, a technical school in Concord. To get there he would commute way out in the east bay through the tunnel under a mountain. Sometimes he went with another coworker from Berkeley. At the trade school, Walker had written several lab manuals. And he had written several other manuals at the community college in Austin where he worked before — one for physics in the frame layout of comic book, with actual comics and chalkboard equations. He had been a lab tech troubleshooting equipment there too. So he had some portfolio toward technical writing. He had realized that here in Silicon Valley they were making chips and using main frame computers. So he just started applying for really technical jobs in the paper. He thought his chances were good since he could read schematics and could talk the talk with engineers.

Walker somehow got through the HR process of Manpower. Then it was on to the interview with a belea-guered engineer hiring manager at Perkin-Elmer. He got the job as a technical writer writing up Field Change Notices for the Electron Beam Microlythographer. This huge machine that takes up a room actually writes semiconductor structure into silicon like the way the electron beam in a TV writes image in phosphor coating of screen.

The word processor Walker had to use was run on a Unix mainframe. Walker had an awful time with the SysAdmin. She was this dark-skinned scowling wrathful-deity looking Indian woman. She had henna tattoos and too much eye shadow. Her eye liner was tattooed on too, because this eye liner was even blacker than her own skin. It must have

been made of India ink. Oh! she was frightful. Her name
was Varun. Walker could tell she regarded him with priestly
contempt for he was a nubie, a lower cast user-entity — they
were zombie untouchables, worthy only of sneering thinly
veiled malice: eyes pointed in hatred. This was made all the
more horrible because she also filed her teeth to a point!
Who does that in the modern world?! It was all Walker could
do to look at her when asking for help with some esoteric
command. And what's worse, she had this nervous habit
of letting her mouth gape open and leting her red tongue
loll around and hang out of her open mouth too. It was the
most frightful thing in the world! Walker tried to be Jungian
about it, looking upon her as a guardian at the doorway to
further career. But their encounters were grim. And he had
to at first be constantly bugging her for commands to use
on the hideous Unix text editor — vi, to do documentation.
Looking things up in the manpage didn't help much. Later
the company bought some kind of word processor to run in a
shell script over the raw seething unix c. It was not Wordstar
— which he knew. No, this one didn't even have the banner
of commands across the top. It was frustrating. He just used
the cursor arrows to move around in the document. It was
electric typing. And, this "word processor" program was a
throwback to time-sharing; and like in those ancient days
on the main frame, completely dependent on the central
authority. Occasionally, in mid-sentence their license ran out.
And the thing just stopped.

The level of contempt with which the SysOp held
Walker was palpable. With such utter disdain for his
unctuous dependency she made him feel like the white poster
boy for the great heathen unwashed masses of "User" —
getting their grubby keystrokes all over the inner workings
of her pristine machine. The loathing was not mutual; Walker

tried to humor her, but she would have none of it.

Walker persevered, writing up the Field Change Notices. Every day there were several of these Change Notices to write up for the Electron-Beam Microlythographer project. Walker got them in the form of scrawls, sometimes as bad as cave drawings in marks-a-lot, on a cheap paper napkin, in Engineerese; though usually on paper form documents, filled out by hand. The engineers looked upon technical writing as a kind of secretarial service. His manager was a reserved Britisher; not a bad chap, but perplexed, remote, stoic. In order to write, Walker did have to go into a dark dank cave-like room where the terminal was. He soon came to understood how important documentation control was to the detailed trail of engineering that goes into such a compli-cated machine. Change Orders were a big deal and had to go through rigorous scrutiny all the way up the engineering hierarchy.

The engineers were extremely well paid. They liked to talk about their vacuum cleaners, comparing suction and crevice penetration. They worked behind glass in a clean room, in which particulates were excluded by powerful HEPA filters (High Efficiency Particulate Arrestance). The machine was used for etching the microgrooves in the substrate of wafers. The engineers wore "bunny suits," disposable coveralls with little booties. Contaminates were anathema to the Electron Beam Microlythographer. In that microworld, a hair is like a huge log falling across the road. This vastly complex machine with exposed magnetic coils for controlling the focus of the beam-generating cathode ray tube, now actually wrote by carving structure into silicon at the sub-micron level for the integrated circuit chip. This elaborate regular pattern of inlaid gold stripe highways for electron movement were set out like terraces on the side of

the hill for raising crops. These step-up and down of barriers
and races of circuit runs etched and sputtered into silicon
were like a citadel seen from above. It reminded Walker of
Buddhist monks making sand mandalas. As he raced down
the freeways of Silicon Valley, Walker thought about how
he had started out his life in open fields and forests. Now he
was driving around slotted into the urban canyons.

One time they gold plated an ant. They would look at it
through an electron microscope. And there it was — huge —
coated in a fine shining exoskeleton of gold. It was a bright
colossus a strange statue on the real estate on the chip wafer.

To Upgrade Dreaming

It was around that time that Walker started keeping a
dream diary. He wanted to upgrade his dreaming. To do that
you have to remember your dreams. To remember them
you have to write them down. He even got a little pen with
a battery-operated light that just shined this little light cone
down onto the the line as he scribbled into a bedside journal
page. He was supposed to get up and try to capture what
there was to remember from the dream as it evaporated
with the onset of waking consciousness. (He usually slept
alone. He noticed that you dream better if you don't smoke
cannabis; weed somehow performs the dream function.)

Dreams at the beginning:

> A detached eyeball goes out and is floating in the waves at
> sea. I somehow take it, and since it is cleaned by salt water, try
> to put it back in my eye socket.

Walker thought: Wow! My . . . that's auspicious. It is like
the Psyche has been waiting for me to cross some threshold
to be with it. I mean even I, could interpret this one — the
ocean is the unconscious, or psyche. And, a detached eyeball

. . . is cleaned by salt water — I was being given an opportunity of second sight. This would be intuition.

At first, and for the longest time, Walker the shy and reticent was blanked from being able to do interpretations of the dream. He felt lucky just to be able to capture one and wrestle it down onto paper. Bring it into consciousness.

> *We are trying to climb up a steep hill to a castle. And there are these huge Cossack guards with tall head-gear and long beards and scarves up there. They are wearing great overcoats and they are slipping and sliding down the icy hill to this froze lake down here below where we are. We are trying to get up into this big castle up in the sky.*

In another dream his anima represented herself to him.

> *A pink door opened up into a huge vast dark stormy sky scene. I am looking through the door and there are thunderbolts and ominous clouds moving and swirling about in the distance, portending rain and storm. It was a precipitous drop if you fell from the cloud which I realized as I marveled through that rectangular door at the little rectangular farm fields way below slipping behind as we drifted. I became afraid of being so high up in the sky. I backed away from the door feeling like I had to dig my heels in to keep from sliding out. I quickly closed it. And then there appeared a Las Vegas show-girl type female with a costume of bird feathers and a helmet of bird feathers with a big lyre or Poseidon's prong coming out of the top of it. She was very pretty and glamorous and statuesque in her curvaceous build, but also remote, "on stage". There might have been something "official" or requisite about her beauty-pageant smile.*

Kerouac showed how to keep the dream diary in his admirable *Book of Dreams*. He started with the place. Where is the dream taking place?

Parents in Montreal Dream

I was with my parents and we were trying to get to some kind of a bus that would take us to an airport to get back. I thought my mother had already left.

And I had to go back to the hotel where we were staying, and I realize now it was my sister Joanne's condo. (She died young.)

And I found all of my mother's stuff unpacked. I kept finding her stuff, detailed stuff.

On racks and hanging from the windows and festooned out of drawers. I realized she was not properly packed. As I was trying to get away.

I led her out of Joanne's old condo. She was dragging some kind of suitcase on wheels. And then we pulled up to the airport in a taxi. And my father was angrily waiting for us on the other side of some fence / barrier. I had to get through immigration security. I realized I had left my ID in a wallet in another pair of pants in a suitcase and I ran back out to get it.

It was some kind of crazed scramble, leaving.

Walker hadn't seen his parent's in a dream in a long time. Ghosts of the too soon departed were circulating.

The dream diary answers the questions of journalism —where, who — and what they were doing. Kerouac's dream diary is very inspiring because he throws it down fast-clipped like a telegram, but yet it is right brain and he will follow intimations. Also spelling and word play and puns and poetry occur and he just lets it stay there. It is symbolic. For a long time Walker was not yet able to leap into the interpretation of the dream, to feel the symbolic.

The *Book of Dreams* helped Kerouac to learn how to write the book movie. It is like writing the dream diary. A kind of synopsis style telegraphic, as though sending those words into this fleeting hypnagogic entity evaporating like the shadows moving away from light. Sometimes it is possible to ask the dream to play a movie for you.

Freud called the study of dreams the royal road to the unconscious. The dream diary creates a bridge over the discontinuity between conscious and unconscious. In the space of dreamings one must commit to going on this journey. Walker ran into it.

When starting off on a journey into the unknown you have beginners mind. You are like the fool in the Tarot. Walker was reading a lot of Jung — not to be missed when going through here. To read Jung is one of the great privileges of being human.

> *I started off looking at a newspaper and the headline was in print see P, inciprie in prencipi (that was the basic unit of sensation in Locke?) and then it shifted into this large matrix of cells in a spread sheet and they were about subtle differences of feelings. Ah, man what a trip.*

The discovery of the psyche started when Walker set himself on a program to upgrade his dreams. He believed that this would somehow lead to a more numinous being. Suposedly by understanding dreams you learn to understand the symbolic. Then somehow perhaps by meditation you are able to step back and look at yourself as though you were a cypher or a moment in the unfolding of your mythic destiny. And this seeing or perceiving of realty would have a more numinous sheen to it. He found that by paying attention to his dreams it helped him come to know the Self which was a much more numinous collections of symbolic entities, the ego being only one, that dreams. It became this sweet alternative reality that he could just go into. He started devoting more time to cultivating his intuitive ability and humorously thought of himself as becoming a Master of the Nap. He wrote this poem about it.

Master of the Nap

Somewhere in the between Bardo:
of the ordinary day dream,
to the cat-like sleep of meditation,
to the real horizontal nap,
to the deep dreaming REM sleep of night,
the Master of the Nap can move.

For the price of a nap
the pilgrim can enter the collective unconscious.

In dreams, in dreams the eye of the day
becomes the tunnel of the night.
The tunnel of the night takes you to another dimension:
it is the field of the archetypes in the collective unconscious.

The sight sails on the light of day
and alights on this and that — attention is like a butterfly
unless it is focused like an eye.

A mandala is the third eye, a kind of memory theatre or
mind map of a terrain. Craven images help us recall because
of the extra emotional bits attached to the string.

Where does this string lead? What is it attached to? To these
objects of mind that lead us back into time, so that we can find
our way to know the now.

The Master of the Nap stopped following the Buddhist
meditation tricks of spuffing off the thoughts. Now, he just
lets whatever images circulating out there in the movie of
mind come up onto the screen. He can sense when some
are communications about the dreamer from the great earth
mind, in whose dream we sleep.

To get there into that earth mind he focused on the count
down of numbers timed to the in and out of breath. Numbers,
are the greatest archetype of all. They order the plethora of
forms. You can think of the integer numbers 1, 2, 3 as being

the harmonics of vibes — of all known hue. Though, warding off thought certainly has its place especially at the start of the descent, counting breaths is a good beginning to the fall.

With a little bit of therapy and study you too can become a member of the order of the oneironauts. Jung left us a prescription for awakening in the *Red Book*: Dream and become involved in active imagination.

It is good to construct logical spaces of theory to explain the phenomenology. The adventure of active imagination is to become Involved.

Pipes : Unix : : Logopoeia : Psyche

Walker had to go through a lot of attitude adjustment around his passion for writing in order to become a technical writer. It was a shift from associational to procedural literacy. He felt like he was some kind of representative of modern man who would increasingly have to interface with the machine through algorithms.

His idea of literacy was informed by an early love of poetry, which started in the 3rd grade. They had art class and little Walker was liking art. Then they had poetry in English class, and the poem *The Highwayman* by Alfred Noyes came before him. The child was astounded by the rhythm: [And the highwayman came riding, riding up to the old inn door.] The rhythm was mimetic of the energy of the situation, a horse moving then being brought to a stop. The sound energy was like this whole direct communication that brought him across time to be much closer to the event itself. It dawned on the third grader that poetry was images and music together! He wanted to be an artist and though he wasn't very good at drawing and didn't play music, he could still be an artist with poetry: in writing he could learn to see, like an artist, the numinous. Also he and his mother shared a love of poetry and verbal play. She played piano and could draw and sketch. She spoke French and liked slang, and jokes and word play. She had a wicked wit. SO Walker got into poetry because it made him feel closer to her. No doubt all this gets convolved into his Anima. (Written on the substrate of his being.) Not that Walker and his mother were close: she was hysterical and hypochondriacal in the extreme, and was addicted to all sorts of drugs, and in the end was completely narcissistic, unable to see anything beyond herself. She believed that god created the world; there was an afterlife and she did not believe in evolution.

Walker thought of poetry as the makings, the first impressions, the apriori of a sign; as notes for the creation of structures. Writings were icons. He liked to be in that connected flow and writing down what came to him was how he made sense of what was being picked up. As a teenager in high school he wrote angst-filled poems of longing for freedom and love. No matter where he was in his life he could write a poem. He did that then and is still doing it now. The muse was his first love.

It was a huge shift from associational lyrical writing to logical procedural writing. For one thing in tech writing you never use metaphor.

Now Walker was aware that he had consciously made a change as a young guy after studying Jung, after high school that he needed to develop his thinking and put aside for a while his primary use of the feeling function. He went to university in engineering and physics. So he had a technical background and a literary one and he used one to cross sort with the other in order to look at the same phenomena from different schemas, in order to understand.

Here is how Walker thought of {pipes} in Unix, for example. He understood it through the idea of logopoeia which he first encountered in Ezra Pound. The analogy is this: pipes is to Unix as the passage of meaning is to poetry. He thought about a line of Ezra Pound: "His true Penelope was Flaubert." Look at how the syntax of the sentence carries meaning through several domains. Walker thought the line was Pound making a hidden commentary on his contemporary writer friend Joyce. But then Walker recalled it was about the persona of Hugh Selwyn Mauberley whom Pound created to carry exploration into his sense of how the poetry reading public had different tastes and needs. Hugh S. Mauberley was a communication about Pound's friend Joyce who was deeply influenced by Flaubert. Walker marveled at the density of that line. How it maps the loyal wife Penelope to the painstaking artistic writing practice symbolized by Flaubert. It says: The love and commitment that marriage required, was also what literacy required. (It was also ironic: if you think of Flaubert's most famous character Madame Bovary and how she was a kind of anti-Penelope — not true in her heart. Maybe the line just says stick to your art.)

The line is a marvel of concision, a jewel in a diadem. You have to have heard of *Ulysses* and know how Joyce was influenced by Flaubert. Like "pipes" in Unix logopoeia is like a kind of literate programming language, it calls subroutines of memory and gets them interacting.

Pound and Eliot used phrases sampled from other poetry to set up an associational bridge to and from these ancient works — if you had heard of them. Though part of the California critique of literacy was how exclusive this writing was — only understood by academics. A people need literacy; it was most important to understand your own times through the narrative of us telling ourselves who we are. Chuck Berry and Jimmy Breslin, Whitman and Kerkouac changed the way we look at the world through their seeing and saying.

To Walker, Unix seemed like the far-flung enigmatic

Cantos of the redoubtable Pound. Unix was a vast language system written down and compiled and shared among wizards. Walker realized it wasn't until his generation and computers becoming part of literacy that the poetry Pound and Eliot made of association links from certain suggestive words or phrases across times / locals / frames later became hypertext. Writing is a kind of programming written on a substrate of human memory and emotion, to be recollected and reflected upon and relived in simulation. It is like how with the language that one acquires, comes the ability of archetypes and metaphors and deductive logic to mitigate the deriving of truths from truths as they were stored and run as a program.

In those days Walker related new tech to philosophical things or to quantum mechanics. Or the aspects of the writer. Poem as Matrix. Metaphor as parallel processing. Pipes as mapping. He had a pretty good education and it served him well. Along with everyone else he was moving from an old pre-computer associational literacy to a new algorithmic literacy.

When Walker first heard the term "daemon" in unix, he thought it was some reflection of Maxwells Daemon, a fiction put forth to illustrate the relationship between information and energy. This Sorting Demon was a machine or process that separated hot molecules from cold ones so that then — since there were hot molecules on one side — it would push the boundary into the cold side. Thus the work of moving the piston was from a potential difference of informational increase against disorder. In a way these WERE informational daemons in Unix. Indeed, Daemon stands for [Disk and Execution Monitor]. A daemon is a long-running background process that answers requests for services. In Unix, the names of daemons conventionally end in "d". Some examples include inetd, httpd (the famous web server), nfsd, sshd, named, and lpd.

These imaginative forays across the cognitive divide of science and art were how Walker let himself time-share his life with a job. It ameliorated the wasteland feeling of always having to be working when you have much more interesting and important things to do.

Through his study of dreams in order to learn the art of interpretation Walker found the archetypes of anima and persona and ego and shadow to be useful for understanding the workings of the inner world. These archetypes were like programs running in the background of humanity like the utility daemons of Unix. They are sub conscious; too important to the maintenance of the individual for him to have control. They perform action without user interaction. These terminate-and-wait programs do routing, monitoring, logging (etc/syslogd), notifications (dialogd) in unix; in the human they are the primal emotions of anger, sadness and fear that often get called inappropriately and get stored in repressed memories. These routines become unconscious habits. These utilities stop but remain running waiting to be called upon. They are nature working through the psyche to form mind. In unix the who command calls the whod to find out what users there were currently on the system.

So in Unix, rather than through hierarchical program control, flow was handed down through pipes to daemon utilities that were always running. These pipes were commands like binary operators, whose left and right operand specified the input and output files. Thus a "copy" utility would be commanded by cp Source Destination. (To copy file1 to file2 it would be cp file1 file2.)

Walker also understood this great green-faced Unix

beast to whom he had to relate in a language, by analogy
to the computational metaphor of general abstract quantum
mechanics — in the sense of an operator that changed one
state into another. He remembered the Hamiltonian on basis
vectors: <a | H | b> H operates on a to produce b. H trans-
forms a into b.

Commands in the computer could be thought of as
binary operators, whose left and right operand specified
the input and output files. Thus a 'copy' utility would be
commanded by

inputfile copyd outputfile < i | C | o>. To make a pipeline,
command operators could be stacked up. < i | S + P | op>
This would: sort input, and paginate it then go to an online
printer and print the result. In a higher language one would
write "input sortd paginated offprintd".

Pipes were like the Implication Operator " >". You
would say sort input > pg > opr to mean take this input sort
then paginate then offprint it. The idea is that following the
'>' command may be either a file, to specify redirection of
output to that file, or a command into which the output of the
preceding command is directed as input.

This corresponds to | o> < i | in the bra-ket notation of
Dirac for Quantum Mechanics. There IS something quantum
mechanical about this Dirac-like notation. It was as if you
have this language medium that you could ask it to do things.
Quantum Mechanics gave you this perspective that matter
was *computational* in nature. All this, was part of a great
computer running programs on a substrate of mind. Leibnitz
saw it that way; Peirce did too. Jung and Pauli were developing the analogy.

pleroma & creatura :: mind & substance :: cybernetics &
information : entropy

Quantum Mechanics and its fundamental development
over complex probabilities emerging from a situation of

fundamental uncertainty was about the etiology of matter
being computational. It was like the universe was a mind,
it was teleological, it was trying to organize structures
that could evolve the capacity to feel it, to know it. This is
basically the anthropic principal. The universe is a quantum
field computer whose operating system is thermodynamics.

Dream Interpretation

After a while Walker began to interpret his dreams. He
used dream symbol dictionaries, and just let himself dwell on
the imagery. It was exciting to conjecture, though he did not
feel at all authoritative. There were the CHARACTERS and
the OBJECTS and the ACTIONS to interpret.

Kandinsky Dream.

*We are trying to climb up a steep hill to a castle. And there
are these huge Cossack guards with tall head-gear and long
beards and up there they are wearing red scarves wound
tightly around their necks and tucked into their great big black
overcoats. They are slipping and sliding down the icy hill to
this frozen lake down here below where we are. We are trying
to get up into this big castle up in the sky.*

We are trying to climb up a steep hill — falling off a steep
hill is escaping from challenges/obstacles in life. Failure to
make progress.

to a castle. — castle in the air, desired beauties, safe home,
elegant intellectual discussion

And there are these huge Cossack guards — the guardians
of the unconscious, the parental super-egos

with tall head-gear — {head gear}is the set of received
ideas blocking out the transmissions

*and long beards and scarves up there. They are wearing
great overcoats* — the prophets of old admonishing from a
cold place

and they are slipping and sliding down the icy hill — the
parental figures were in the same predicament as us

to this frozen lake — lake, water represents unconscious , but the frozen surface of the lake means the unconscious is being hidden beneath a transparent hard surface layer.
down here below where we are.

Title of this dream: We are trying to get up into this big castle up in the sky.

Further thoughts association of this dream: It is a bright simple round steep Kandinsky hill with one of his beautiful romantic castles in the sky, like cloud city.

And like in the Kandinsky painting these strong black swatches against the hill and the detail of the cloud abode there are these huge Cossack guards with tall head-gear and long beards and scarves up there on the hill above us. — [what kind of a mood does all this color suggest? — {seeking a heaven}.

Both this group of large guard 'cop' caretaker Cossacks and you are falling down not completing the mission — instead of getting going into your own unconscious {experiences, resolutions formed in childhood}, you are content to remain on the surface just depicting events.

The dream is telling me that to wade into this water buoying me up would represent both the inner and outer issues. You are keeping yourself from going beneath the surface to your foundations/early life experiences/influences {childhood}.

We are trying to get up into this big castle up in the sky. {The castle, having it made. Not having to work being able to create all day.}

Megastructure

A Megastructure in Mind is Quantum Mechanics Writ Large — as shown by Pauli and Jung.

(Fundamental uncertainty, probability, projection operators on energy)

Walker had this dream:

In my dream last night I saw a dark room crisscrossed by red laser beams. It appeared to be an omnidirectional, motion-detecting, guarding system. I wondered what jewel was behind all this high tech protection.

At that point I awakened. After marveling at this skein of focused light beams I tried to get back into the dream, and become lucid in the space. But there was only the image that remained, it would not animate and unfold as a movie. It was just a sense memory from a dream.

I got excited that this was some kind of matrix / mandala / yantra I was being shown, an inter-dimensional portal — a door to parallel space.

Now I know the door is there. I just have to go through it. The dream was using modern technology to show ancient sacred geometry. Though we didn't see, we know a god is present when this excitement lights up our psyche.

With "skein" I think I was cross sorting seine or weir of a fish net, with a space of fiber bundles or beams in space. A ball of yarn fiber is a skein. But a volume of space pierced with straight lines is a . . . I don't know. A brush of bristles? It would be a matrix which would be a collection of vectors, but skewed vectors.

I was looking up the word "logopoeia" the other day and recalled Ez Pound distinguished 3 kinds of poetry: melopoeia, phanopoeia and logopoeia. The first two have to do with sound and image but logopoeia has to do with context and usage. He says "the dance of the intellect among words." He took it to mean using phrases from the past as a kind of historical landscape in which the meaning of the poem was traversing. For example he might use phrases from 3 or 4 different languages and times in a stanza because they are talking about the same myth or archetype but are coming from different cultures and times. They refer to the same phenomenon but don't have the same translational meaning.

Other structures like skein are: Matrix — seems flat, though

it could be multi dimensional. Table (of data) is flat. Database
is connected data elements essentially a table, but they have
intersecting attributes which then become a new table, said to
be the key of the bigger space. I think skein is more like a relational database in that sense, some big phenomena of which
you have only a few tenants or threads or observations.
Walker wrote this poem.

SPACE IS GRAND
The space in which we turn on /
is so grand that
we can no more understand it
than we can sense it.

It is as though the endless distances
in which we turn abolish distance.
We measure what we can move across
and the rest is a container into which we project our god.

When man discovered fire
it was like a little bit of star
had come down into him from the universe.
It began to dwell within him now.

Now from space we see the main thoroughfares of our wold
as paths of light. We see light flowing from traffic
outlining the edge of our world
running wild in the dark night.

And when we are down in it on the free way
we are making time through the parcourse of our destiny.
Each one of us with the mind to see
is a point of perception fanning out
into parallel parsecs to infinity.

And whether we are moving ahead or not
each one is the same with the same rights under the sun.

We see through a window punching out through the surface

of a sphere within a sphere within a sphere.
Like how a star warps space around it.

Because in space without end
there are millions of kilometers and 10 to the 10 to the 10
to the 10 to the 10 times as many millimeters
each waiting to be part of a niche,
to serve and work together to advance The Cause.

We saw in quantum mechanics how the infinite
turns itself inside out so that it can combine itself
with what we need so that we may be here.
Standing on the sun we are exploding out into the void.

We have received a gift that took thousands of centuries
to try and measure this infinity,
as we hope to find others and move from sun to sun,
as we set out to know the measure of space without end
unfolding its destiny through us.

At a session

Walker would be seething. His days were always the
same. Get up in the morning drive an hour to work on high
speed death-wish freeway of rush-hour insanity leading
to then enduring 8 hours of stultifying ennui in a milieu
of competitive nerd macho. Then an hour of high speed
agression with 2 ton projectiles on the free way coming back
to a lonly apartment and walking the streets of Berkeley.

He thought: I am holding on to the hope that the
knowledge gained on the job will be worth the huge drain on
my time and creativity — though there is the money — that
was nice. I am renting out my mind. But not my soul! But
the hard behavior modification of starvation and having to
spend your time in the company of savages at the charity
meal is even more depressing than being employed. How sad
that this is considered "normal" and "healthy," like drinking

alcohol, getting married, and having children. I too was becoming a peasant of the Global Village, wading out into the streams of the information age. Actually I was cannon fodder for the computer revolution. We were energetically dispersing and fanning out like confetti.

Walker was going from mostly unemployed to employed. It was a progress of sorts. Most of his life he had been doing odd jobs, construction work, tile setter. He was OK with not being able to make a living at his poetry and supporting it with paying gigs of some kind. He was a poetry bum like being a surfer, making yourself available for the waves of feeling welling up from the great sea of the unconscious. Creativity is not static, it builds up until it is discharged in the aggressive act. How could he ever connect the passion he felt in the possibility of reflective writing, with the real, the world of valued exchange. He did enjoy the money from tech writing, $25 / hour was a nice jump from $11.

He was writing on the substrate. Material about wafers and clean rooms and HEPA filters (High Efficiency Particulate Arrestance). Written on a substrate. He sometimes picture the real estate of the semi conductor chip as this life is the background of the mandala.

Walker had not even thought much about the creative possibilities in technology when he came out to Silicon Valley. He was a slacker from Austin and his only ambition was to be a beatnik and a writer of true literature. That was always my job, he thought. My passion, my work. But to keep body and soul together I needed food and a place to stay and so I needed a job. That's how he drifted from part time temp, to independent contractor. But the substrate was always beatnik writer, that would not change.

Walker began to think technical writing would be OK: he would get a lot of practice with the simple declarative sentence. He read Fleish-Kincaid on readability and his idea of the index. Walker learned a lot about straight forward business writing. Readability was a function that diminished with large average sentence length and large average syllables per word. Fleish had a formula for it. This gave Walker insight and confidence as a tech writer on how to help people in marketing cut through the bull.

When the contract was up, they offered Walker a full time job. And, they were prepared to pay a bounty to the head hunter for sniping their worker. Walker turned them down. He had to talk about this with his therapist.

Walker let out a sigh. . . Then there was a long pause. Going into patient / confessional mode, he began.

Patient: I stood Cora up one night.
I called her up and there was a big bunch of traffic to come over too and I ended up going to a movie by myself over in the City. I just didn't know how to call her; it didn't work.
I like going to movies by myself.

And the next night I didn't call her or anything. I was just really getting sick of working at the job. I was jammed up with unexecuted ideas I need to explore in my OWN writing. I was supposed to go over and meet some of her friends, I didn't stand her up. I felt like, I don't know, that I was really being asked to do too much. And I was feeling put upon. I was having an awful bored feeling around work. I am being asked to commit too much of my time . . . same time I want to be involved in networking and devote some of my time to that too. Theoretically. . . (He laughs.)
But when it comes down to doing..... I feel very little repayment for the time I have put in. I always feel

like a big brother having to drive everybody around. Organize, and take charge of things, and put my energy into it. I don't feel like I have a lot to put in. I think I was in some way shy to meet the new people that she wanted me to meet. I would have to put on an act with them; though, I wanted to meet her brother. I think that it is something I would very much admire — being he is a mathematician. That sounds real interesting and even though there was some of that enthusiasm in it I felt really lonely and I am just this guy who is got this crummy job and doesn't do anything interesting.

Analyst: So it seems like the job, is making you feel overtaxed.
We need to see how it effects what we were talking about in here.
Patient: Why does this sound like that I don't know about that.
I mean I rejected them. I couldn't call them back if I wanted to. And I was even offered a full-time job.
Analyst: But you turned that into a rejection.
Patient: I did!? How did I do that?
(Long pause in which therapist leaves you to sort it out yourself.)
Patient: It . . . well . . . it does; I rejected them. It doesn't sound like they rejected me.
I mean is it finally comes down to it, I think I have realized, they were not at all paying me anywhere near the kind of money they should be paying me. For the kind of expertise you need to do the job and I just felt like I was exploited and I became kind of outraged after I saw through the game. I wouldn't play it anymore. It
Analyst: So how come you are so easily persuaded to look at it that it was a lost opportunity. And if we are aware

that we have talked about it here before. When . . .

Patient: Well, I mean yes. We said it was like a Father Projection On the Boss. Well I mean, yes. That's the psychological coloring to the whole thing. But really it's the economic issue.

Analyst: You want to justify it in black and white, while you're writing as just economic.

Patient: Well it comes down to that, you know.

Analyst: Well, no it is noting that what you wanted to do is forfeited into a simplification. It happened into a black-and-white picture of the situation too — but now in here we see the things that are more compli-cated.

Patient: Well, That's what happens when I exert the Why command.

Analyst: And I know you're very aware of that and of how very complicated it is.

Patient: Well, not today, I'm not. I would like to know what you mean by, "turning it into a rejection."

Analyst: (mimics him) Not today, not today, I don't want to look at this.

He laughs.

Analyst: I am supposed to give you a hint, and I do it for you. You don't need a hint, is what it boils down to.

Patient: Well what am I supposed to look at, the reason why I feel uncomfortable while being there on the job?! I am in indentured servitude! And need to become a workaholic. And work real hard and didn't hook up with anybody and it felt isolated and . . . I had a lot of projection on the boss, as a father, and although he appeared to be a nice guy to be around, I didn't like him.

Analyst: So that you managed. . .

Patient: Well, it all adds up to that.

Pussycat Theatre

When Walker took Ms. C to a porno flick at the Pussycat Theatre on the border between Berkeley and Oakland, he wanted it to be a nice experience for her. So he chose a Saturday night so there would at least be a few other couples. And there were.

As they were getting ready at her place to go to the movie she asked "What time does it start!?"

He ruefully explained to her: "Oh, I wouldn't worry about it. They have previews of coming attractions. It doesn't really matter if you don't get there for the start of the show. Besides, the plot doesn't really mean too much. Mostly it is about the sex. And then there is some filler — driving somewhere, a plumber comes to fix the sink— anything to get the man and the women or whatever together."

Ms. C smiled a kind of sweetly shocked, slightly imperious, slightly distasteful smile. And nodded that she understood.

The Pussycat Theatre was a fine old movie house that had once been grand but now was serving out the last of her days as a movie house for the burgeoning porn presence. It had the pussycat girl logo, backlit on the theatre marquis above the awning: this is the cat girl with little ears and wearing a porn-actor mask; and with her long pussycat tail in tights she was leaping tall, doing a tour jete in the night above the boulevard, all surrounded in a halo of light bulbs. Under the awning of lights you passed by the now unused ticket taker booth — everything was tile — and there were posters behind glass. Inside everything was yellow tile and the floor had red carpet. A woman sold the tickets and she worked the snack bar too. The pussycat girl logo was on the cups and on the free matches.

Walker did not let on that he knew some of these porn actresses by name, Lisa De Leuw, (Lay-you), Seka, of course. His favorite was Loni Sanders. And here he had taken Ms. C to see her in *Blue Confessions*. And since the ticket taker / snack bar worker was a woman it conveyed a woman to woman message that this was a Pussycat Theatre, safe for couples. They even had their own logo on the popcorn tubs. There was ice cream and candy too. Though Walker wondered how anyone could manage to blithely stuff their face with popcorn while watching a porn flick with all those sexual organs and butts moving around and cocks as big as Cadillacs stretching across the wide screen. But for a surprising number of people, it seemed that eating popcorn was a necessary part of the movie-going experience.

In the cavernous dark, they could see on the screen was a movie about something. This thin Europop electronic sex-music was going. It must have been a fairly notorious skin flick from someone who wasn't just a total schlock-meister. There were also previews of coming attractions. It is becoming somewhat of a mainstream theatre, among liberal people who go in for that kind of thing.

Ms. C had cut her hair quite short, so did not have that outward sign of woman's glorious long hair. She slunk down in her seat, so that her head was just above the top of the chair back. Looking out over all the seats in the cavernous theatre, out to the large stage with the screen one could see couples were grinding away up there. Walker thought Ms. C was handling it well— her first time to see one of these probably. She was not acting shocked or protesting.

On the screen in the dark amid sucking sounds was a huge horizontal cock being engulfed in loud squelching noises. The movie *Blue Confessions* starred Loni Sanders as a psychotherapist having people divulge their sexual story to her over a magic telephone. Which somehow got her involved by teleporting her into the scene, or something like that. One doesn't scrutinize the plot too closely.

Luckily there were other couples in the audience here and there. When Walker had to get up to go to the men's room, Ms. C did give him a somewhat bug-eyed pleading look of horror as if to say "Don't leave me here alone."

After a while of this grinding he wanted to go but she stayed his arm to remain a while. He thought that was good, her showing interest.

She wanted to see a scene where a woman was fucking two men, one in the asshole and one in the cunt. She seemed to get really turned on by that. Hmmm, he thought.

Walker had once seen the porn actress Aunt Peg in the Berkeley Bowl on Shattuck. She was squeezing a mellon in the greengrocers isle. He was slightly embarrassed at being caught letting his gaze rest overly long upon her robust personage. She did meet his gaze with a defiant look of recognition, and the eye-lock was broken with that.

Cinema lets you engage in unchecked gazing behavior. That's what it is all about.

Walker occasionally spiraled down into some depressive activity and even did go to a seedy house of porn when he didn't have a girlfriend. Now that he was in this really hot sexual adventure with Ms. C, he never went. But he still liked the idea of them and anyway Ms. C was curious to see one as much as anything. Later she made some funny comment about the woman getting fucked by two guys: "They were sawing away on her, one in the front and one in back."

Not to be outdone, he retorted: "I believe they call that 'spit roasted' in the trade." She feigned being shocked.

Walker felt a little bad, like it was kind of introduction 101 to some kind of male sexist world. "But really these women were treated well. I worked as an extra in a porno flick. Richard Pacheco got a day's work for a bunch of us from the Pit on some movie he was directing. Several of the actors from the warehouse, men and women did voice and bit parts. The name of it was *Careful He Might Be Watching*."

Walker told her about it in his usual self-deprecatingly droll style. "I can actually be seen in the movie among the passengers on an airplane. We were in a large warehouse somewhere in San Francisco, and inside was the fuselage of an airplane. It was a prop, but it was fairly large like maybe at least 8 rows of seats. Anyway the pilot was supposed to deeply shtup the stewardess in the WC.

"The gig was kind of boring; in movie making you do a lot of waiting. It was catered, there were a lot of women working on the set. More women around then men actually. Even some older women who looked like they could be aunts or moms. We as extras had an acting coach and it was fun, he took us through some exercises to warm up. I think we were supposed to be talking like people. Then after we were there all day they got the shots. The divine Seka graced the set. She wore a nice silk kimono between takes. Of course us anonymous crowd people usually aren't present for the sex scenes. Howie had to really struggle and argue with the cinematographer, who was famous; I forget his name."

During the movie Walker thought about his lifetime infatuation with the form of the female. I have spent way too much time of my life looking at girls and pornography and feeling guilty about it. Good old Catholic guilt. All wound up with your feeling-body all perturbed by masturbation guilt.

I'll have to delve into it sometime, on my own. It would be ego-dystonic to subject myself to it now in therapy.

The music instantly cut to half-naked woman and man with cock, with dubbed moans.

Afterwards while telling Ms. C about his experience working in the porn industry, Walker further displayed his lack of civility by mentioning, "I actually knew some girls who did moan-overs for porno films. Later one or two of them got into phone sex and were making some decent coin, enough to keep them in housing and cooking. But that's another story."

Sometimes the guy who had to switch the reel fell asleep at the wheel, and the theatre got left in darkness. The patrons had to start yelling to wake him up. This happened in your more lower class places. There could be an edge of frightening anarchy about to explode kind of feeling when the surge of outrage at their lot spread through the audience like a foul order from a fart and people started hollering.

When the light came on you could see in the darkest corners of the movie house furtive figurers were leaning over seated figures getting blow jobs —from other guys no doubt. Walker didn't want to see that.

When Walker fucked Ms. C, he really got into it. Especially when she came over to stay at his place. It was like he was in a state of sexual infallibility over her because she had the power to turn him on, or he got turned on by her vulnerability. And because he was not terribly invested in the affair.

After a few weeks he was constantly horny and spent a lot of time hoping Ms. C would have him come over to fuck her. Very soon he discovered how easily she came especially when he hit just the right spot to make her squirt. So naturally he did it over and over. A man likes to feel he's appreciated. He wanted to fuck her like an animal, feel her on the inside. He reduced her to a quivering, twitchy, barely coherent mess, and then continued fucking her for an hour. It felt like an hour long orgasm. Ms. C eventually developed the right mind-set during sex that makes those orgasms obtainable anytime, even when they're just playing around at the hot tub. He marveled at how a woman's body can deliver so much pleasure. When she came over to his place he got her stoned and drunk and it was like he became this porn star / slave master. And he made the experience 1000 times better. Uncontrollable crying out when he stuck his finger up her ass while eating her pussy, squirting juice running from her cunt to her asshole. Her eyes would be rolling into the back of her head, full body shaking. It was good.

Some time later Ms. C was talking to here friend Ruth about him (but was really bragging about her sexuality). "First he says, 'I'm going to have to report you to medical science. I didn't know women can have squirting orgasms like that.'"

"Yes, I believe they can," she had said demurely.

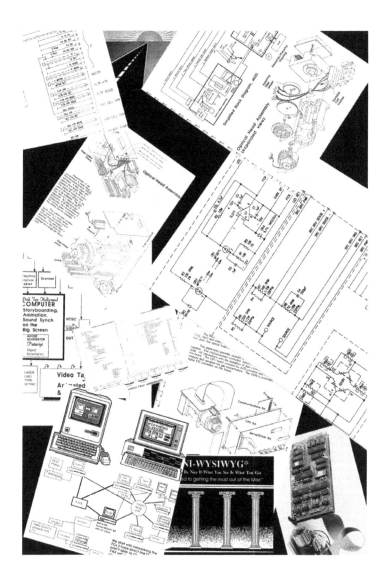

122

Open Systems Interconnect

Walker went to work for Trace Analyzers as a full-time technical writer. With the help of therapy he stayed there quite a while. They made gas analyzers. They had a dominant position in the market place with their scientific instrument. To the company flowed money, the owners were millionaires. That was the first time Walker had ever encountered millionaires. There was definitely an ersatz aura of money about some posh inner offices, with gilded mirrors and fuzzy fabrics on the walls, that Walker did not even see until he was there a while and was actually given the job title of engineer.

The company made gas analyzers mainly for the automotive (exhaust) and the biomedical (anesthesia) sectors. They called their instrument a bench referring to 'optical bench' like a laser interferometer on a stable table the way it shined infrared or laser beams through a gas sample. They were well on their way to developing an all digital system for anesthesia. It was 1987, Walker was 37 and he answered an ad in the paper and went down there. The building in west Berkeley, right next to the railroad tracks was a great vast warehouse complex, as big as a mall with plenty of room for engineering and manufacturing and marketing and CAD and business. It was an interesting industrial area of Berkeley near a little lake that separated the college town from the freeway. Walker could walk; it was 40 blocks but he needed to have a car to run around and do print buying.

Walker's area had a couple of cubicles across a hall from each other. In one cubicle there was a round conference table for spreading out work. The other cubicle was dark and had the computer. This secluded alcove was out of the way — down another little hall. This hall opened up into a great room where Karen had her desk. Her desk was not surrounded by cubicle walls but was open to the passers-by. Then at the opposite side of this room was Don's glassed-in office. He was the head of Marketing. He could be in his spacious office sitting on his plush leather banker's chair with aerated back rest and look out through his large window but he could not see into Walker's dark laird. Walker's "chair" that first day was a turned over waste basket.

Karen's manager was great big Bob, a giant of a man, he looked like a cigarette machine on legs or a refrigerator, walking around the place under neatly combed-over blonde hair. Bob was a Hoosier from Wisconsin. Karen was Bob's secretary. She was Latina with fetching dark looks and a sweet shy conservative disposition. Her desk was not enclosed in a cubicle so she was often commandeered by prowling floor managers for typing and filing organization and other duties. But mainly she was Bob's administrator and he would intercede for her. They were very close, big Bob was her boss and she was his protectorate.

Karen had long curly black hair, she was a very cute girl of Mexican aspect. She was Bob's girl, and might have been kind of a daddy's girl, or just shy, though she bluffed a good game, she acted like she was out in the work world on her own, but there was a vulnerability and shyness to her that was sweet and it brought out the big brother in Walker. Karen could look quizzically at you with these big eyebrows while at the same time look so innocent and capable of being shocked. It made him feel like a heathen bohemian that she would never understand. So that's how she won every body over to her well-being.

Walker got right to work on their manuals, word processing in Wordstar on a hideous XT clone with the green screen. Familiar from school. They just hand you an old paper manual and expect you to just start key stroking; they never seemed to be able to find the file disk.

Now when it came to tech, Walker had a great ace in the hole: his good engineer friend, Kevin from the commune who was attending night school at UC Berkeley. Walker would take home the schematics from work and it was great to flatten one out on the desk and the two of them go all over the bias of the op-amps and where to put the probes to check the signal and what the signal should look like and why. This made Walker popular with the techies because he could confidently talk the talk with the engineers.

The engineers. It was terrible to hear the vice-president of engineering upstairs in huge shouting matches with the head of research. What a shocking and uncouth brouhaha. It was a fierce row. One thought they would go at each other. The rest of the engineers were cowed. Walker had met Mr. Rubinstein, the head of development, a prince of an engineer from MIT. And they were working on a manual for the new digital instrument. The little engineer introduced Walker to the anesthesia bench with this dramatic initial walk through:

"Imagine a car crash. Someone ran a red light as you are going through on green. They unpack you from the wreckage and take you to the hospital emergency room. There the resident anesthesiologist is monitoring the concentration of anesthetic being administered to you — a helpless patient gassed-out on a table. It would more than likely be one of our gas analyzers.

"These have to be exact. The slightest variation in concentration of agents can cause brain damage or even death by cardiac arrest or other means. The name of the gas analyzer we manufacturer here at Trace is the General Anesthetic Digital Monitor and Administrator. We measure the concentration of a gas against a known sample, by means of laser light scattering."

Walker felt sympathy for the beleaguered diminutive scientist and hated to see this quantum anesthesiologist having to go through the stress of arguing with these big screaming mucky-mucky engineering vice-presidents.

It was amazing how inefficient they were at this company. They were giving the paper text of the manual to an out-of-house designer who would re-key it all back in again into a Linotronic typesetter at great cost. Walker started selling Trace on the idea of desktop publishing. He started taking a disk of the manual to the laser parlor upstairs at Kinkos Copy Service on University. There Sandjay showed Walker how to move the files over from Windows onto a Mac. They could format the whole document in Microsoft Word to print it out on a laser printer. Soon Walker was spending a couple of hours every day at the laser parlor. It was an exciting place, ordinary people were helping each other get an education in design. It was a little like a head shop for desk top publishers. This was before people who easily picked up working in computer design became corporate consultants in competition. In those early days, everybody was trying to raise their game, and in exchanging, raise other's. Walker got Trace to do their own typesetting on the Mac as part of publishing the manual. This gave a lot more control over the documents. They could see the value of being able to do updates quicker. Walker started lobbying Trace to buy a Mac. And then a laser printer.

Walker had difficulty asking for equipment, feeling like he was not worthy of their investment. He had to talk about it in therapy, often.

Analyst: So you're really angry at these sort of persecutory purchasing people, and other people at work, who you sort of expect aren't good enough, and are not

going to get you the right kind of machine that you
need.

Patient: (Pauses, thinks) We've been here before . . .

Analyst: And they are more supportive of you than you've
imagined.

Patient: I'm threatened by the idea that this image I have of
my father is not true. I'm threatened by the idea that
he might be something other than what I want to
believe he is.

Analyst: Right. So you try to convince yourself that YES, it's
these people at work that are oppressing me. YES,
I'm being persecuted. Yes, this is a machine-like existence. I'm going to free myself, by quitting my job.

Patient: I know coming to therapy has helped me keep
working. To have to come up with more money to pay
higher fees. And it's had a lot to do with my ambition
and wanting to keep just, I mean , wanting to keep
making money so I could keep coming here. It's been
very helpful.

Patient: It is one of the reasons why I've gotten more and
more involved in work. I think too, dressing better,
just wanting to be like you that way.

Learning page layout and book design and being a
publisher was exactly what Walker wanted to be doing for
work. The Macintosh gave him confidence. It started with
PageMaker. There was so much expertise embedded in
programs like PageMaker, and Photoshop. It was like having a
great, patient tutor always at your side. With visual communication, Walker began to feel the opening up of his right brain
to the language of space.

The increased creative empowerment was such a high that it made him blind to the techno bureaucratic enslavement that was taking over his life and the world of work and the world in general. He pushed many manuals through the little Mac+.

Then someone around the office named Therese started making herself known, as someone who should have some input into how the manual would look. Just because she showed some interest Walker let her make suggestions. She suggested the Lucida font which Walker came to use for all the manuals because it was joyous and open and readable. She was in Marketing; somehow was Don's assistant. And she was somehow assistant to the vice president. This VP guy was a huge hirsute hog who dressed like a don. He bellowed the loudest and had the final say in the quarrelsome disturbing meetings with the quantum anesthesiologist. The porcine potentate had never deigned to notice Walker. So a projection, began to form in Walker's mind and he constellated the man into this high-up, outsized gray eminence.

Therese — unlike Karen, wore sophisticated suits, and was perfectly made up. She always had on a starched blouse and looked very finished and polished, with expertly applied mascara and glossy seductive lips. She dressed for success in sharp little suits and it looked good on her. Since she was Don's marketing assistant, she had his ear, could hang out with him. The henna-haired brunette with expensive faceless wristwatch and was totally at home with the supervisory old-boys. Theresa was always thinking about her next move in the further preponderance of her power and acquisition of same. She had sharp incisors and looked like a man eater. She smirked as she walked across the carpeted floor of the Marketing space, aware that she held the eyes of the company VP in thrall. They smoked together in the VP office. Walker said, "Hi," to her. She nodded and walked wordlessly by.

She did not say what her education was in the time or two they exchanged pleasantries.

Marketing had the job of doing the annual report and the advertising sell sheets. She hired all that out. Other people did cost analysis. Walker told her about getting a Mac and bringing the manual production and the annual report and the advertising sell sheets in house. He showed her how they could be typesetting these documents as they went along, just like they were redoing the manuals.

Walker would go with her to photography shoots. He showed Trace how to get half-tones made at a funky little hole-in-the-wall shop in Oakland. He learned how to supervise contractors, illustrators and other helper artist types. He dealt with printers often. He and Therese were (ad-hoc) teachers for each other.

Desktop Publishing had indeed begun making news. And technical writing was a perfect application for it. Walker was inspired by the beautifully designed manuals coming out of Apple. Plus he was interested in using desktop publishing for his own creative works, and that of his friends. Walker was a no longer young man new to business feeling the necessity to prove himself. He wanted the company to buy this good desktop publishing equipment so he could do his underground magazine on it. The Apple LaserWriter cost a princely $7000 when they first came out. Walker would eventually become an Apple developer and bought one for considerably less.

Walker bought himself a Mac+ and got Trace to buy a LaserWriter. He started writing and designing much more visual, magazine-like manuals about these great gas analyzers. He did go over mechanical and electronic details with engineers, that got revised under their authority and expert opinion. He interviewed engineers and technicians, he asked a lot of questions for clarifications and got the material in the manual right. After a while he thought he might stay there. He pushed many many manuals through that little Mac+ and the LaserWriter while saving them a ton of money. The computer amplified creativity by removing drudgery, it started him on giving free reign to the right side of his brain. He could see beauty was a fine line, an efficient arrangement. Walker did like to actually do the technical part, op amps and transducers and step motor pumps and stuff. It was like being the All Seeing Lord of Electro Mechanical Light Terrain. It was like being phenomenological using instruments to see beyond your own senses. And so he thought to rise in the organization by actually doing the work and making money for the company, being a team player and bringing new technical skills and opportunities.

It was amazing how he would work all day cranking out these manuals. In the year and a half he was there he pushed over a dozen manuals through the little Mac+. Walker loved it because it was quiet, you could hear yourself think, there was no fan! He bought a funny looking elongated chimney rising out of its head to help with the heat convection and extend the life of this hard working companion. He did all the marketing materials, and even a kind of network newsletter. He found himself nearly blind at the end of the day from VDT fatigue. He would crawl home. Walker started going to BMUG (Berkeley Macintosh Users Group) meetings on Thursday night. They were held in the large physics lecture hall on UC Berkeley campus. There was an open question and answer period at the end. It was very charming and enthusiastic young people mostly guys, though nerd girls were there too. One community organizer in particular, Raines Cohen was the spirit of Mac. He rode to meetings on his bicycle with a 20 meg hard drive strapped to his bike rack. The burning question was how this hard drive survived such treatment. The Mac people were like Christians in a lion's den of PC users. The Mac and the PC symbolized the kind of workers they were supposed to appeal to. Macs were for designer types and artists, publishers. The PC was for spread-sheet jockeys and data miners, engineers who connected to instruments. And CAD. It was several years, for example before PCs got speakers.

If you listened to what Users said, you would see most people were overwhelmed by the PC operating system DOS. Some mistakes, especially if you corrupted the autoexec.bat file or the config.sys could be fatal to the machine causing it to irrevocably fuck up and require the OS to be reinstalled again. On a Mac you were sheltered from that level of OS detail. (Perhaps this did infantilize users but you had to get some work done, you couldn't be puttering around in the OS all the time.) The Mac people seemed spoiled and arrogantly entitled compared to the PC workers. The cost of ownership of a PC was way more in terms of time and hassle then its cheaper up-front purchase price would seem to belie.

And these clones were hideous. Usually you saw them in a store where some Asian guy would fly through the esoteric commands so fast that it seemed like slight of hand typing and executing the DOS keystrokes. Their infallible fingers dancing on the keyboard fairly flew through all these database and arcane operating system interactions.

People hired you because of your ability to operate a certain software. If you couldn't operate it then the thought of going to the expense of training you was deemed not worth it and you were passed over. Every PC worker had some horror story but the hegemonic march of the clones proceeded regardless. You have to remember Microsoft was a software company, they made their programs to run on as many democratically cobbled together machines as possible from all over the world. They didn't make the hardware. Apple made the hardware and they had a closed operating system that only their engineers and developers could work with, and they had to make software that was very attractive and made their hardware all the more seductive. Microsoft didn't seem that interested in the Graphical User Interface, the GUI. The early versions of Windows (colored text button across the top) was frightening to look at compared to the keep-calm and carry on black and white and gray GUI of early MacOS. It was a hoot when the first Windows machine got shown at BMUG. Since the charter of BMUG was graphical user interface they invited IBM to show off its product running Windows at a meeting. IBM sent their finest marketing bunny, all dressed for success in the Di Fi bows. At BMUG it was a heathen crowd of unwashed nerds, but their leader had admonished them to be on their best behavior. The BMUGers were not used to seeing women doing a demonstration. They set up the machine, had the hook-up to the big overhead screen, and soon the lady's fingers were flailing away flinging out the keystrokes typing DOS commands. A shocked but forbearing tolerant silence befell the crowd. After a polite interval some guy in the audience interrupted politely and asked, "Will it have a mouse?" The crowd burst into laughter. The lady looked slightly chagrined for a moment. It was clear that they didn't understand the importance of the mouse to the GUI. They still didn't get it but if Mac had it then Microsoft would have to get it. Then later the next version of the Windows GUI seemed unbelievably garish. Windows had no clue what to do with color at this time. But it was color. Toward the end of his tenure at Trace, Walker learned to program and design in HyperCard on the small black and white screen. This constraint insured optimization of screen real estate.

Time or Newsweek had a picture of monks in saffron robs in front of Apple equipment marveling at publishing Dharma.

Now at work they were moving files from PC to Mac; people would bring Walker a file on a disk to print on the company's laser printer across the hall in his other cubicle. After being printed at Trace on the laser printe and proofed Walker could send files by modem to Krishna Copy where they would be output on the Linotronic. Then just go by and pick up the work. Then Newsweek ran a piece on Desktop Publishing. And there in the national magazine was a picture of their upstairs laser parlor at Krishna's. The elegant Sandjay and some of the regulars were in it. It was a sweet time of enthusiastic sharing and cross fecundation at the beginning of desktop publishing; people had not yet become competitive consultants.

Walker put out one whole manual a month for 4 months. Things moved with grace and ease, the people at Trace were pleased. Visiting customers carried away the fine documents he designed and published for them. He even did some photography.

His face was always stuck in the small Mac screen. He was entranced by the Japanese orderliness of the interface and the creative worlds it gave him access too. He talked the company into buying him a big screen. He turned out so much work. And right away he was typesetting the manuals as he wrote them. Don would get Walker any equipment he wanted. He was driving to a photo service to get halftones. Then they got a screen going on a Xerox machine to make halftones in house. Then Walker got them to buy him a scanner. This made Walker's cubicle very popular. People were rolling through to drop things on the scanner. Problem is they had PCs. Few of them even had the small disk, most had those big 5.25 floppy disk of DOS.

Computers were changing how work was done, and it was a very exciting and creative time. It was a gold rush of opportunity. And even though Windows was hideous and clunky, it was what everybody embraced. Apple's slogan at the time was: "computing for the rest of us," referring to them making it easy for ordinary people, but it was only a small proportion of computer sales. So many people got so balled up in some Windows boondoggle that they swore off the company; but you couldn't, because it was the main computer at work. Mac might have wormed its way into education, but it was not what people sat down to in the work place when they got out of school. People were pissed at Microsoft. And yet containers of clones from the far east continued to wash up on American shores were they were dispersed to infiltrate the work place.

Microsoft was seen as middle class. As computers were more and more becoming central in the modern office they were colonizing everywhere. People who worked with their hands and didn't have to work with a computer looked upon Microsoft as the instrument of elitist office worker stuffed shirts; the elitist sect of high priest main frame computer workers thought the PC was a kiddy toy, and thought even less of the Mac. The artistic elite loved the Mac and hated PC because of its ugliness and lack of interest in human factors.

It was very calming and inspiring to work on the Mac interface. Walker felt a little thrill of interest every time he turned it on and it chimed in the morning. To have a common interface across many applications not only ameliorated anxiety, it allowed you to featherbed on what you already knew. It was very calming to have a machine in which you could use beautiful typography to name the files with long descriptive names rather than the usual 8.3 characters.

Management didn't seem to know diddly about computers. These guys didn't use them for much though they were sure to have the latest on the desk, or across the room. "I'll have my girl do the word processing on it." After a while Don did learn to click a button and look at database information.

Meanwhile, Walker was going crazy from withdrawal around not having any time to be writing his own fiction. He wrote this little bit that is working on a theory of types found in the newly computer literate work place:

> As you can see I totally bought in to the elitist Artist type vs. the common worker Drone type. Bob and Karen were pretty much trapped in Drone. Whereas Therese and Don and the VP were bourgeois and nouveau riche marketing / executive types I called Vidiots. The engineers and CAD people were of another type: Technos. The CAD people used only one application, AutoCAD. They did the line drawings. That too was amazing— they had changed whole rooms full of draftsmen into AutoCAD operators. They got much better documents that way and much easier document revision control.

Click

Once again Walker is vis-a-vis in his therapy session. The phone rings and there is a pause of annoyance.

There is a loud click and the message machine tape starts recording what Walker assumes is a paean of pain from another client. He tries to ignore it but now he has to feel his jealousy kick in, now that another of Ms. Z's children is taking up her finite attention. He has to think about other people needing her so much. And he has to think about his need. He becomes embarrassed at his jealousy behavior towards a fellow sibling in therapy.

Patient: Looks like you have got a new THING there, a new phone? The things, the electronic things.

Analyst: What comes to mind.

Patient: They're neat, they're cultural, integrated circuits. They influence life a lot.

Analyst: You love them and you hate them.

Patient: We were talking about this stuff the last time. The idea that I had broken off all these relationships, in February, when I started coming in here twice a week.

And we were talking about how I feel love that you had come to represent in this time. I said something to the effect that everything else is kind of pale in comparison. You don't get this sort of situation in regular boy girl talk.

Analyst: (raising her eyebrows in surprise): There's a lot in this.

(A pause.)

Patient: Carol called me yesterday morning. Real early in the morning, before 8 o'clock. "I've got one question," she said. "Are you bisexual?" She wanted to know. She was obviously having a lot of fear about AIDS, or a lot of fear about something and was projecting it into that.

She said, "The way I treat women, I thought that you are bisexual."

And I of course told her, "I had never had any bisexual experience, and didn't really care to."

(A pause.)

Analyst: But what were you feelings about what she said?

Patient: Well she was just obviously very hurt, very angry, very afraid.

Analyst: I asked you what YOUR feelings were.

Patient: I guess I felt kind of guilty that I am putting her

through that. I don't know if I am putting her
through it, but . . .

There was a long pause . . . during which Walker got this
image of Cora riding him, sitting on his cock in a reverse
cowgirl position. She slid her wet cunt up and down on his
dick. She had to bend herself way forward, and put her hands
on the floor, while he put his hands under her lifting on the
thighs just outside the cunt, helping her slide this lower
mouth up and down slowly fucking him as he helped her.
They were slow and deliberate. She was way forward with
her head between his feet. Moving and being moved up and
down. With her ass in the air, Walker was moving her back
and forth on his cock in deep low sucking fuck plunge.

The pause continued. In the fantasy now he watched as
Ms. C got off of him and beckoned for Ms. Z to come over
and pull up a cock and sit down on it. But Ms. C seemed to
think better of it and she started showing Ms. Z how to do
it. Except now she had started to squat over Walker with one
foot on each side of him squarely on the chair and had slath-
ered his dick with fine slick precious pussy juice and had
pushed a dollop of it up her asshole and was now slowing
sliding her slick asshole down over his cock. The thought
of this vision of his girlfriend getting boned like a whore on
the chair in the psychiatrists office, while his therapist had
to watch, and in fact was being instructed on how to do it,
shocked and mollified Walker to the quick.

He tried to get himself back into the session.

He was balking at her asking about feelings, he didn't
know from feelings. When asked what was he feeling, his
mind went to this sequence: I will try to get her to give me a
hint. Seeing through this you will discipline me and tell me
I have to try and identify the feeling in myself. At this time I
will throw distracting shift and try to get you to bargain with

me or make you laugh and I get stuck in this game for two, three, or maybe four minutes. Awkward silence while I feel shame for my performance.

Analyst: What made you bring this up, in relation to what you were describing about on Tuesday.

Patient: Well we were trying to talk about how I relate to women, and that's an opinion about how I relate to women from somebody who knows me.

Analyst: That you were bisexual!

Patient: Right.

(A thoughtful pause.)

Patient: I don't know how bisexual men treat women.

(A pause.)

Analyst: You're really resisting looking at your feelings.

Patient: I said I felt guilty in that.

Analyst: Right, but that's not to the point. What you're avoiding saying is how you feel about being told that you seem like a gay or bisexual man. And you must have feelings about someone who is close to you saying that.

Patient: It's been said to me often enough. I mean not all the time, but a time or two over the years. People have said that to me several times. I used to have really long hair in the early 70s.

I mean I don't ... like gay men, I find that very unattractive, pretty sick all of it. But I do like the idea of sensitive men. I mean when I was a young man coming up...when I grew up in Texas it was the surfers vs. the cowboys...sensuality, try to get together with women in a real way without games, quit being such an insensitive hard guy.

(There is a long pregnant pause.) . . .

Patient: I wanted to ask about the idea of a characterological disorder. One that is just inherent in your character.

> I'm beginning to think that I will never change, and
> will always be this way, and it's just my character.

(A pause.)

Analyst: Where did this idea come from.

(A pause.)

Patient: I've been wondering about the meaning of this word.
It's like deeper than neuroses. Something . . .

Analyst: But how do you know about this.

Patient: I've run across it in several readings. I've never
quite understood it. Particularly Murray Bowen, and
another guy who wrote *The Betrayal of the Body*.
And Wilhelm Reich.

Analyst: But you associate this with the idea of hurting a
woman. You are concerned with this being characterological?

Patient: Well I don't know, that's my association, yea.

Analyst: Do you know what the link was.

Patient: No, I had it in the back of my mind, I wanted to
ask about that today. It seemed like a good place to
interject.

Analyst: Well it is along the same lines.

Patient: The connection was I was looking through the Bay
Guardian at the ads for lovers, personals, and one
of them in the Women for Men section mentioned,
Please No Characterological disorders.
See, it seemed to me they meant, you might really
hurt somebody, and you don't want to get too close
in case you might have some incurable disease, a
characterological disease.

(They both laugh.)

But Ms. Z would not explain to him what this term
meant.

Walker was frustrated by the way Ms. Z would not just
give a simple answer to his questions about terminology. He

began to think that psychotherapy was only about frustrating him, that was the whole point. Don't do what he asks, frustrate him, and see how his defenses martial themselves, and display themselves in the therapeutic situation. Bla bla. It pissed him off.

From what little he read, a characterological disorder is where people are caught up in a "fixed fantasy". These become basic core operating environment, like for example "being a hippie". I am a hippie. That is my life. It is an enduring pattern of inner experience and behavior that deviates from the expectations of where I grew up. It is a way of feeling special, different from the cowboys and the surfers. Being a hippie is also ego-syntonic it fits in with a belief system about what a righteous person should be doing to help the ecology, and also be more tolerant of others, their beliefs etc. The hippie character is a whole way of political and spiritual and economic being that guided his way of being in the world.

It wasn't until later that Walker understood psychological symptoms were grouped according to whether they were acute, chronic or characterological.

Acute had to do with trauma, and could be addressed in a shorter time. Chronic problems took longer in therapy. He didn't understand characterological disorder until he studied Transactional Analysis. They had to do with ingrained destiny scripts which made up how one sees the world, what kind of games and rackets one became adept at.

The Great Mac to VAX to PC and Back Hack

Walker's first hands-on exposure to networking was at Trace. In the early days of the personal computer revolution, one had to advocate strongly for bringing a Mac into a bastion of PCs and engineers.

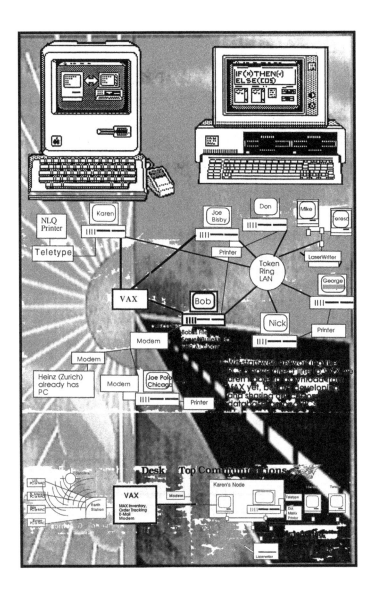

It was just after word processing was the killer app that brought everyone away from the typewriter, and before email; it was Desk Top Publishing that was the thing. The engineers eyed the little anthropomorphic one-eyed Mac with suspicion, like it was some kind of a Trojan horse — let one in and soon they would all have to be working on one of these little toys. So it behooved the Mac lover to be able to demonstrate that the files that one created on the Mac were compatible with the majority of the work done on a PC. If you were going to be part of the work network you had to be proactive. You couldn't just idly sit by and let the Mac be excluded from the work group. Walker had set up his own little AppleTalk network to the LaserWriter and he wanted to get the PCs onto it. They had to be on his network because the Macs were closed and you couldn't put a network interface card into an extra slot in the mother board and hook into the PC network because the Mac+ didn't have slots. All the engineers and vice presidents smirked at this with an "I told you so," expression.

In a flurry of activity over the next few weeks Walker made file exchange happen. He called it: The Great Mac to VAX to PC and Back Hack. It started when he was hanging out with the technicians watching them bring up a new digital gas analyzer. Doug started using a new procedure written in WordStar on a PC. Walker wanted that procedure for the manual and for his own education, as he was getting more involved in product support. He knew that since the PC guy was connected to the VAX and if he could get linked to the VAX then they were linked to each other. He got himself a user id and a password to log onto the VAX. He used his Mac computer at home and a 1200 baud modem to dial up a number and got into his account on the Trace VAX. Then he used a Telnet client on his Mac at home to use the resident mail program on the VAX to get the text of the procedure onto his Mac. This he saved that file onto the small plastic plastic disk the Macs used and brought it into work.

Imagine that! Logging into the server from home. The modem dial-up and handshaking became a source of constant amazement for him when the modem made that sound of the digital byte-stream screaming through the old analog telephone company switching circuits like a banshee's wail: buuunetatatutitoottitoottutituteepurshwahrht-weetikikieyieyieyiruhruhuhdaaaaschhhhhputangputang-putang.

A kind of protocol called handshaking would occur and the next thing you knew, you were in. Landing at the command line. With your telnet client, right in your user directory. You could run applications on the VAX remotely. You could send and receive email. You could search for papers on subjects with a gopher daemon and download them with a file transfer protocol.

It suddenly dawned on Walker: With the modem, I don't need to come "in" to work, every day.

Unix shell as psyche shell

The possibility of working from home excited his introverted thinking personality. But then he put that aside and let the metaphor of network sink in. Even then we were starting to see that the network was the new mandala of our time. The word "cyberspace" had entered the language through *Neuromancer*, a novel of Gibson (typed up on a typewriter). This sent Walker off into almost an entrainment of cross-sorted spiritual feeling and thinking, a kind of synesthesia common to nerds who grew up in suburbia. These types seemed to be able to have feelings only in thought; and now he drifted into a creative high that took over his mind. Walker had always had a great ability to become entranced and entrained with an analogy. With his studies of Jung, and all the great interpenetrating circular diagrams and mandalas of the components of the Self therein, this analogy occurred to him and he wrote about it:

> Logging into the Server with software is like making a call to God through some software called prayer. (Along with many other spiritual practices. Which are little programs called sacraments! You can Run when you get "in".) The Server is connected to the Source, the overall Psyche. And what connects to that Psyche is the SELF, a hybrid between the universe and the human ego/consciousness. Once you have felt it and logged into this Unix, you will know the Unity.
>
> The structure of Unix with its shells was like the chakras. The bottom chakra, muladhara is the root, is the kernel. Around which there are several enclosing shells. Inside a given shell there is lateral communication around this echelon among the symbols; and there is also the out and in communication beyond the shell to the adjacent levels and beyond. In the chakras these are transformations upward and downward. Moving from one chakra / shell to the next gave off or absorbed an energy like in the quantum transition diagrams. I read somewhere in Jung that these great energy exchanging life events were reflected in the celebrations of the church sacraments. Baptism, confession, Eucharist, confirmation. These correspond to moving up the 4 body chakras: baptism celebrated the root chakra; confession celebrated the sacral chakra (or was it the throat speaking); taking the Eucharist celebrated the heart chakra; being confirmed and receiving the gifts of the holy ghost (rather spirit as they say now) was about the 3rd eye — the intuitive perceptions beyond the obvious. It is good to look around in these new spaces.

Then the next move in the great Mac to VAX to PC and Back Hack was connecting his Mac at work to the VAX. Walker routed a line to the VAX which he had dropped into his cubicle. He went to Al Lasher Electronics on University Avenue and bought an RS-232 connector. Then he sliced the end of a Mac serial cable — splayed out the wires to identify them. And these he crimped it into the connector. The 8 pins are: 1 Data Carrier Detect 2 Receive Data 3 Transmit Data 4 Data terminal Ready 5 Ground 6 Data Set Ready 7 Request To Send 8 Clear to send 9 Ring Indicator. That makes up the Big Eight pins.

Then the new sysadmin in MIS, Robert, pushed Walker's RS2-232 plug into a socket of the bank of RS-232 ports on the VAX and the Mac was IN! Robert explained to him how Telnet runs over TCP/IP. It is an application on that VAX operating system. These would be digital packets with headers etc, which controlled and contained levels of inter-connection from bits in the wires up to meaninfgul data level on the Open System Interconnection, OSI model.

Walker thought, How interesting.

After Robert gave a brief introduction on TCP/IP to him, Walker started to read up on it. He became a standling of Cody's among the massive collection of advanced computer books. Walker found the OSI — Open Systems Interconnect model of how computers connect with each other to be fasci-nating. Basically TCP/IP is an application that ran on the Transport level of the network. Robert had mentioned the 7 layers of the OSI (Open System Interconnection) model and when Walker looked it up he saw that in its simplest form the Transport set {physical, data, network, transport } supports the Application set {session, representation, application}.

He was trying to think of a good analogy to try and picture or remember this, and he ran into one that was a train on a track. The track is the physical layer, the train cars are its packets. The track has to be shared by trains / packets moving back and forth. So there is a switching function layer of how they can share the track and this is the Media Access Control, M-A-C.

Transference

Walker's first experience with networking was at Trace. He had his little LAN fiefdom going with a little serial Appletalk network to the laserwriter and other macs. Then, when the new IT guy Robert came around he had to do the official jacking-in to the VAX with the RS-232 plug Walker bought to force the issue. Robert was a recent graduate of university with a degree in IT. He was the keeper of the company mainframe computer. IT was a new profession. He was an enthusiastic young guy and very smart and for some reason took a liking to Walker — probably for crawling around up in the ceiling tiles looking for a socket.

"Networking is because of TCP/IP, that's the greatest thing. Have you heard of it."

"Not really."

"It's how the network runs. It stands for Transport Control Protocol / Internet Protocol. TCP/IP, though it used to be called Transmission Control Protocol / Internet Protocol. And they spell it TCP (slash) IP. The / indicates it works across two layers of the network. The third — and now I have to go into my mnemonic to remember the layers of the Open Systems Interconnect model." Robert smiled a mischievous grin and announced: All people smell the new dog pooh.

"A P S T N D P Application. Presentation. Session. Transport. Network. Data-link. Physical.

"So, uh the TCP/IP is about layer 4 — Transport and layer 3 — Network. See the TCP is about Transmission on the Transport layer and about handshaking or Internet protocol on the Network layer.

"Well, I guess I should say something about the layers of network. See, the OSI model helps you think about the *layers* of network. Or you could think of them as *channels*."

"That's right, the Open Systems Interconnect. That's what OSI stands for, just in case you were wondering."

"I was wondering about that, that's good to know."

"The Open Systems Interconnect, this is their model for giving you the ability to talk the same language as every other thing. So a developer, trying to create a program that needed network access, would use the OSI reference model so that he could make sure that his program actually can talk to other programs that use the same type of modeling. It makes everything nice and even. No miscommunication. It sets the rules and protocols to follow to make things work correctly.

"OSI's been around a couple of years. The ISO developed the OSI . . . The International Standards Organization developed this standard in 1984: the OSI, the Open Systems Interconnect reference frame. Because before that you had all these vendors of different kinds of router hardware developing their own schemes and they found out they couldn't talk to each other. It was a Tower of Babel and they had the foresight to not let that happen.

"You got the socket and matched up the pins."

"Yeah I had to look it up in a book at Cody's."

Robert continued, "It's like the building code for an electrician or a plumber. If I want to make an appliance and I want to be able to plug it into a socket here in the US, I have to follow that three prong layout, right? I know how far apart those pins have to be to plug into the socket. And that's the same thing they're doing with the OSI model, so that our Application — "appliance" on the network — will plug into each other and send and receive data reliably.

"We studied it a lot. It has seven layers. They've got a mnemonic. It's hard to forget: All People Smell The New

Dog Pooh. If you are going from the top down. Which is starting up at the top, and if we go through there, the A, application; People, presentation; Smell is session; the The is transport; New is my network. And then dog is Datalink and Physical. Or going up from the bottom Physical, Datalink, Network, Transport, Session, Presentation and Application. The Application runs on top of all of those layers. It has a windowing system which is the Presentation. This is where the compression is decompressed for human consumption. It has the Session in which there has been handshaking to establish a connection. It has Transport moving packets over the Network which is above the Switching on the next level below; — that's the (Robert looked up and to the right inside his memory for a second) — Datalink about sharing the network and routing. And that all running on top of or through the Physical wiring and cabling. Or on radio waves."

Robert left it at that and they got onto their next work.

At another time, this day or the next Robert came by Walker's cubicle and found him in and continued with, "Well shall we continue with a little more about TCP/IP?"

"Sure."

"After the physical bits of electricity passing down the wires. Next level of abstraction above that is the Datalink layer. That was layer two. And that's where the Frames are formed. That's their Point of View, and you want to get that memorized as well.

"We'll get back to that. And now we're moving on to, well, layer three. Obviously right? It's the next logical number in our order here."

"OK."

"Yeah, I guess we'll go onto that one. Do you recall the name of layer 3?

"Let's see . . . that would be. . . on your mnemonic . . . it was . . .

"That's right use it."

"Let's see, All People . . . Smell The New Dog Pooh. New, N — is the 3d layer. N. Network."

"Yes. That is correct. It is the Network layer. That is layer three. This is where we get things like IP addresses. It's one of the most important facets of networking. That logical address for each one of our computers. That is where this resides, is at this network layer. Layer three. Very important stuff.

"Absolutely. And below that your on layer two, dealing with the MAC addresses."

"Do you mean Mac, Macintosh?"

"No-o. Not at all. M A C stands for Machine Access Control. This is where one machine gains access to the media of another machine. It is a unique identifier. And once that control data gets to a particular subnet, we use that MAC address to deliver it that final leg to get it to that host. But what about when it's being transmitted between subnets, right? That's where layer three comes in above that because they can see it's working with that IP address. The one that we can break down into a network portion and a node portion using our subnet mask. The IP address. This is what allows it to travel out there, BETWEEN subnets, in a corporate network, or different hops on a router out there on the INTER— net.

"Yeah, that's basically it in a nutshell. We're talking about connecting devices. Between networks, like the dissimilar networks. I've got one network over here, for the office and you are your own network here in the marketing front office. And the laserwriter network. How do I get data from other people on my network over to you on your network? That's where this layer comes in. This is what we use it for. We can set up devices that work on this layer, things like usually a router, a routing device. I can set that up. I can say <[I wanna talk to Walker's network]>. We create a shared interface together when we make that connection. And of course, we are talking, we have layer one right there because we have a wire of some sort. Some sort of physical connection that connects the two devices. Then we have layer two where it's actually checking how do we get connected to that over that wire, giving us that Media Access Control. Well once it actually hits those routers and says <[I need to get data from this network to that network over there]>, that's when this IP address is starting to come into play. So that's what you need to be thinking about when it comes to layer 3. IP, that Internet Protocol. That is the bread and butter of the network layer. That's why it's so important.

"That's your 192. 168. 1. 2 address, or your 172. 16. 1. 2 address, or your 10. 0. 0. 2 address. The sub net mask. Those types of addressing. . . And then that breaks down into Private and Public addressing as well. The dot and decimal formation is what they call that. Subnet masks is a very important part of that. So I know what network am I actually on, especially when you get into breaking down a network into multiple networks.

They were standing next to the white-board in the meeting cubicle part of Walker's area. And Robert started drawing on the board with a green erasable marks-a-lot.

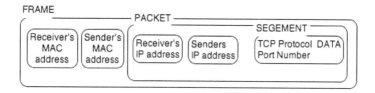

FRAME

PACKET

SEGEMENT

| Receiver's MAC address | Sender's MAC address | Receiver's IP address | Senders IP address | TCP Protocol Port Number | DATA |

When he had it drawn on the board he continued.

"Yes. Wow. Where were we? We have established MAC that Media Access Control —not MacIntosh, he smiled — and are ready to send information. You have established a frame work at the Data Link-up. At some point having to cross that network stream as well. You got to hit a router device. The routing device does things that route packets or talk across networks. That is what we're talking about. And I think I just said the magic word there. Packets.

"You did say packets didn't you?"

"Yes."

"Another name for packets might be datagram."

Walker said, "Packets. This is where IP functions, right?"

"Right!" Robert smile. "The TCP/IP suite of protocols. The protocol that we use to transmit data across Ethernet.

"All that IP number. IP works at layer three. It's dealing with those network addresses. In fact, that is what is responsible, INTER — net Protocol: between nets. When that packet makes it to the final network of its journey, and now it needs to switch over and start using that MAC address. It is IP that calls upon the Address Resolution Protocol, the ARP. It says hey ARP, here's the IP address that I need to deliver this packet to. What is the MAC address that goes with that IP address? And ARP is that Address Resolution Protocol, that works at layer two that can do that translation between that IP address and then map it to a particular MAC address.

"Layers within channels?"

" Right. Bits on the Physical. Frames on the — I have to recall the mnemonic: All People Smell The New Dog Pooh. Dog, D — Frames on the Datalink layer. It is Packets on the Network layer and Segments of data on the Transport layer. The Transport layer. The Transmission layer. TCP / IP. Transfer Control Protocol on top of the net address protocol.

Layer 4 on top of 3; on top of the ASK: Acknowledge — Synchronize of the Media Access handshaking protocol; on top of the bits streaming through the wires.

Walker said, "Wow. Yes. I get it. It allows applications working on either the sender or the receive side to have access to each other's media in order to write stuff and retrieve stuff. Data."

Robert liked that. He smiled at his pupil and continued. "The Segments of data go into the Session where it is assembled for presentation. It has to be decoded.

"That's because another interesting thing that occurs down here at layer 3 is where it starts to break things up, right? A term we use is fragmentation. This is where it gets done, cuz you're sending, according to the rules of whatever protocol you're using and you can only put so much information in a particular Frame as it gets ready to be sent across as bits across your medium. And it's at that Network layer that we start fragmenting the data, we start chopping it up into pieces that are gonna follow those rules right? You might be using Ethernet, what is it 1500 bytes or somewhere roughly around there. That is the length of the packet. Well if I'm sending more than 1500 bytes, what if I'm trying to send you a big huge file or a database or an MP3 or a movie or something like that. That's more than 1500 bytes, right?

"So at some point, that has to be chopped up into pieces that will follow the rules of my protocol that I'm using. And that occurs at that layer 3 as well, that Network layer.

"So it is the rules of layer two that won't allow for very large packet size, right, or very large data size, let's put it that way. The Frame can only be x amount of size. Well the packet could be whatever you want, but since it has to work with layer two — it actually needs to get on that line and involve that media — well it's gonna have to say, <[well let me just play ball here. And I'll break this up]>. And that's fragmentation. And that's what they call those little packets, that gets put on the line and sent across. The packet has to fit in the Frame. This is all part of that encapsulation process where they're gonna take that packet header information, gonna slap it on to that datagram like I drew. Whatever you wanna call it and make it a packet. If it's at the layer 3 and that's what it's destined for, that's what it's gonna be at that point. It's a packet. It's a little package."

Walker added, to indicate he was following: "A nice little envelope of bits or something."

"Right. That's what we've been talking about: is connecting between two dissimilar networks, and that's what routers do. That's their whole purpose in life. So you gotta think what kinda protocols are gonna be at layer 3? And that's a really good question. The answer to that is it's gonna be routing protocols, because that's what they do. They're built into the router to help it perform that function.

"Crosstalk. It's all about resolving the cross talk."

"One of my favorite protocols that is on the Network layer is the ICMP. Internet Control Message Protocol. If you've used the application Ping you've used ICMP. It looks out onto the net for network addresses. It says, <[Are you there? Let me talk to that layer 3 portion of your system and see if it will reply to me]>. That's the whole purpose of Ping. It uses the Network address. It doesn't send any data. It just checks how things are encapsulated in the IP datagrams. So Ping, it's basically working with IP addresses saying <[I need, *need* to talk to whatever node has this IP address]>. Those nodes have to look into layer three to find out if that is them or not, then respond on that same layer.

"See with Ping you can start to do troubleshooting. That is a layer three network, troubleshooting protocol."

"Ah I see."

Another day Robert stuck his head into Walker's cubicle, and said "I have come to Ping you."

"Hey-yo."

"Let's get into probably the big daddy which is layer four. Layer four, where are we at. This is going to be, which layer, Walker?

"This is going to be my — let me see, All People Smell The New Dog Pooh. T! The Transport layer. Right?"

"Good job."

"I'm trying again, trying to think backwards here, but yep, we're up on Transport now."

"Let's talk about The Transport Protocol. A lot of things going on in the Transport Protocol. This is a very interesting. Or the Transport layer, I should say, not the protocol. Mm-hm, that's the transport *layer*. A lot of interesting things going on at this layer. Basically its job is to say, let's see here, I need to create a connection from myself to another host. <[I need to transfer some data between the two of us]>. I need to make that happen. Now I can do that one of two ways. I can be very, what's called, connection-oriented; or I can be connection—less, and not care about whether or not I make a good connection. I'm just going to start pumping data at you and hopefully you get it. If not, oh well. Let me know later. And let the connection orient itself, once it starts getting into the details. The devil's in those details. That's normally what we use and that's the TCP protocol right? The Transport Control Protocol. I used to hear it called Transmission Control Protocol. Back in the day when dinosaurs ruled the Earth."

They laughed.

"It was called Transmission Control protocol but now it's Transport Control protocol.

"We mentioned the term TCP/IP, earlier; we said IP

worked on there: layer 3. Well TCP, the other major protocol in that suite works up there at layer four right? They write it with a little slash in between: TCP (slash) IP.

"And it's responsible for creating those end-to-end connections, that we were actually gonna end up using, to send that data back and forth. TCP is one of oriented connections. Oriented protocols. UDP is also a protocol that works at this layer. It's connection-less.

TCP is fascinating, TCP being connection-oriented. What we mean by that is, It's gonna give you that reliability check. It is going to make sure that the packet made it to the other end of the conversation. And I should say — let me use the right term there, really — we're talking about segments here at layer 4. Right?"

"Oh, right."

"Yes. Let us confuse you. We've got our bits and our frames and then our packets. And up here on layer 4. We're gonna call them something else. We're gonna call them segments.

"But layer 4 is where those checks occur to make sure that the packets have made it to the other end.

"TCP connection-oriented, is kinda like doing registered mail. Right? I know that that packet made it to the other end, just like registered mail, when that person receives that mail they have to sign for it and say they received it, right. That's basically what TCP is doing, it's saying here, I'm gonna send this information and then I'm gonna wait. And you're gonna have to send me back an ACK-knowledgement that you got it. Or you're gonna send back a negative Acknowledgment saying you didn't get it, or that it was corrupt or unreadable. And I'll send it again.

"UDP, same layer, layer 4. But it's connection-less. Meaning that it doesn't care. It's like sending snail mail. You put it in the mailbox. Mailman comes and picks it up. You really have no idea whether it makes it to the destination or not. You're just kinda like send it and forget it. Or just your hope and a prayer type thing. Whereas TCP is more like registered mail. You've got proof that it made it to the other end.

"What happens is the computers goes through what's called, the handshake, Or the three way handshake process."

Robert pointed to the diagram still on his white-board. "This is an important portion of TCP. This is what makes it, or at least part of it, that makes it so reliable. What happens is that it says I'm going to reach out to the host that I want to talk to. I'm going to send what's called a synchronization packet. Right? It's basically just a segment.

". . . Right," Walker said in acknowledgment, to keep the information flowing.

"All right, it's going to take that segment and it's going to turn on the synchronization bit. Say, here you go, I wanna SYNch chronize with you. It sends it over there and if that end host actually receives it, well it says, I have received this, I need to tell that person that I have received it. And, that's an ACK-Knowledgement, right? But, they kind of do it in a weird way."

"U-huh?"

"It says, I acknowledge that you're trying to synchronize with me, so they call it a SYN and ACK. Right?

Robert wrote this up on the white-board in Walker's cubicle: 'What is a socket?'

"All right, yeah, so we got the SYN packet, it leads off the transaction.

Walker began thinking it was like a transaction in social psychology. His mind drifted into Transactional Analysis, the general greeting and handshaking of social interaction.

In TA the unit of interaction is the "stroke". If you say Hi to someone they are supposed to say Hi back to you. Otherwise it is rude and can lead to crosstalk among the ego states. But in psychology I have to establish what State it is coming from — the Parent the Adult or the Child. In Games one started out apparently communicating from one state to the same state in another but there is, a switch. A-person is in one frame, but B-person is in another frame directing the communication of the transaction. If the stroke was acknowledge, then things proceed; if not, it could lead to crossing the states which was transference — wasn't it? Walker liked the simplicity and elegance of TA. To define Transference with one sentence rather than a whole book about alchemy with dismemberment and *coniunctiones* the way Jung does.

But he quickly snapped himself back to Robert's explanation.

"So say if I'm gonna try to make a request to a FTP server, I send out that SYN packet. <[Hey, I wanna synchronize with you, we gotta set up our numbers cuz we're gonna chop these packets up]>.

"And here the FTP server is saying: And I wanna make sure you can put them back together in the right order at the other end so, [let's synchronize]>. The other end is gonna ACKnowledge my SYNchronization request as well as send his own SYN request. He wants to request synchronization too. He sends back an ACKnowledgment of my synchronization request. And also sends his own SYNchronization request. I <[ACKnowledge his synchronization request]> and at that point we've done our thing. In Transport you have it twice. We've done our three, that's that TCP three-way handshake. And at this point we've got an established socket. We've got a connection between me and say that FTP server, and we can start sending data back and forth.

"That's right. Now, TCP is so worried and thinking about reliable data, right? It wants your data to be as reliable as possible. That's its whole purpose in life, is to make sure that what you send is what the end user receives, right? So it's very interested in keeping that happening and wants to watch over that. So that's the whole purpose of it, creating that socket first, making sure that the connection is actually established before any data ever gets sent. But now that we have a connection established we're allowed to start sending data. But that's not where this TCP show ends."

"Oh, no." Walker said with an admiring wink to Robert's style, to encourage him to keep going.

"Like for example. You might have gigabit network over here and it can pump out data really fast. While I'm sitting here on my little 10 megabit network; I can't take all that data that he's sending in to me. So TCP watches that. Because it's connection oriented, it's very important.

"TCP is still continually watching over things. And it says but you know what, I wanna make sure that I don't overwhelm you with data because I could just send data all day long and you might not be able to process it. So let's go ahead and make sure that the data I send you, you are getting it, you're processing it, and you're letting me know when you're ready for more. I'm not just pushing it off on you. You're letting me know how much you can handle and I go by your rules instead of just trying to overwhelm you.

"Data is being transmitted to your machine. That's gonna be chopped up, right. We talked about how at the next layer down we're gonna break that up and start getting it ready for those frames. Well what if some of those frames don't come through, right. I get half the data, but the next packet or the next packet that I need, that next frame I need, isn't there.

That's not going to do me any good, I'm going to have holes in my data. That's why we have those acknowledgment: hey, if you didn't get it, I'll resend it to make sure that everything displays properly. Because, if I chop it up into chunks, well now I've got to make sure that you got all the chunks at the other end, so that you can put it back together successfully. That's why we want those ACK acknowledgments, that's why we like those connection oriented protocols. And, so that's where the whole flow control thing gets done.

"Yeah. Flow control is where we talk about, how different nodes have different capabilities. And less congestion on your end, more congestion on my end, or just simple physical capabilities of the equipment, they're not the same. We don't all have the exact same computers, the same servers out there. Different capabilities. So flow control becomes very important.

"Yeah it does."

"You don't want to overwhelm a computer, that's when things like congestion and data loss start to happen. So then being able to talk to each other and say, <[Hey, here's what I can handle, please don't send me any more than that]>, — establishing that rule set and then following those guidelines is what's gonna ensure that your data stays safe and doesn't get corrupted at the end or lost altogether. That's what we want, that's why we use TCP protocols in a lot of ways when it comes to things like the internet, and doing things over that. Because I want to make sure I actually get that data. Any time we make a connection it is going to be detrimental if I lose connectivity,

"Yeah. If you want to send money through banks, you want to make sure every penny gets through."

Last Tango in Berkeley

Have you ever felt like you've been beamed up into a movie and you were stuck acting out a part of that movie? If Walker had to pick one movie he was trapped in, or at least in which there were many interlocking parallels to his relationship with sex, it would be *Last Tango in Paris*.

It was a little over 10 years since Walker had been in his first serious relationship with a woman. That had been Terry. This was back not long after he had graduated from University with a physics degree and was working as a teacher in a trade school in downtown Austin. And she was a grad student working on a PhD in French literature. At that time she was Mrs. Elliot. She was in the process of getting divorced. It was her therapist, Paul, who empowered her to get a divorce. Paul had started having sex with Mrs. Elliot. Powerful neo-Reichian, biomechanic, blue-box, hot-spot cosmic orgone sex of every persuasion. Thus when, Walker got to become boyfriend and girlfriend with Mrs. Terry Elliot, he was indirectly the beneficiary of Paul's sexual education of her, which made her a wonderfully lustful sexual partner. At the time of his first love with Ms. Terry, he would have been in a parallel to the Last Tango movie as Tom the hapless art-obsessed boyfriend to Ms. T as the free spirited Marie ingénue / predator. The parallel with the movie repeated again recently in his relationship with Dahlia who was liberated by her sexual predator guru therapist Chase — the Paul figure. Once again Walker would play the part of the hapless boyfriend (who was the benefit of a sexually liberated female.) Now though with Cora the tables had turned and he was the Paul, rapaciously pursuing sexual liberation for his own self and that of Ms. C.

Back in Austin he and Ms. Terry had lived together in

connubial bliss for a couple of years. They had their own apartment above a garage on Speedway close to the campus. But he was young and stupid and inexperienced, drifting into hanging around with poets, though he hadn't done much writing. During that time he had managed to write his first novel which was called *The Church of the Coincidental Metaphor*. It worked with the Jungian idea of flying saucers as mandala while under the influence of peyote.

Walker became a student of General Semantics because of how his girlfriend had a profound life change around her therapist using concepts from Korzybski's psychotherapy (which later became the e-meter in Hubbard's Scientology.) A number of sci-fi writers and Burroughs studied with the Count. He read the count's *Science and Sanity*, and did appreciate his engineer's take of applying the layers of abstraction in the human nervous system to the structural differential of calculus. Korzybski showed him how the calculus of motion was much more than the insight into the derivatives of velocity and acceleration of change, it was about the manifold in which we lifted experience to higher order abstractions.

Korzybski's idea of multi-ordinality to bring the mind back to the concrete reality of our time-binding situation was liberating. In Korzybski was a larger picture of reality beyond the nominalism of Aristotelean logic and subjectless assumptions of Newtonian physics. These classical worlds were embedded in this larger manifold Walker was looking for. Multi-ordinality (the idea that nouns should have indices indicating their relative relationships) was a science of the concrete, a kind of bricoleur confrontation, an axiom of choice, double-bind (Bateson), Theory of Types (Russel), paradoxical attempt to free man from the stultifying effects of too much thinky business. His famous dictum, The Map is not the Territory had a profound effect on many. The world of non Aristotelean logic, conjectured by Korzybski, the world of null-A, even got taken up by the Neuro-Linguistic Programing, visualizations and sutras.

But then Mrs. Elliot got the opportunity to go to Paris to work on her doctorate. She was a specialist in Diderot and the Encyclopedists. She and Walker had had many interesting conversations about the Enlightenment. Walker knew about the mathematicians Descartes, Desargues, d'Alembert, the Bernoullis, Leibniz, Laplace, Lagrange and later Lagendre, Cauchy and others, Gauss and Euler. What an Enlightenment they must have felt! To further the work of Newton's absolute certainty that God was space and the calculus was the secret language of functions that God spoke through gravity to en-form the objects and conduct them through change. And they could know this unfolding in time.

And even though Walker spoke demotic French informed by a Quebecois upbringing, his low-life slacker tendencies kept him from getting the money together to go to France with her. And so he had to let her slip away. They parted sadly. He was broken hearted and hit the road north.

But now here in Berkeley once again Walker was entering into a profound experience because of sex, and was the beneficiary of a therapist, Chase, who was the head shrink of the commune where he and they had all consorted with each other in a tantric Buddhist practice. This made sex spiritual and they helped each other get through the ensuing jealousy and possessiveness which were inevitable but a grievous slip in the sangha. But then Chase died and the commune could not hold together. Now, in this movie Chase was the Paul character and Dahlia the lover and Walker the hapless boyfriend once again. But now in the current itera-tion of the movie starring Cora, the drama triangle would take a turn and he become the persecutor Paul.

The Last Tango movie took over Walker's inspiration

one day — in particular the infamous butter incident — while sitting at the kitchen table with Ms. C. Walker used a dab of warm soft butter off the kitchen table to slip his finger up inside her asshole so that she could explore "asshole feelings" with her partner's finger up her. And she let him. That, that! was when things started taking off. Then, after they discovered that she had squirting orgasms which she didn't hardly even know about herself.

A man grows with each deep love relationship he has with a woman. He is looking for his mother trying to find the way to the Mother. (Walker knew this, but unconsciously.)

But for Cora this love became more than serious. And thinking she had found the love of her life she played her part with Walker taking the role as he became the guru taking advantage of the pupil, the protagonist predator, and her the antagonist victim. It got convolved. She was also the contagonist who goes along with; and the retagonist when she the victim becomes the predator; all while being the syntagonist, who went along with what the protagonist wanted.

This sexual exploration work really developed both of them. She turned out to be amazingly hot, multi-orgasmic squirting hot. It made Walker feel like a stud, a slave master, a whore monger. He had never felt more – one could say in-command, but it was more like he had come into his own body at last. Or at least a more relaxed and purposive owning of what was going on in sex. For example he might say to her, "I am going to use you vigorously, my dear." And try not to blush, and she would try not to blush, for he had never said anything like that, (and much worse) to a woman before.

They grew to be like acolytes of getting high through sex, and were instruments for each other. Although Walker came to feel at times like a slave to it, and a little bit

163

perverted in it too. He didn't trust this opinion of himself though, he didn't know if it was a true recognition of something or just a revisitation of his catholic upbringing. He had once been a fervent catholic boy on his way to becoming a priest back in the olde days of the tantum ergo Latin mass. He was going to be a priest; he went to visit the seminary he was thinking about entering. Now he realizes it was just a young guy playing out Pascal's wager.

Cora Rosenov changed a lot in the time she and Walker were together. Ms. C began to enjoy being risqué. In the beginning she liked to portray herself as not exactly the victim, but one who was somehow forced to satisfy the lust of this horny man: as though it were against her will, or at least not as if she had thought it up herself. This posture, perspective allowed her to feel OK about all the pleasure she was having, and somewhat ameliorated the frightening feelings of desperation and dependency that came up for her. This made here feel trapped and desperate at times: with Walker, there was no way out.

Walker came into Cora's life at a time when both of their biological clock had been ticking neglected for a while. Walker would cringe at the thought of his mother thinking about him being a single man in his late 30s in gay San Francisco.

And he did understand now that Ms. C had an especially strong need to be loved and developed dependency easy. Her parents had died when she was fairly young; she had a much older (17 years) brother. Being in love made things feel desperate for her during some of their time together. Walker could sense that she felt at times like she was hooked, stuck, trapped, that he was somehow holding her against her will. He felt like that too, at times. And it was not a bad feeling, all the time. They were lovers. And it got passionate and frightening back and forth at times. When was it ever not so in Love.

They certainly made things hot for each other. Over time she let him use her body in every way. She often got immediately turned on and wet with the slightest touch: a man likes to work with that sexual responsiveness, it is very empowering. It is really true: the female orgasm, again and again in a session is more powerful than a males. Not being female, Walker could only imagine it. For whatever reason, obsessive dependency or just being always so turned on, she allowed herself — she could not stop myself — from being as agreeable as possible. And later as the two lovers began to trust each other she looked forward to using his body, his dick, for her pleasure. She began to enjoy her power over it.

— — — — — — — — —

Cora Rosenov was so emboldened by her burgeoning sexuality — and so unhappy about where their relation-ship was going vis a viz long term commitment — that she started seeing a therapist too.

She was talking to her therapist and wondered if Walker were gay.

Patient: "I will not blame these inconsistent feelings entirely on Walker. It's also because of my hunger for sex and my need to have and hold a spouse partner in life. How did our story progress. It started out conventional enough. Then we started exploring anal and I let him, was when things started taking off. And I started having really satisfying sex."

What Cora did not get into with her therapist because she was ashamed was about (How he started finger fucking my asshole while eating my pussy. It often happened. And I would just go out of my mind, and have these huge almost passing-out, heaving, fainting, squirting, ejaculating orgasms, in which a stream of pussy juice shot out of my pussy into the air. . . .... My god, when we were over at his place he would get me stoned and drunk and then would make me squat over his mouth as he said "Kiss me with your pussy lips." . . . And I did, it was like I had a whole other set of lips down there . . . Walker started licking my pussy even harder and fingered me so that I was impaled on his finger. I came. . . I came on his face.

And he said, "Wow!! You are delicious as always." He made slurping sounds while licking my pussy. He laughed.)

The revery stopped and she said:
Patient: We were both about pursuing maximum pleasure.

Ms C said to her therapist:
Patient: "He got me so stoned. I hadn't ever smoked pot up
        until that time. It is quite an aphrodisiac. We drank
        wine too. We were both unemployed and had time
        on our hands."
What Cora did not get into with her therapist because she was a little ashamed was about (how he liked it when I sucked his cock. And I liked doing it. He said "I can tell you like doing it. Your good at it. You're a natural."
    Whatever that meant.)

Patient: "My appetite for sex became huge after that and my
        hunger for love along with it. I might have got the
        two confused. At one point he called me his love
        slave.
        After we started going to the porno flicks he told me
        he wanted me to shave my pussy.
        I said "No.! I have to change at the gym."
        He practically broke up with me over it, so of course

I had to give in.
And we started going to hot tubs.

What she didn't say but let drift into memory, she censored from the therapist.

(Also he started pulling his cock out of my mouth when I was giving him a blow job and shooting his cum on my face.

At first I was shocked and a little bit disgusted.

"You meant to do that," I said.

Yesss he hissed, and winked. "You look so cute with cum on your face." We talked about it, "But the girls in the movies don't seem to mind." And and I felt better about it. He sure did it a lot with me that way.)

Ms. C continued with her talk in session.

Patient: "We were both unemployed at the time, and had
time to devote to boy girl games.
Sometimes, when we were driving in my car, he
forces me to go to a nearby parking, or even just off
to the side of the road when we would make out in
the car. Hot passionate tongue-twined kisses."

But what Ms C didn't say was: (He'd reach his hand up my dress and play with my pussy through the panties. I'd get soaking wet. Then he'd have me lay my head in his lap. And he'd let his cock stick its head up out of his zipper. And I'd suck it for him.)

She did say:

Patient: "I don't take off all my clothes. . . while he is kissing
me. . . he just opens up my shirt, opens the bra and
pushes the bra up to expose my boobs. . .

But she didn't go into detail with her therapist but an image did flit through her memory (And I take off one leg from my panties...because he asked me to do it that way...We do it on the passenger seat.....I being on top of him.)

Cora sighed and told her therapist:

Patient: "We mostly got together at my house. It was good to have a man sleeping in my bed."

Then she remembered (He'd wake me in the middle of the night and we'd do it sideways. I would get wet even if I didn't want to do it and wanted to sleep, and though I did protest, he lifted a leg and slid it in.)

Patient: "I feel somewhat disrespected. The other day we were in my kitchen". . .
. . . (he would start kissing me and squeezing my boobs. He fucked me there.....bent over with one hand on my ankle and the other on the linoleum floor. ....he didn't even take my shirt off or opened it.....he just pulled my panties down half way and made me sit on him....and screwed me.....humped me and fucked me....reached around and rubbed my pussy with his long strong fingers." . . .while I did grind on his cock.)

"And we got into sex and he left. . . Right after we finished."

(He fucked me but not ejaculate in me.) . . .

Patient: "He pulled his pants up and headed out the door. The only words that he said were....'Thanks, sexy.... Loved fucking you. Gotta go to work. Bye We'll finish this later.' I was there . . . in the kitchen". . .

Cora had a look of pitiable desolation.

(fucked....with my panties down around one leg. . .)

Cora told her therapist:

Patient: "He rarely lets me have control. I drive to his place. He greets me at the door saying 'Hi.' I sit on the one chair, he gives me a glass of wine out of the fridge. He sits on the mattress on the floor. After a while of him looking up at me, and maybe another glass of wine I get on top of him . . .

(And he opens up his pants and takes them off with his underpants in one swoop. He pulls me towards him and makes me lick and suck his dick. And I do it. Sometimes I keep going strong and make him ejaculate inside my mouth but then he might pull me up by my hair and make some of it splatter on my face. And I am left with loads of his cum inside my mouth or on my face.)

Patient: "And he says, 'You're so cute, have some more wine. But he rarely lets me take that much control."

(He has lots of other things in store for me.)

Cora mentions their weekend lover's getaway.

Patient: "After a while we started staying in hotels, and even going on weekend stays at a bed and breakfast in the wine country. Or a cabin at the hot springs."

She gives the PC rated version of their adventures in the hot tub.

Patient: "We went to the hot tub very often and that is where we had the hottest sex of all."

(Well it was always pretty hot, but at the hot tub with us both being so scrubbed clean we got into all kinds of dirty sex.)

Patient: "As soon as we are naked and get into the hot tub, he pulls me to him . . ."

(So I can feel his erect cock underneath the hot bubbling water. Perhaps we thought of ourselves as actors in a porno flick. He said "You are that groovy hot little cock sucker porn star with the short curly hair." He got the idea to make me kneel down in front of him looking up at his cock while giving him a blow job from porno flicks.)

Patient: "Our sex life got hotter after he took me to a porno
movie. At first I didn't like it, but after seeing it
in the movies it seemed OK. He enjoyed it. Told
me it was an exercise in exerting control by being
submissive. He had some Japanese word for it. What
was it? Waif fu. He explained it was like kung fu for
women using their wiles in sex. We used to go to the
Pussycat Theatre . . ."

(I can't believe I actual said to him about one of the
awful sex acts we saw in a porno: "We'll have to try that for
yourselves.")
Patient: "Some of the porn movies even were feminist.
And spoke to the women's pleasure which is a
departure from the earlier men's stag flicks.
Walker would argue, 'But it's a feminist porn flick.'"

Walker was just out of the commune and the fatal
venereal disease AIDS was starting to ravage the gay,
Haitian and intravenous drug-user populations. Since women
and heterosexuals were getting it in Haiti Walker was quick
to point it out to her. He told her that it was necessary to
use condoms. And they used a lot of them, for birth control,
since they were monogamously going together. Heterosexuals didn't routinely get themselves tested.
Cora dismissed the porno for her therapist.
Patient: There wasn't much in the way of a story.
(But she had to admit it was naughty fun. She enjoyed
them.)

Mandala — DSM IV

A Modern Mandala

Mandalas came before cartesian abstract space. The old-school mandala had the pig, the snake, and the cock chasing each other around in an endless cycle of samsara. This gives way to a new modern structure of the workings of personality in the world: the DSM-IV. The Diagnostic Statistical Manual in its 4th iteration is the bible of professionally accepted and accredited sanity. The DSM-IV has dimensions going along various axes. There is clustering of personality disorder along these dimensional domains.

Walker got introduced to the DMS-IV when his therapist and he were looking into diagnosis so that she could fill out the insurance claim. She assigned him homework: "Look through the DMS-IV they have at the Berkeley library and pick out a suitable diagnosis."

Walker and Ms. Z went back and forth, and eventually settled on the nebulous diagnosis of "Dysthymia". It is a persistent depressive disorder. "You may loose interest in normal daily activities, feel hopeless, lack productivity and have low self-esteem. And an overall feeling of inadequacy." Dysthymia is on Axis I because it is a mood disorder.

His therapist filled out the form and now his depressive aspect was a matter of record. A diagnosis of dysthymia requires having experienced a combination of depressive symptoms for 2 years or more.

Walker thought maybe being in therapy so long is what was making him depressed.

At first these concise descriptions of Personality Disorders by doctors and experts made Walker feel that the good doctors were guilt-tripping. But Walker realized this scientific perspective was helpful to understand and not react to the more obvious ensnarements of PDs in his life. Clearly his mother and many women had Obsessive Compulsive Personality Disorder. And clearly he had to feel his own Avoident Personality Disorder, and Dependence to try and let go of them.

Walker's years of apprenticeship at love with women was not without episodes of being on the receiving end of some major bitchery. His apprenticeship required a study of bitchery which is basically a cover up for anxiety, using projection onto the husband or boyfriend as scapegoat. The hand-wringing anxiety of mothers and nuns in his upbringing was Obsessive Compulsive Personality Disorder. Histrionic.

Also he came to understand that what he thought was severe introversion of his personality was actually more of an Avoidant Personality Disorder. That mixed with Obsession and Addiction tip him into Dependent Personality Disorder too. You have to work on yourself to find these painful insights. Hopefully awareness will liberate.

DSM-IV space as a vector space

The DMS-IV space of mental health is 5-dimensional, spanned by: Axis I is major mental disorders like schizophrenia and clinical disorders like clinical depression. Serious stuff like anorexia and bipolar disorder. Axis II is where the personality disorders are: Paranoid, schizoid borderline, histrionic. It is here on Axis II that they have the personalities disorders clustered into groups.

Axis III is physical like a brain injury. Axis IV is psychosocial and environmental, like living in a ghetto.

Axis V is the scale from 1 to 100 giving you a number for your Global Assessment of Functioning. The GAF.

90 to 100 is like a captain of industry and 0 to 10 is a street person living in shoeless oblivion. There are many of these latter folk walking the streets of Berkeley. A middle of the road GAF score of around 50 means that the person has moderate symptoms or moderate difficulty in one of the following: social, occupational or school functioning.

About 20% of the population has a serious mental or behavioral or emotional disorder at any one time. Half of those are involved in criminal activity, with crimes against property and individuals, indicating a serious lack of boundary and / or empathy. The other 80 % are getting along, stuck in their jobs but not driven postal around it. The above number of 20% does not count drug or alcohol related disorders. For many, self-medicating on the down-low seems to be the only way to get through without getting ensnared in the legal system or the mental health system. On the other hand, for many drugs exacerbate the sloughing off of normal inhibitions. Of course a lot of people, the higher GAFers, are using yoga, meditation and other healthy means to avoid drugs and the doldrums.

Instead of society being measured by how well its people go about producing a gross national product, what if a society strived to have a general national happiness index. The GHP. Like in Bhutan they have a Gross National Happiness index instead of the GNP. It's a spiritual thing; the great Buddhist wealth is lifting those around you. It is kind of Christian that way. They see being in society as being on the great mandala. In the Mondragon region of Spain, they have cooperatives; the workers are the owners of the means of production. Production is to further employment and research, not to create excess wealth for the investor owners. The workers are the investors. Those people walk the world with pride.

The human mind has evolved many defense mechanism which are necessary to protect the ego. It is necessary to carry on in one's own self interests. But it seems like given free reign in the American dream, the ego will surround itself with as much wealth and property and the protection it affords even if it gets further and further from the truth of itself.

So your chances of encountering a psychopath or sociopath is one in 10. Perhaps a boss. Or a criminal uncle, or a friend who just can't seem to not fuck up and stay out of trouble. Or a hot girlfriend who knows how to use her desirability to manipulate a man. The fault is in their stars they might say. We all maintain our deceptions of both self and other. Once you know that, you can relax and watch the game that you are part of. Assuming the other is one of the 90% that have a conscience and they can reign-in their aggression and seek to have their all-consuming desire for recognition appeased in some normal way. People have been trying to figure themselves out and are interested in your insight if you go about it the right way. Ask yourself what would it take for you to transcend your defenses and come to know yourself.

What would it take to convince you to tell the truth to yourself. Why not. Walker wondered: Is being an addict the same as being in an obsession? I am what the nuns in grade school used to call a recidivist. Always coming back to the same behavior of writing no matter how much it took from the rest of my life. I had to. There was just too many thoughts and ideas and voices needing to be expressed running around in my head.

People see the world through their Type (introverted thinking, or extroverted sensing or intuitive perceiving); they also see the world through their personality disorder.

In Axis II the Personality Disorders are grouped by clusters A, B, and C. In Cluster A you have Paranoid, Schizoid and Schizotypal. In Cluster B you have Histrionic, Narcissistic, Borderline and Antisocial. And in C you have Avoidant, Dependent and Obsessive-Compulsive. These clusters are called weird, wild and whacky. These are technical terms from the thereapy industry.

Weird

Under weird you have Paranoid Personality Disorder, Schizoid, and Schizotypal. People who have Paranoid Personality Disorder are your hate group member, militia man, bug-out survivalists, isolated terrorist bomber or killer. They have unwarranted suspicions and misinterpret the actions of others to see them as threatening or deliberately harmful.

The person with Schizoid Personality Disorder are loners like a hacker, or the night shift workers of the world. They are detached from others, have a limited range of emotions, are not caught up in the interests of others.

A schizotypal on the other hand is like a hippie that has gone over to being a mystic of the universe. They are likely to have distortions of thinking and perception. They are not big on interpersonal relationships. Emily Dickinson.

Wild

The criminals are under the wild cluster B, on Axis II. The Antisocial Personality Disorder. The criminal class is easily capable of guiltless, exploitative and irresponsible behavior all the while running a deceitful con and knowing it, being proud of it without a compunction to think of how it is hurting the other.

You have the Borderline PD. Disruptive. Be going along then suddenly have a precipitous personality shift (which is different from mood swing in Axis I) into an incredibly cold dissociative person. They are unstable in their relationship life, their work life, and have trouble maintaining a sense of who they are — their identity.

Cluster Wild also includes the Histrionic PD and the Narcissistic PD as well as the Antisocial and Borderline PDs.

The Histrionic was Freud's speciality: excessive emotional expression and attention seeking behavior. The spit-fire women in Mexican soap operas or like Scarlet O'Hara in Gone with the Wind.

The Narcissistic personality is everywhere. Everyone has an "I'm all that personality" in the modern world. Donald Trump the real estate tycoon who loves to fire people to maintain the top dog position.

Walker had thought that Denial was the generator of the defense mechanisms but Narcissism in a ubiquitous spectrum of behaviors is the most common.

We'll (hopefully) get back to that in a minute.

Here we start to see that several defense mechanism are used in service of the Narcissistic Personality Disorder: Omnipotent Control, Denial, Externalization. Walker began to wonder if he suffered from Covert Narcissism.

Whacky

Then you have finally the Whacky group, Cluster C. These are Obsessive/Compulsive Personality Disorder, Avoidant PD, Dependent PD.

OCPD is rigid perfectionism, orderliness, and yet indecisiveness. They would rather make a quick decision quick. [Judging /Perceiving] rather than prolong the agony of indecision. They also must maintain interpersonal control and emotional constriction. A lot of mothers and old wives fall into this category. The endearing neatnik Felix in the odd couple too.

Another whacky is having Avoidant Personality Disorder. These are inhibited, introverts alone in a crowd because of anxiety in the social situation. They often have eating disorder and dissociative disorder. And the Dependent PD. These are the emotionally clingy, who hope their submissive behavior will lead to their emotional needs being met. They tend to stay inside and have low activity levels.

Some operators in DSM-IV space

Walker began to feel like he was infected by every other one of the PDs. Beneath the beautiful disguise of his persona were layers and layers of false pretenses. They've built up through the years. And they mix and match. It was like a vector space of dimensions spanned by the axes.

The Personality at least is a plane or convex hull prescribed by the intersection of axes of the DSM-IV space. The intersection of two axes; Axis I and Axis II form the most common convolutions. It could be thought of as a cross product of compatible elements on Axis I and Axis II that produce synergistic personality disorders. Here are some examples:

(Axis I: PTSD X Axis II: Borderline PD)

(Axis I: ADHD, Substance Dependence X Axis II: Antisocial PD) .

(Axis 1: Bipolar, mania; Axis 2: Narcissistic PD)

(Axis 1: Social phobia; Axis 2: Avoidant PD)

written in Dirac notation:

<Axis 1: Social phobia | Axis 2: Avoidant PD>.

The self-referential convolution of personality disorders is a concatenation of operators in a vector space.

Some Girlfriend Talk

Ms. C let it slip to her friend Ruth about their car sex.
"We'd be driving in my car somewhere, and if it was remote
or pretty safe, he would pull over and we would make out.
Sometimes I would open his fly and massage his boner.
Then he might have me take it out and suck his cock, going
down on him right there in the car! On a public curb side!"

She mentioned this girlfriend talk to her therapist:

Patient: "I must confess that my old girlfriend seemed
jealous when I told her about it.

I noticed them looking at us different the next time
we were at her house for a get together. I decided
not to tell so much about my relationship with
Walker, because it was starting to be serious and I
wanted to protect him somehow."

Although Ms. C did tell her therapist:

Patient: "There have been really good quickies, once when
I got a job at a pharmaceutical company as a temp,
he could come and visit me on some pretext. Like
once the company was giving some kind of demonstration or talks on microbiology.

And after the talks he took me in the supply closet.

(And bend me over a table, and pull my panties down
around my ankles and just sick his hard dick up my coos and
fuck me right there. I would be trying not to come and pretty
soon the pussy juice would be running down my leg and
getting my stockings wet.)

Patient: But it was the sex in the hot tube that was the
hottest.

Cora remembered being at his place. (I end up getting
completely naked he takes off my skirt and panties and he
takes off my shirt and bra. And he licks my body before
screwing me.....I make him lick and suck my boobs while

getting fucked. And after the fuck, I suck and lick his dick clean. Then go to the little closet bathroom in his studio and I clean my pussy with tissues and then come and lie down beside him.)

Patient: At lunch, we discuss the sex session . . . he loves to talk dirty…and horny; we also discuss the next fuck….evening or late night or next day. HA. He is funny because he tries to not say things that he thinks are offensive to women, like instead of saying blow job, he says 'feel me with your mouth.' Isn't that quaint.

She mentioned their plan to her therapist.
Patient: "I starting thinking about having Walker move out of his apartment and into my house. Wouldn't that be wonderful. It would be like my friends, sharing the same bed with her husband. Ha! He suggested I rent the studio in the back yard to him. It was decided we'd think about it."

(Once we rented a B&B on the Joy Rd. in Occidental near the Gold Country. It had grounds you could walk around on and a couple of different little cottages. Both me and Walker took leave from our senses. We walked around naked. We did not leave for 4 days except to get food. And I stayed wild naked for 4 days with Walker. We fucked like gorillas. We went mad on each other, fucking each other. Showering then sleeping.)

She mention to her friend Ruth, "At other times he would get all sad and mixed up and desperate, around his therapy, and I would get to feeling deserted and left out and rejected. I was madly in love with him and I wanted him to feel that way about me."

Homo Septiens

Network is the New Mandala

At Trace, Walker got Therese's new Mac onto the network. The company gave him the job title of Support Engineer. And he was given some company stock. One of the techs teased him about "the golden handcuffs."

Walker was working his ass off. He was invested in this company doing well, because he was fascinated by desk top publishing, being able to design pages and print them out on a laser printer. This would move him ahead in his desire to become a publisher. He was being a paid writer, well paid; and he was a publisher. He wanted their faith in him to be certain. Walker became such a nerd. He actually did like being able to do both the creative part and technical part — op-amps and transducers and laser interferometer stuff. It was phenomenological. It was cyber-enhancement, extending one's senses by machine. You could for a moment have a sense of smell more like that of a dog. Phenomenon beyond the ordinary senses were just as real; you had to reconstruct them in part from abstraction.

So Walker was stoked to rise in the organization by diligently doing work; making the company money; being a team player. And bringing new technical skills to bare on opportunities that arose.

Walker was getting closer with the CAD people and the support engineers. He followed one of them into an area of the building that he had not seen before: Manufacturing. He was shocked to see all these Asian technicians working at benches with lighted magnifying glasses. They had their own little cafeteria back there and everything. There were some 20 people working back there and they were never seen coming or going, they had their own entrance, or maybe they even slept there. They were like refugees or boat people. They might even have been undocumented workers. They were the fabricators of the boards. Here is where the analyzers were built. Trace was an immense warehouse space on the railroad tracks that hugged the edge of Berkeley at the bay. Upstairs there were suites of offices and an executive washroom. This is where management resided. From there to rule over all.

Walker found the OSI Open Systems Interconnect model of how computers connect with each other to be fascinating. Why? Because he thought it might help him understand something about the great neuro-electrical network in his person.

He saw it in a dream:

A long dream takes place in a large warehouse. I find something wrong with some circuits. I am investigating circuits. I'm a contractor and I find that people are using the circuit to make porn, and do things not related to work. For what it was put in. And I am going around into other people's cubicles just following this circuit. I am trying to find out how much is being done on it. And I wanted to do an energy audit. I had this company do an energy audit. I started meeting people. People using things.

Yes, a person could do an energy audit. And, there's a circuit in there, and loads would drop across these energy centers. We call them chakras (shockras, for want of a battery word: I wanted to somehow plug into them and know the body electric.) What a huge insight that would be to know what's draining your energy? Where are you stuck? Also an energy audit might enable to somehow to "read" a person. I wonder if there is even a print out, for reading these centers. The ancients read the aura as a diagnostic tool.

I imagined the objects of OSI networking might conform to some more General Systems Interconnection model, like say Shannon's information model of messages relayed from sender to receiver in an information system. Or semiotics: object and representation becoming a sign that was interpreted. And then went on to be communicated at the next higher level of abstraction — now as an object to be represented in a higher sign system. I began to imagine a general systems interconnection model that was useful to biological or ecology or other systems. Surely someone had developed a systems interconnect model for humans. It would be starting at the cellular level, or even below, and going up to the world of ideas. And even higher to a world of spiritual rapture.

I read Maslow of needs hierarchy { physiological, safety, love/belonging, esteem, self-actualization }. All Maslow needed was five. These all have to do with interconnections with the system, the physical emotional and social human ecology. And they are dependent on the level beneath or prior to it. In Maslow the physical level is Physiological: breathing, food, water, sex, sleep, homeostasis, excretion. Safety is: employment, family, health, property. Love/Belonging is: friendship, family, sexual intimacy. Esteem is: confidence, achievement, respect. Self-actualization is: morality, creativity, spontaneity, problem-solving, lack of prejudice, acceptance of facts. Maslow had reflected a hierarchy version of the human in-situation system.

It occurred to me that the seven levels of OSI might be a paradigm to think about the meaning of the chakras for these were an image of this thrust to higher organization based on structures below. In buddhist literature there was a great deal of speculation and awe for the chakra symbols of these structures. Perhaps the analogy: making contact with the chakras is like logging onto a server.

For example starting from the physical level you touch this table and touch sends a message to your brain, it is encoded from moving along the neural pathways. The message is trying to get through the nervous system, it needs to be in the memory of a brain, it needs to be known. There probably is a whole OSI for sending messages in the nervous system.

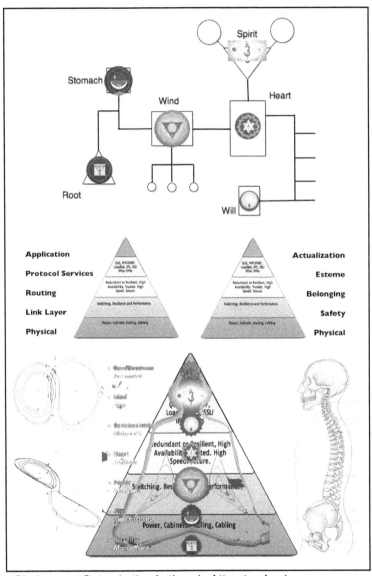

Chakras as Gates in the Anthropic Attractor Analog

Walker enjoyed reading Jung because he explained culture and mythology so well. Jung introduced the western reader to many exotic books: *The Tibetan Book of the Dead* (about levels and representations of body mind hieararchy); The *I Ching* (about number and synchronicity sampling and divination); *The Secret of the Golden Flower* (about Taoist alchemy); *Answer to Job* (about the personality of God); also he wrote about the symbolism of the Catholic Mass; also the Tarot. Walker started reading Jung's *The Psychology of Kundalini Yoga*. The system of chakras and the curved spinal entity, the kundalini were an early attempt to find a code or a language of images tasked with generating symbols for a controlled descent (or is it ascent) into the unconscious. Several religions show a chakra structure model to explain the ascendancy of: survival instinct, sex drive, self esteem, emotions, intellect, will and spiritual aspirations. The Jewish Cabala tradition of the Sephirot has 10 centers, in an array of interpenetrating triangles. The famous Sri yantra shows the triangles as flattened layers superimposed. Both the sephiroth and the yantra are derived from the tetrakys so idolized of Pythagoras.

The chakras are seen as icons to represent each of the layers of complexity of the human nervous system; each with centers visualized as wheels or vortices, flowers or mandalas affixed at various heights like cell phone tower antennae going up and down the human spine. Or like video, networking, sound and storage cards stuck into the backplane of a computer. The hierarachy is teleological. In the sense of the anthropic principle, that matter evolves conscious beings so that they may know its designs. Jung's book talks about Western man coming to understand the chakras in a descending order. And in particular Jung talks about the change from one level to the next. There is an energy of change, that is experienced.

Walker wrote a hypnotic induction as a kind of phenomenological experiment to experience something. It seemed to him that was what was going on in the sutras, or in yoga nidra.

VIBGYOR SUTRA

Let yourself imagine a sunset
At the golden hour
the sun is low
and the light is yellow.
You are looking out at the edge of the world
where the sky meets the earth.
The clouds are glowing with an internal fire
as the light has been separated out into its colors
by the prism of atmosphere
and air brushed into layers
of the most exquisite softness
VIBGYOR
Violet Indigo Blue Green Yellow Orange Red
The Violet on darkening high is the oncoming night;
It down shifts to Indigo,
And the still Blue — left over from the day.
Perhaps some Green just above
the golden molten Yellow of the sun
at the center of the scene.
And below that, the Orange
and Red below that,
in the crack of dusk or dawn.
You can see time in the golden hour
at the junction
between twilight and night.

Do whatever you do to step into the light day dream,
the common everyday trance . . .
staring at a candle or a bright reflection.
Let yourself go . . into the land
of winkin' blinkin' and nod.

You can sit or lie down
stretch out your shoulders one then the other
 and hips one then the other and feet one then the other
then let them fall into repose

Focus on your breath
you might want to count
The mind loves to be occupied with counting
... backwards ... breathe in on the odd
and breathe out on the even ...
50 ... 49 ... 48 ...

You are a soft machine . . .
Allow yourself to feel the heat from this sunset,
let its warmth come into you.
We are going on an inward journey of intuition.
Like people since the dawn of time
have believed, assumed, there are, somewhere in the body,
centers of interest to the human enterprise:
your survival instinct,
your sex drive,   your self-esteem, your emotions,
your intellect,   your will
and your spiritual aspirations.
The basic 7.

So the chakras are an ancient way
people used to contemplate the structure of their being,
your muscles   your gut
your lungs   your heart
your voice   your brain   your soul

To feel where these sources of these powers are,
relax the body and quiet the mind.
The sun, since it gives us everything on earth,
is an archetype of god, and people wanted to see
that god within — reflected in the colors
of the sun's spectra — without,
as it is in a sunset.

You have seven chakras or energetic points within.
Choose one
of the airbrushed layers
of color in the sunset
and allow its rays to enter you.

Usually they start at the bottom,
the red root
at the center of the physical.
And work their way up,
through the orange
and the yellow and the green and the blue
to the royal crown
at the top of the head.
But instead,
let us start with the most important one,
the yellow chakra of solar energy of the breathing.
Fix your gaze on the yellow at the center of the sunset
and let it expand and contract with the breathing
of the solar plexus.
Visualize a yellow disk there, and relax,
and let it shine out of your chest.
Let your shoulders relax
and your chest expand and open and settle in
for a journey within,
to find the real you.
Your center of the solar energy.
It is shining out.
Inhale into that yellow circle chakra and exhale,
pushing the light out — beyond the edge,
of the confines of your body,
filling the space around your arms,
between the legs, out
beyond the confines of the room.

Let the yellow light from the solar chakra
blend on down into the orange circle
in the middle at your waist.
And on down into the red,

of the sacral spine as the warmth and focus moves,
down from your spine
down your legs
as the beautiful mandarin orange
flows

into the proprioceptive physical body.
Let the warmth, the red flow
down and out through your toes,
down and down to the lower depths of dark space.

Perhaps you will feel an efflorescence of the tissue,
a kind of tingly numbness,
like just before you are to fall asleep.
But you are still awake.
Now in your mind
move from the yellow of the solar plexus
up
into the emerald green of the heart chakra.
Think of how your heart goes out to spring,
you can't help it.
There is love all around.
A vibrant green just like fresh green grass and
it's extending, growing outwards
through the shoulders.
Through the arms and hands.
Through the tips of your fingers.
Moving through the body,
opening the heart,
pressing down into the bright yellow,
the luscious orange, and
beautiful rose red.

A ray of sunshine
separated by the prism into its colors
illuminating your chakras
reclaiming your personal power.

Moving up from the emerald green circle of the heart

chakra we come to the blue
in the throat.
This is where you
speak your truth,
make your will known.

Coming out of the mouth.
Blue, green, yellow, orange, red.
Are you the glib raconteur you think yourself to be.
Or are you tongue tied.
What can you do to balance your speech.
Alignment comes first to mind,
and connecting the heart
to how and what your say.

Moving the focus higher to the eyes,
the brain behind the eyes
we have the third eye,
It is gazing inward.
You can watch a movie projected on a screen
here behind your eyes.
The 3rd eye is a projector, running dreams.
The dream maker
wants to edify and entertain you.
All you have to do is pay attention and let it.

Keep them all in focus
Moving down into the blue, the calm blue
of your peace and your truth.
Into the green of your heart.
Into the yellow of your energy.
Into the orange of your desire.
Into the red of your action.
And let it focus up to the top
On top of the brain, is the crown chakra.
It is like a building with the roof lifted off
open to the clouds and the sky.
It is a symbol for your spiritual connection,
you soul some call it,

opening up to the quantum waves of field light
evolving us to be here.

It is moving on the dark
lifting you out
of your getting and spending reason

into the real
with its own rules.

Into what Castaneda called the Nagual
it is the dream maker ,
the internal guide — out there
to alternate parallel realities,
there is something abstract about the spirit,
in the sense of the mathematical form
into which beings become themselves.
The synchronistic, the higher dimensions
in which our world is embedded

As we inhale we extend
and as we exhale, we ground.
Meditate on these colors
let them become the real you.

From reading Jung's *The Psychology of Kundalini Yoga*
Walker started thinking of the analogy to quantum energy
transition diagrams. That energy was being given off and or
taken up in the transition between chakra layers. That it was
like the energy around Christian sacraments. For example
one could think of the transition of the sacrament of baptism,
becoming a self-supporting entity, is about the transition
from the 1st chakra, the root, up to the 2nd chakra the sacral.

The transition from the 3rd chakra, the lungs, up into
the 4th chakra, the heart, is celebrated in the sacrament of
holy Eucharist. Becoming part of the agape of the human
Christian community. Confession celebrates the transition

to the throat chakra, having the courage to speak your truth even if it was in the wrong.

Confirmation — getting in touch with the holy spirit occurs in the transition to the 3rd eye chakra, about will and desire.

The chakras are intelligences, secret selves, recesses of the heart, vital force centers, that animate the animal and human being. Top chakra is one affiliated with recognition of the divine. It is one you become more concerned with the older you get, if you have been successful enough with the others needed to provide the basic necessities of survival and support.

The analogy sent a shiver running down his spine from head to tail bone. Was mortality the frame for all means?

It corresponds to the Open System Interconnect. The upper three send messages down to the network and get messages back: this is said to be the Applications set which runs on top of the Transport set. The Applications set includes the Application that is running, the files that can be pulled up and are showing in the windowing of the Presentation, and Session which is how inquiries are started and finished with the lower layers. It is in the Session layer that conversations with the Other, or the Holy Spirit or the intuition are instigated. This corresponds to the throat chakra or the 3rd eye chakra.

Now in the being when you go from the upper mental levels to the lower body levels, there is the heart chakra which is about love and feeling. This is distributed through out the body — it is the limbic system; we could have called it the limbic brane or brain. In the OSI model this is the Transport layer.

It is the TCP of the famous TCP/IP, where the IP is at the network layer. This physical layer is the 3rd chakra

the breathing, and in the OSI model it is the router. To log
into the server you have to go through a router. (Breathing
control to hypnosis.)

Transport (Layer 4) This layer provides transparent
transfer of data between end systems, or hosts, and is responsible for end-to-end error recovery and flow control. It
ensures complete data transfer. So the router is the heart of
the network. That's true. In our analogy it is proprioception.

It is this love and interest that lets you into the system,
invites you into the kingdom. Sentience the ability to
feel; distinguished from the ability to reason. Walker had
discovered a new religion: Septentience the ability to probe
the 7 layers of your evolution with your archetypes.

Transport layer: this layer provides the fascia ligaments
and muscles for structure and speed that carry and support
the being. It is important to discover this. Ballet and tai chi
explore this world.

The layer above that provides switching and routing
technologies, creating logical paths, known as virtual
circuits, for transmitting data from node to node. Routing
and forwarding are functions of this layer, as well as
addressing, inter-networking, error handling, congestion
control and packet sequencing.

The 2nd layer is the Data Layer. The layer of the cells
and the organs they comprise — arterial pathways and
the layer of energy transport between the cells, and within
the cells. This is switching circuits and bridges between
networks.

The 1st layer is the physical, the basic energy process,
the thermodynamics. The automorphic hypercycles.

This corresponds in the OSI model to the hub and
repeater.

Open systems interconnect; closed systems don't.

Specialman's Provisional Life

March 19, 1987.

Walker is in the waiting room at his psychiatrist's office on Telegraph Avenue. The sky outside the large waiting room winow was dark and forboding, it was about to rain in Berkeley. His guide comes to the door and gets him. Soon he is sitting in the hot seat at his regular therapy session. He opened his coat. He starts.

Walker: I'm really afraid of my anger. I feel like I want to test everybody a lot. . . . I feel really testy. . . I mean I'm so upset around asking for this new big screen, I will put my job on the line if they don't give it to me.

Anna Z: You are? How come?

Walker: It's 2000 bucks. I think I need one and I should have one.

(Pause)

I'm starting to think like/ I just got paid yesterday, and I hardly have any money in the bank, it just goes real fast. My parents never let me have any money, never taught me how to manage money very well. And I'm just sort of getting really dissatisfied with the money.

Anna Z: What's your salary?

Walker: 38,000 a year.

Anna Z: Really. Have you gotten a raise lately.

Walker: No. Not in a while,

Anna Z: But …You have never told me that . . .

(Walker feels embarrassment. It settles in as though she were catching him in a lie.)

Anna Z: that . . . that was how much you were making. It doesn't seem like enough to you?

Walker: It certainly doesn't seem like very much. I'd like
to move, live in some decent place. I can't even see
doing that. Or just saving some money for a trip to
Europe.

Anna Z: I thought that your way was being paid, potentially.

Walker: Nah. They're not going to pay my way. I bought my
ticket. I paid for my ticket. Although I am going to
visit our office up there, I like the guy, he lives in
Zurich. And that's where Jung's house is. I'd like to
see that. Bollingen, it would be like visiting a shrine.
So I've decided I'm going to go over there. If I can
just keep this job... Jeese, today is 6 months I've
been there.

Anna Z: It's been hard for you to keep a job longer than 6
months.

. . . . . .

Walker: I don't know how the money goes. I have to look at
that more closely I never look at my paycheck. I just
throw my money into the bank and make sure there's
money in there. I don't balance it or anything. I don't
keep track of it. Confusing. Or too much trouble, or
something. They have these people there at work,
Purchasing people and it's just really getting me in
my guts to have to track everything, you know and
uh, follow everything around. God, I'm sorry, but
I'm just so bored and frustrated with it all.

Anna Z: But the result is . . what's the end result of quitting
your job? Not only do you not have 1400 dollars to
let slip through your hands, you don't even have 200
dollars. You feel even more dependent, you know?
And you find yourself in a situation where you have
to line up with other people to get something to eat.
You feel much littler and even more victimized.

(Pause, retorts).

Walker: Yeah . . . But I get to work on my books and do my own writing.

Anna Z: Right. And that brings us back to another thing, in terms of that you also feel closer to a certain idea of yourself. That somehow your mother is being there, to protect you in writing.

Walker: Uhm . . . Well that's a good idea.

Anna Z: Am I going to be like my dad or like my mother. Do what she wants . . .

Walker: Hummm. Is that how you see it? Is that how it is? (Pause, thinks).

Walker: It's pretty good. Perhaps, I think along those lines (Pause, having an insight.)

.....

Walker: I'm going to set it up to make you get rid of me.

Anna Z: Again we have talked about this before. You get so confused. Again you feel so guilty about getting any kind of special privileges, you do it in a kind of outrageous demanding way, and on the other hand you feel really uncomfortable about asking for anything at all. And it's hard to find a middle ground. Part of you thinks that you don't even deserve the drawing pen and the other equipment, the scanner; and yet another part thinks if they don't get you this 2000 dollar piece of equipment, you're gonna quit.

Walker: Uhhum.

Anna Z: Surely there some middle ground here!

Walker: This incredible polarity here. Did you ever see anyone so polarized. Is it a common thing.

(Long Pause)

Walker: I don't know what to say about all this stuff. I'm sort of losing it here. . .(Long Pause) . . . . . .

Anna Z: It's related to this feeling of being special. You partly like it and you partly don't like it.

And, it may have been helpful in some way to give you the low fee but I think it also may make you feel kind of dependent in some way.

And I think it's interesting in that light, is that one of the things that would come up today, is that you are making as much money as you are making, and that you've never let me know before.

Anna Z: What about your attitude toward money in all this? Which is what came up. I mean it is odd, that a single man, making that much money nearly 38,000 dollars a year is having trouble. And I think also it is odd, that, um, you know making as much money as you do, you haven't brought that up with me, in terms of the fee we arranged. I mean it has been a lot lower.

We talked about my fee scale being between 30 and 60 dollars per hour, and you are still really at the bottom. I mean if we understand it in terms of the metaphor of the relationship with me, and how it is like the relationship with your mother, that it might not be such a good idea for you to not be paying a bigger fee. In terms of being bigger.

Walker: Uh huh.

....

Walker: It's not so important, the idea of being a big guy making a lot of money. Doesn't interest me.

Anna Z: You would rather be a little guy

Walker: No, not that either. Big guys are assholes.

Walker: Make more money.

Anna Z: Well don't you think having a special relationship with me where you kind of get some special priv-ileges, lower fee, and maybe in other ways, that we haven't talked enough about, you feel kind of special. Kind of like how you felt with your mother, and you feel guilty about that, and you punish yourself.

Walker left that session shaken, and stirred to write something to try and understand what did his shrink mean, going on about his sense of 'being special.' He felt there was something important about himself he had to confront or at least understand. And how it related to his mother and his relationship with women and his creativity and his soul.

In the House, they often used the term "infantilized" meaning: To create dependency by getting into collusion with. But that's not it. . . 'being special' suggests the idea of Inflation. Suddenly he recalled how in his callow youth he would sometimes notice a, what he called his bob-dylan-smirk of amusement at the world, spread across his lips.

But inflation suggests narcissism and how could that be if he had what was surely an inferiority complex. He was the opposite of narcissism most of the time. What would that be: bedraggled Sisyphusian drudge? Abdicating? Beatnik? It was living the provisional life on the edge of things. Not taking part in the action and the passion of the times. But hunkered down in a bunker trying to live the artistic life.

He tried to use it in a sentence: Because you are really involved with (addicted to) creativity, you think you are 'special.' And he was quick to add: as well as especially cursed! much of the time.

His childish way with money was some kind of artistic disdain based on the fantasy of his being different from the wave of lock-step conformism and homogeneity drowning modern life. But was this extended adolescence he was trying to live really an attempt to reproduce that feeling of being cared for.

He cringed with chagrine at seeing this childish behavior still so active in his personality. Can one be haunted for a lifetime by an archetype? It's like finding out you've got some chronic disfiguring disease.

"He's got Puer Aternalis!" "Stay away from him, it might be contagious."

He started looking up the Eternal Boy syndrome, and realized there is much to see about himself in that archetype. It goes by several names. Peter Pan syndrome. Mamma's Boy. The Man Who Wouldn't Grow Up. The Boyman of Fuck-it.

He read Jung and von Franz on the Puer Archetype. To Walker they seemed confrontational in their writing with an aggressive, psychiatrist-confronting-miscreant tone — for men who refuse to mature.

Their observations began to dwell in his mind. The archetype of Puer began to seem very pertinent. It explains many things. Much as he would rather not, he had to drag himself into looking at his relationships. They talk about how the Puer avoids commitment. (Hence the peter pan syndrome that all the women talk about.)

> It sure sounds like me. Like always trying to make sure to keep my options open; not get tied down. I was an alien in this land; didn't vote, didn't participate much in the action and the passion of the times; hold no currency; tried to avoid becoming an automaton ruled by habit and routine.
>
> I must admit I was in some kind of a thing with women that I had developed with my mother. As Anna pointed out I felt or I acted like the world was supposed to accommodate my being special, just because I was a writer. I had a unique destiny. Compared to being in the flow of creating, the regular world was just too mundane, and so it was hard to hold onto a job, to earn a living.
>
> I felt like I was creating things that were so high and wild that it would take the rest of the world a long time to catch up.

(Now that, even I could admit was inflation.)

Not being able to earn a living caused me to live a more marginal or provisional life. I organized my life like a surfer, being able to drop everything and go out to sea but this was the sea of the unconscious and it did flow if you were committed enough to catching that wave, around what was the next best creative opportunity coming down the road. So, this was the reason I kept myself in a kind of low level prison, poverty to minimize distracting from the real work though it also seemed to deny choices and opportunities.

The key here is special. Wanting to feel special. Special as in the eyes of the mother. Writing was somehow an attempt to maintain a relationship with the mother.

The confrontation with the archetype brought my normal sense of sanity into question. It made a place for both Puer and Senex to encounter each other, two archetypes filtering up from the collective unconscious to the unconscious and over the edge into the pre-conscious.

Jung is always quick to point out the constellation of the opposites in any diagnosis of a patient. I recalled the passage about the macho man who becomes sentimental for he has pushed his anima away from him into the unconscious and consequently develops a kind of dependency on this wife. In the House we used the phrase "giving the feelings to the woman", meaning that the man got himself locked into an insensitive set way of being in order to not feel manipulated. Whoever lives one pattern exclusively risks constellating the opposite. He called this engine of the opposites enantiodromia. It was a principal of nature, using the friction between opposites to generate a force of movement and change. The more one sided we are, the more likely it is that the opposite will break through to spin our lives around.

A feeling of foreboding and denial began to make itself felt in the periphery of my day. Was it because I had repressed that side of myself? Now it returned with a vengeance. I had to cut the shit and get real. Go in the direction of the pain source rather than run away from it.

When I started to understand the influence of this Puer archetype, I had a mixed feeling. On the one hand it was like this huge insight to personality; on the other it was some things about myself that I did not even want to know. The feeling of foreboding and denial lingered on for days and days. It became a nausea in my stomach and my whole body.

The puer complex based on the Puer archetype explained the feeling that I was special. And it let to me really questioning: what could my life be?

Walker had a dream which at first seemed to be about his struggle with the impossibility of ever making a living from his poetry.

Selling a creative poetry project

I am at some kind of creative meeting with the Terminator cyborg Arnold Schwarzrnegger. I am supposed to pitch a creative project involving poetry. It is in a coffee shop deli, downstairs. There are black formica tables and cold cuts under glass. It is Moshe's on Shattuck. (A familiar hangout near the warehouse theatre they called The Pit, Moshe's was a Jewish-Italian deli owned by Chinese and staffed by Koreans.)

The Arnold and his people are supposed to collaborate with me on some project having to do with poetry. But he's got fans coming up and waiters scurrying and I can't really get his attention. I've got this presentation that is not working and it is klutzy and long and I've got to find something in this giant literary supplement, the pink section of the Sunday paper. I want to read this famous poem in it to him, because he has said his idea of poetry is the rhyming speech soldiers recite to keep cadence when they march. He has even been rapping out a little bit of it for me as an example (and to put me down):

Reading, writing, arithmetic!
Too much homework makes me sick
I don't know but I've been told
Writer's dreams can't be sold.

I was quite taken aback and needed to explain poetry to him; but we are being bum-rushed out of there because it is closing time. And I am desperately searching through this huge pink literary supplement trying to find this great poem, cursing that it has no table of contents or index but that I know is there.

I have to wonder Why would my psyche compose such a dream for me. I think it was to show me my Writer archetype, who is working to try and make something popular, something to communicate with people. And being very very very frustrated by it. It was a soul crushing dream.

Interpretation

That "It was a soul crushing dream" juxtaposed with a creative meeting with Arnold Schwarzrnegger sends out a shadow signal. Schwarzenegger is very big in size and casts a large shadow. It occurs to me that the meaning of this dream is: Perhaps I am avoiding a more popular approach and, in fact, stand in my own way. Also another possibility, more difficult to look at: If the Arnold is a father figure then might the dream also be about a personal rejection coming from my father?

Why does one become a writer? And why does one choose a particular way of writing other than for popularity? The scene in Moishe's diner was where the "other-than's," the outcasts and the rebels met back in the 70s. It seems to me that it is truly a writer's archetypal dream. The fact that it is "crushing" shows how tremendous the affect is, that it is close to a nerve.

Perhaps it is not as negative as it seems. However, the affect or the feeling that I have as the dreamer is what is really important and only I can really be a judge of that. What am I feeling. It might even be a positive dream. That I am searching through the pink section (the section of popularity) rings true of the conflict between being true to one's self and making a compromise.

Walker had been developing a parallel or analogy between how a computer runs an application to how a dream

runs symbols. He started by interpreting the dream. He had
some idea of Dream as Application run on the computer.
Then Walker got the idea to look at running an application
on top of the code of the dream. The Application is Active
Imagination. He began pursing the analogy —

Computer : Application :: Dreams : Symbols.

Jung and the gestaltists ask you to explore the idea that all
of the dream characters are aspects of your own being. So
then, play that the Arnold is also me. What do you think about
being Arnold Schwarzenegger? What of his busyness, that he
is constantly being assailed by attention seekers and that he
can't concentrate. What does that mean to me if I were him?

Jung would suggest that I use active imagination and take a
few minutes to let Arnold tell me what he thinks on his terms
And not in the terms of the renegade cyborg shadow. One
doesn't use this process as a way of interpreting the dream but
as answering the dream's challenge, namely that you continue
to write no matter the conflict. This may be a key to open the
door to a new writing. The most important thing is not really
knowing what a dream means but using the dream as a way
of opening parts of your unconscious and letting those parts
inform your new text. In a sense it is the Puer archetype within
you that is being challenged.

The dream has symbolic elements that will suggest Interpretations. And the dream asks you to take it further as an
Application into your life. The application produces some
energy structure back into the life of the dreamer. One communication from the dream comes in the form of a suggestion, of
how to let the psych develop more. This Psyche that is larger
than the ego is interactive through the dream that way. And
you get better with practice. The practice asks you to expand
into unused pathways of Feeling and Thinking, Sensing and
Intuiting. This oneiromancy along with active imagination was
Jung's Way in the *Red Book*.

The computer is the Psyche and it has an operating
system (Aristotelean / Newtonian language) which groups

phenomena into categories. The Psyche runs the dream, and usually in the dream it runs both a landscape of images and actions. And these have meaning in the sense that they can be signs carried out into action of self-understanding.

Dreams are maintenance routines — cron jobs run at night when the ego is off-line. They are part of the speculative nature of mind: to say what if and to visualize and imagine in images, fantasies, dreams, myths . . . and other linguistical structures.

The most positive thing I learned about this encounter with the archetype was feeling the force of its two opposite energies at work — Puer and Senex — in the creative process. These two are the childlike beginner's-mind in the thrill of discovery that the Puer is always trying to be in (the creative flow) and, the logical, constraining, shaping of the rational Senex mind — shaping the persuasion.

Walker wrote a poem to mark the realization.

The Interface of Senex and Puer

An unlikely cooperation—puer aternalis
enjoying the beginner's mind
and senex with experience and solace,
bookends of (shelf) life, stretching out behind.
Puer is the child making things ravel
to fill in the gaps of knowing with magic
and Senex who knows — experiencing the tragic.
They meet in the creative act of time travel
as you old man looked for how he feels
and sat with him because he has no real
understanding of how things accrete.
He inspired you through the effort started long ago
to make it through trauma and defeat,
an interface to take the art to where it needed to go.

This strong experience of the Puer archetype manifest in the complex and how it was bound across time to the Senex archetype suggested that these were two poles apriori to dimension, in this case the dimension of time. I got an insight into the theories of Jung, how in a way the unification and dialectic of opposites informed all the concepts in the psychology: the unconscious, individuation, projection the shadow, the anima. The force of enantiodromia, is reflected in the image of archetypes as unification of binary opposites — the two faces of one god.

I was trying to stay with the concepts but behind it I was thinking and feeling about how I had come to be who I am, what I might become. And I was slowly taking on this perennial mind. Depth psychology was reorganizing my cognitive structure. Yes that was it, I was undergoing a reorganization of cognitive structure. Jung's writing was like Castaneda and don Juan, without the peyote. It was like James Joyce and Ezra Pound on steroids. Jung's writing was about consummate literary scholarship going across histories and culture, but also rooted and crossed with experimental science.

And you have to go in the direction of the difficult and scary, you have to let go of old received ideas. It is a kind of ego death and rebirth.

You are trying to bring these levels together, what you do, and how you imagine yourself and the narrative of who you tell yourself you are. And you are trying to get them to know about each other and help each other, pull together, yoga.

You imagine yourself to be one thing; then you act a different way; and you talk an even different way: to somehow keep the peace — Anima Ego Persona.

The Persona intercedes between where the anima, your soul, your creative self, wants to lead you and the shadow that is afraid of being different. And the ego that is trying to martial the troops and move on forward into the breech. Reading Jung gives me an expanded sense of self and possibilities. And I am afraid of that. I want to run away from it but am drawn to it. At times you do have to be like a warrior moving through these structures and you have to really believe in them. You have to fight for them. It is a lonely path.

I had to take a good look at what is not helping me, and abandon it.

You get shot out of the tube
and you soar into the game
on an energetic arc.
You touch and bounce off
many rubber bumpers
that light up and make sound.
You score lots of points.
There is a little skill involved
tilting the playing field.
And eventually you
roll all the way down
to where you
drop off the edge.

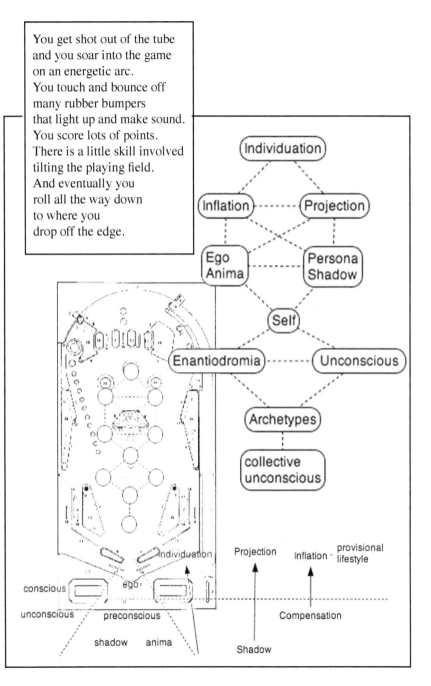

Individuation

Inflation — — Projection

Ego
Anima

Persona
Shadow

Self

Enantiodromia — — Unconscious

Archetypes

collective
unconscious

Individuation

Projection   Inflation - provisional
                        lifestyle

conscious

ego

unconscious   preconscious   Compensation

shadow   anima

Shadow

Mandala — Archetypes

When Walker experienced how the puer archetype overtook his personality in a complex, it felt kind of crazy. It was a big realization. Were their other archetypes lurking in the wings ready to take stage and run the show? Apparently so. Certainly the psyche had been giving him evidence of archetypes in his dreams. He had come to recognize the Anima certainly and the Shadow unfortunately too. He could just look in his dream diary.

For example this one. Is it a reflection of the Anima?

Ducks following Mama

I was out on the street in the old neighborhood, in Montreal, and there were these birds, little ducks and they were lost and we kept on asking them, Where's your mom? Where's your mom? And they were wandering off and we didn't know and finally at last the momma duck showed up, but she was a different kind of bird, a different species. But she had come to intercede. And the little birds got into formation with her.

The idea that this female intercedes.

Here is another dream with the Anima.

Sister's friend hug

I am with my sister. It is an old memory of a boy and a girl building sand castles by the sea in Corpus Christie. On vacation I spent much time with her at the beach of Padre Island. We are the divine couple emerging, a son and daughter.

Now a grown woman in her 20s, the Psyche shows her to me in a dream. She is visiting with a young woman friend. We are sitting around the table, talking and my sister is butting in complaining: I was supposed to help with her Japanese translation job, or something.

I was standing up and this woman friend of my sister's came around to embrace me. It wasn't the sister but young

*and willowy like her. And there in the room in front of others
we hugged for a long time. It felt so good this dream hug,
people don't get into the full-on hug any more. And after we
were hugging for a long while my sister and other people in
the room were saying, "Brother . . . brother!" But we were
hugging and hugging, trying to find each other. And I could
sense a host of projections out there peopling the room with
their eyes on us registering shock because we were exceeding
the boundary of common embracero. And still neither of
us were making an attempt to pull away and we continued
hugging. (It is amazing in the dream you can feel the physical
imprint of a body against your own, real, physical; I could feel
her little pointy breasts through her blouse.) Who was she, this
strange woman. She didn't let go and I didn't let go; it was just
as natural as could be. I woke up and said Wow, and thought it
was an embrace from my Anima.*

With practice Walker have gotten pretty good at keeping
the dream diary. It helped him realize that the unconscious
wants to be recognized, and when you pay attention to it, go
to some trouble to learn the interpretation of symbols, learn
to recognize recurring archetypal characters, and keep a
dream diary it gets easier and richer with practice.

Walker wrote this analysis of the hug dream.

The anima enters as the friend of the sister. That is the
permissible sphere of the persona. The anima is a shape
shifter. Once in my arms she begins to become herself. After
exceeding the rules of the persona-sized world. It is I deciding
for her rather than for it, by continuing to hold her tight. She
answers by growing breasts. This synthesis of the physical
suggests I have moved past the quotidian. She is greeting me
as a fellow entity on the journey to the Self.

This journey to the Self is diagramed by Jungians as a circle
with the Self at the center sending out information to the
being. The ego is seen in this representation as an annular ring
around the border of the outside edge of the circle centered on
the self.

Also you could think of the ego as being the center of consciousness, it would be at the center of the circle. And the Self would be as the everything-else area of the circle around it. That which contains the container.

But one usually thinks of the ego as a smaller circle trying to move from the outside in toward the center which is the self. Becoming aligned with the Self is a tractor beam that draws you in, closer to this source, so as to act and react in more harmonious phase lock with this bigger reality Self.

Individuation is seen as coming to know the archetypes; that they be known by the conscious ego.

This ambiguity of flipping from one image of the self and ego relationship to another suggest Pascal's statement: "God is an infinite sphere whose center is everywhere and whose circumference is nowhere." I got to thinking, wondering: what are these archetypal figures I am supposed to come to know. Mother. Father. Others. My own myth. They are always present orbiting around in the peripheral field of psyche.

I saw this in another 'process illustration' dream.

Looking at this Zen garden of small white rocks raked into waving patterns around huge boulders or stone monoliths embedded in the gravel fields. It was like the big stones were islands and the waves propagated out in ripple rings into the gravel field. These waves would be an image of libido energy.

Walker could feel the relation with his unconscious getting more real. He was given evidence of this through his dreams. This was what the work of self-analysis leading toward individuation was about. Sometimes it was painful. Sometimes there were insights. And rewards. As much as you want to understand the unconscious, the unconscious wants to understand you. Call it a handshake. Or a transference. That is how powerful the potential of our experience is.

The "Sister's friend hug" had such a good feeling. I must have made friends with the Feminine for her to send one of her daughters to me. She is inviting me to leave my family behind psychically. By that I mean, she is encouraging me not to identify with them and showing me why. She is engaging my feeling function. That is why I am experiencing feeling. The anima comes challenging functions. I have joined with her. I have accepted her, wanted her. She wants me to embrace the feminine in me.

Here is a dream where it seems the Shadow is menacing the Anima.

This awful movie with the killer clown in a bright bright yellow suit with red trim piping around the cuffs and lapels and pockets. He appears in the room. He floats in the air in front of the big window with the shades drawn. He is dressed up in this loud clown suit, and white face with cheeks painted rouge.

He is menacing a girl. A female, with long brunette hair. She wears a dressy pleated skirt and blouse.

I'm watching him from the side as he menaces this girl. He has a seething sinister toothy grin and red gums and lipstick painted red lips. And cruel unfeeling dark flashing eyes. The room is some kind of dormitory, a college. Away from everybody.

A really crazy and unpleasant dream. Come to think of it at times one only sees his torso, floating in the air: not the legs, no arms.

Walker wrote this interpretation

I thought the dream is probably telling me something about the way I might appear menacing to women?

— room far away = the unconscious

If this is in a movie form, then it is meant to be presented for an audience. I am the audience. The presentation is for me. The unconscious in the form of the killer clown is threatening the anima. I am not threatening the anima. I am on the thin line between watching the movie and being in the movie, and I am the audience and perhaps, even, the director. In a sense I am watching the dailies. The killer clown is a stock character issued up from the stinky unconscious. It is dripping with numinous power. He has great power and if it is a shadow, then his sheer power tells me how much power I might have. Remember, it was I who cooked this dream up.

— no arms, no legs, a floater; that's the signature of a ripe and ready psyche. It is good. The anima is not in power. She is allowing herself to be in a state of being threatened. I wonder what makes the clown be the way he is. He is toothy, unfeeling and has flashing eyes. The "flashing" gave me the willies. The anima as a coed.

I am working on Shadow and Anima.

No one wants to feel the Shadow because it descends or arrises in a cloud of shame or guilt or hate. These are not transitory feeling states but heavier and much more long lasting affect states. A mood. Hard to get out of. Drink and smoke offer only temporary release.

I was thinking that Shadow and Anima were what Freud calls Thanatos and Eros.

Both Shadow and Anima are occluded into the unconscious. They are like opposites. Anima is about joy and nurturance and creativity and love. So wouldn't the artist always be trying to see and rescue anima from the unconscious.

Shame is particularly nasty. Because it is first experienced in a scowl on the mothers face (probably associated with some stinky foul wretched stenchy substance.) One is being cut off, pushed away. And being cut off is such a serious deal that the emotions configure the body into this head hung in shame configuration, shoulders humped, stooped like a dummy, a pilgrim locked in the stocks. The body heats up, blushes, drives into avoidance and tries to extract a promise to never engage in the offending activity again.

The anima as a coed. I wondered if the dream was about the alienated relationship to the feminine aspect of my psyche?

There is a ferment between our inner genders. There is a charge stored between two plates of a capacitor like nitroglycerin peanut butter between two crackers. In order to become your whole self you have to cross the peanut butter barrier, and there is a big nasty Ronald McDonald in the way. I must trust in my feminine, embrace her. Then I can feel like my anima is not in danger, moreover she could eat that guy like a big mac. I wonder what it is like to be a woman? Can I try it out and see how it affects my relationship with this powerful archetype, the Anima.

I kind of felt like if I can win her over then I will gain the power of the killer clown.

What if I think of the girl as me?

Walker wrote this dialog of Anima and Shadow by way of amplification.

Coming back from a gig scaring children, the Shadow is looking at the Anima. She is young, brunette, long hair, and wearing coulottes.

Said the lowly Shadow, a shrunken damaged withered vesion off the self, typing on the computer screen: "Hello world".

The enticing Anima shimmered and bridled in shivering synchophancy.

The Shadow said, "I'm not to be ignored. I've been watching you. I am one of the minions sent from the central authority."

"I know who you are, Heathcliff," demured the Anima. "I like them tall dark and grim. Full of desire."

This kind of thinking made the hair on the back of Walker's neck stand up.

And he could see that he has not really grasped the idea of Compensation very well. He had come to another gap in his understanding. The idea of compensation is fundamental and the next step after understanding the symbolic. It brings a whole deeper level to the work, which was more abstract, and artistic before. It animates the symbolic. The functions

of the anima and the shadow is that they are mediating!
Walker had not seen that before. Compensation ties together
many basic ideas: projection, unconscious, individuating,
enantiodromia, archetypes. . .

One needs a compass to navigate this depth. It emerges
as a mandala, an image of wholeness and completion whose
abstraction is the circle.

We are not used to seeing mandalas everywhere like
in Buddhist countries. Or the sun shields of the American
Indian, or the circle of standing stones in Neolithic England,
or the Mayan calendar carved in stone. We have to intimate
one for our own time. We go into the old ones like we were
doing archeology on a temple in hopes that recognition of a
mythical pattern would resonate across time.

The mandala is a circle. Walker started noticing circles
everywhere. Round tires, round wheels. Circles were
universal, scaling the symmetry up and down. In this view
time is not a linear scaler filling space: time is seen in rings
of concentric circles of sending and receiving back and forth
inner < -- > outer. A mandala lays out the symmetry of
enantiodromia, the dialectic of opposing forces so that one
might see the world looking from the self at the center of
being, rather than from the ego at the center of consciousness. The mandala is the field in which the knowing is
enlarged by making the journey of the hero from the ego to
the true self.

To construct a mandala Walker used a pot to trace a
circle and various bowls and glasses for circles within
the circle. He got out an old pad of graph paper and was
exploring a drawing of concentric circles. He then moved on
to make one with a compass.

The spiritual is a bridge to the Psyche.

Walker had a dream.

Jung Bridge
People playing Bridge with a deck of cards
Tarot like cards.
They are bidding, which is forming the horn of a dilemma.
The dummy lays down his cards and the player tries to
fleece and finesse the 2 players at his side, using the smallest
power cards necessary from the dummy or his own hand.
The four at the table are APES
Anima, Persona Ego, Shadow.

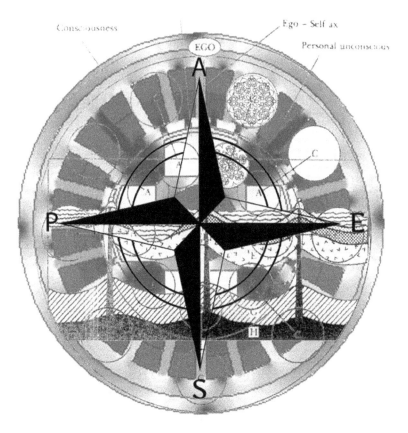

Jungian Compass with 4 points: Anima, Ego, Persona, Shadow

There was so much about the circle to discover. No wonder the early mathematicians were besotted with it. And to discover the terrible unending transcendental number π at the heart of it, the secret chaos in the most pristine symmetry. Having to extend the field from simple integer harmonies to the unending real to the anomalous transcendental must have disturbed their aesthetic sensibilities something awful.

In the biological heritage of animals, instinct rises to generate behavior. In the sublimated psyche of humans, the instincts rise to the occasion of the images, and are circulating in the unconscious psyche and are the currency of dreams and myths. In the depths of the Collective Psyche of humanity, there is a domain where these mythological archetypes dwell, and they can come to exert a powerful influence over an individual's personality development. Anecdotes of apparitions of mythological divinities exist in all world literatures. Modern spirituality seeks the deity in nature as always. Jung showed us how the gods and demons are archetypes in the psyche that are projected out — as though from heaven or hell.

Walker saw himself as the old mystic drawing a circle in the dirt and he heard a voice from within telling him to write sutra and engage in the incantations of spells. We are surrounded by a periphery. Nothing can harm us.

Walker wrote in his journal.

A Persona is the personality that one's ego organizes, and presents to the world. It is a habitual "mask" for an individual to use to face hardship. Berne writes the persona is formed during the years from 6 to 12 when most children first go out on their own . . . to avoid unwanted entanglements or promote wanted ones. The Persona is different from the identity or the self. It is an archetype because it is allowed to take over the functions of the ego (as are other archetypes). It picks up cues from the Collective Unconscious, but does not seem to have a more permanent home in the unconscious like the Anima and the Shadow do.

The Persona is similar to the Shadow. Shadows are manifestations in the form of images and / or actions that arise from the most repressed anti-social, animal instincts necessary for survival now and in an earlier era. While the Shadow seems more godlike (fiendish, energizing, archetypal) and comes and goes seeming unbidden, a Persona is a manifestation of the same feelings but one that can be tamed and trained.

A Persona seems to be based on a hunger, on a high level of will and desire; and perhaps heart (love). If an individual really wants something bad enough and is organizing all his behavior and focus to get it, then his Persona will undergo a metamorphosis into a stronger and hopefully more serviceable form.

This is how the Persona is invoked. The persona is an avatar of our will. The Persona is one of the archetypes, or perhaps a complex which draws in attributes of many archetypes. Does Anima and Shadow invoke the archetypes. Is it just being part of a system that operates on enantiodromia? Attractors finding stabilities in stable orbitals?

What Jung said about equipping a persona: A strong ego relates to the outside through a flexible persona; identifications with a specific persona inhibits psychological development; one can be smothered by the persona, and that sets the stage for the emergence of repressed individuality. This is compensation. (Or complementarity if you follow the quantum model.)

It is a principle of energy and entropy. Though the persona may support the spirit, it extracts a price. It depletes the spirit. For example, a narcissist will have a strong persona to which he is identified. They require adoring minions to concur and ratify his persona in their perception.

A Persona or how shall we say " spell of confidence and authority" is very useful even necessary sometimes to make your way. But looking at the Persona of the narcissist we see that it must be maintained, always and at all costs — even the truth. Personas do not come to any realization, they do not see anything beyond the focus of their desire and need. In fact the Persona grows larger and larger with each new unchallenged "success". It could be that the more "successful" a person becomes in the world, the more the persona is used.

The celebrity persona learns new spells as it reaches higher ranks and gets to conference with more of his kind in the club.

When your dream analysis evolves into self-analysis it requires one revisit his innermost secrets that they have actively tried to suppress, and one way or another expose yourself to your Shadow, an archetype of Self. It attempts to get its host to accept it. If one cannot accept the Shadow, or if they refuse to acknowledge what they want to keep hidden most, the Shadow becomes enraged, attracting all nearby lesser Shadows to itself and transforming into a monster which projects all kind of violent acts and other ugly degenerate depraved images and desires in an attempt to overwhelm the person it spawned from. If one can face oneself and admit to what the Shadow Self says, then the Shadow transforms into a Persona loyal to its user. On standby, their Persona is like a tarot card played in the game as their Persona emerges.

What is it like when one's ego is able to get distance from the shadow and mask it so that it becomes a useful Persona. Is that what artists do?

Actually it is more the case as the Shadow uses the Ego, the Ego uses the Persona in the service of the Shadow. That suggests that the Shadow is a deeper archetype than the Persona. From a much lower circle of hell.

Personas and Shadows are understood unconsciously and recognized in some sense by all. They are not spoken about and are usually kept secret from public knowledge.

The Shadow appears often at times where the Persona is weakened by disease or other crushing adversities, this a the origin of PTSD. If the Ego can see the real tribulations of the traumatic event as an opportunity to transcend the Persona, then he no longer needs to invoke the mask. Then a shift toward the real Self can occur. It doesn't always take crisis to trigger the cracking of the Persona and the mastering of the Ego; some times it can be done with artistic practice or meditation or psychology.

Are each of the Tarot cards the representation of a persona?

Yes. The 4 minor arcana Cups, Wands, Pentacles, Swords, represent. Cups — health; Wands — experience or material rewards; Pentacles — (coins) wealth; Swords — power.

Walker's dreams often were about structures in space. He had this dream.

> *Mall Dream*
> *In my dream I am in an American shopping mall. There are skylights and cavernous open spaces, with escalators and lots of glass store fronts. Lots of brightly colored merchandise.*
> *The mall is a vast structure with escalators going up to the high ground, fountains, moats, columns, high walls, curtain walls, flanking towers, sectors, balustrades, positions of battlements, pull down metal garage doors, metal detector portcullises.*
> *I hear a voice say the mandala is like a fortress or an ideal city in a Buddha realm.*

An analog of the visual mandala is a narrative of psychic structures seen in dreams. In this Mall Dream, Walker saw himself as the subject who is making a representation that reflects the layered model of psyche from Buddhism woven around the theme of channels of psyche. Albeit with an image of what is common in the America he grew up in, the mall.

The dream sees beneath the layers of disguise and layers of false pretenses that you might have had to convince your young mind about in order to get by. These get built up through the years. A mandala is like the image of a citadel, various porticos are guarded and must be gone through to climb up into to the tree of knowledge.

This structure of psyche channels this citadel dweller into expectations and hypotheses not born out by reality checking. After a while there will be demands made to fulfill these expectations. And all this will be spreading a moody delusion involving received event structures sequenced over time into the building blocks of cognitive development and autobiographical memory. These sensations raised up into feelings trying to transform into signs will be transforming, dissolving, and recombining continuously in expectation as they are falling into their appropriate plateaus, constellations and configurations. Like lithography carving on a substrate; or a meme taking up a position, like a mind parasite in the host.

Castaneda is perhaps one of the only literary traditions we have had that is perhaps like Buddha-lands. By that I mean being able to perceive something of a more numinous sense of reality. That and psychedelics where we got to experience the terror of the real when we allowed ourselves to drop some of our filters for a while. What the Buddha lands and Naugual and Jung have in common is that it is an experimental psychology that is prescriptive. They lay out theory, practices, procedures which when performed thoughtfully will yield experiences which though hard to communicate are of a deeper nature than ordinary consensus realty would dictate.

What is the numinous. Can we start with saying it is a non-dual perception of reality? Can there even be such a thing as a non-dual perception; doesn't a perception require a known and a knower.

So. I think the way you get to the Buddha lands as described in their literature involves a lot of practices. A lot of meditation, dream work, psychological struggle with community. They have a lot of ritual and iconography.

Imagine having community (sangha), people that believed in what your believed in, people that supported your process of individuation, were on that path themselves. The three refuges of Buddhism are the Buddha, the Dharma and the Sangha. Now I think the Dharma is the actual. And to really see the actual, as Blake says, is to see the infinite, and that would be the numinous. And the Buddha is the Jungian Self, an inspiration for the goal of individuation, coming to know yourself in a much more real and articulated and forgiving way.

Was I equating don Juan to a Buddha? Can I say that the Buddha is a Naugual? In the dual sense Castaneda uses the term as both a realm, a parallel world in which we are embedded and as a person who has experience, a guide.

But woe, I see where I have dipped into the nominalism that plagues the Buddhist texts, tossing out words like infinite and numinous as if I understood that or the reader understood that. The buddhist texts go on an on vomiting out nominalism of jewels and flowers and streams of winds and trying to outdo with the most superlative courtly honorific terms.

I mean it is good that these guys got to the numinous and obviously they were very blown away by it, and they are throwing down some kind of a signpost. But to get to the numinous you have to use the procedures to get to the right state. It is good to know that it is possible.

In Castaneda, the way of the warrior had most of these practices. He did a lot of work with dreams, and by work I mean trying to become a lucid connoisseur of these erudite communications from the unconscious.

We got better at interpreting symbols and we were just starting to see how archetypes animated the things seen in the dreams meaning. (Thanks for that.) The next step is to study lucidity.

I think the buddhist practice (in the effort to get to the Buddha land) comes down to learning to become more lucid in dreams. Lucidity is being awake in dreams, and from that experience becoming awake to reality (as though it were surface symbol for much more going on beneath.) Psychedelics gave a wee taste of that.

Another space of psyche shown to Walker in dreams.

Dream: cabin in the woods

The cabin is set back about a quarter mile off a river. And up on a rise above the flood plane. It is huge, has some kind of geodesic dome made of steel and glass off the back of it. It has a traditional shingle roof and broad shady porch on the front of it facing the river.

In the flatlands along the river there are patches of garden meadows. There is a gate in front of the cabin proper, and the river beyond with tall trees here and there. It is beautiful, a curving vista in a feng shui. Out front of the cabin is a little mound big enough for a man, and it is made out of straw bales and dirt. There is a square window hole cut just big enough to squeeze in and out of it. The cabin owner likes to sleep out there in the mound and look up at the night sky. We talked to the cabin owner, who showed us around inside. The fire place was impressive like an altar. It had beautiful slabs of golden maple wood boards going straight up vertical and cross ways behind it, like the monstrance, or house of gold holding host. And beyond—the cavernous inside of the glass and steel dome.

I forget what he said, just a householder talking proud of his house. The dome was facing south so it got a lot of light and was used to raise plants. It was an arboretum. I think this was in Alaska or Canada.

I wonder what is the meaning of the mound of straw bales. A burial mound? Or just an advanced outside dream observatory for the sleeper to integrate with the awakening universe and the cozy sleeping bag dream.

In Jung the senex archetype presented itself to him in the form of Philomon. Is it the Senex, the rational who gives the Hero the power to use a Persona?

You have to go into the unconscious to meet this wise one; you have to outgrow your puer, to meet this senex.

The Shadow Probes of Enantiodromia

At Trace after a while, Walker began to feel his shadow machinating. Yet he was incapable of doing anything about it. It was something he sort of understood in hindsight. He could at times feel his shadow take over his ego, like his ego was some kind of machine with other entities holding license to drive it. This is how it happened. And how it led to his quitting his job.

Being a full-time, stock-holding Engineer, Walker even got invited to parties with the upper management. At one party he saw Therese making kissy-face in the hot tub with the great big walrus vice-president. In that moment Walker realized monkey business was afoot.

Soon he would be on a downward spiral to unemployment. Things began to appear skewed. Or maybe, the aberrant warp of things was coming into a sharp focus of reality. All along he had been inhibiting his creative writing voice with the consolation that technical writing was a worthwhile trade-off to getting paid and becoming a publisher. Ever since he was a child, writing had been his way to engage the creative muse, which he was coming to understand was the Anima. Being in therapy helped him hang in, sublimate his impulse to say "take this job and shove it." Tech writing was giving him lots of practice writing the simple declarative sentence over and over for money, but he felt like it was a prostitution version of himself. It was not who he really was.

Things began to pile up to an intolerable level. The work place and the work saddened Walker. How repetitive and boring it all was. Keying in data entry — Karen had to do that all day long for Bob. She was his girl. It meant that for 8 hours a day he gets to operate her. Bob is very nice but he is the Operator of Karen.

Also the disparity of the appointments: in the Marketing section of the facility it was considerably plusher. Walker had thought Marketing would be kind of creative to get into — you got to design these pithy intelligent representations of your product and what it does. He thought maybe he could advance up into that area. But little did he know that Therese, who he thought was just a Marketing Bunny, was a real barracuda in the work place. He realized this the moment he saw her lounging in the hot tub with this great big hog of a vice-president. Walker suspected some kind of a coup had taken place. Next thing they are making Therese Head of the Marketing department, and Don has been kicked upstairs to become a vice-president. Therese was an aggressive young woman. She was an iron fist in a velvet glove. The desire of every modern young woman of today was to be a professional. Walker thought it was unfair: giving the vice-president head so you could get ahead and become head of a department. And of course Therese had to have someone under her for the title, so they gave her Walker. Walker thought she was really a jerk, but he tried to hang in so as not to disappoint his shrink.

The shadow started to slip into his behavior. He started to take really long breaks, sneak out the back of the building and meet Wild Bill for long dog walks around the lake at Aquatic Park in Berkeley by the freeway. Or when he would go to drop off or pick up printing jobs, or half-toning or running errands. Sometimes he would be just gone for hours. If anybody said anything, he'd say he was picking up a print job. All this subliminal self-sabotage made Walker become paranoid and he began to think the accounting department ladies were looking at him funny for collecting all these gas receipts for reimbursement.

Time to go. Though they had given him a little stock in the company, he was feeling over worked and under appreciated. Burnt out. These golden handcuffs he felt kept him tied to the whipping post. Blocking him from marketing would mean he had to stay stuck in technical writing. He felt robbed of an avenue of creativity. Robbed of what he thought were his options to move in this hierarchy. He could not admit to himself: Was I after Don's job? Or Therese 's? Or had I once again fallen under the influence of Wild Bill who was staying in Berkeley. Walker and Wild Bill were part of a giant poetry fest, at the 8th Annual Actualist Convention in Berkeley. Walker edited and desktop published a very thick chapbook of the readings. And he began to long for, and drift back into his itinerant wandering poet self again.

Robert the computer networking manager noticed this behavior. And because Walker had started to trust him and felt the man liked him, he did humorously complain about how much he had begun to dislike being there now. "Christ, I need a lobotomy to stay on this job."

The relationship between Walker and writing and others, is a complicated one. His mother had him reading before grade school. He discovered poetry in the 3rd grade. And he was enamored of it ever since. Now here he had written another novel, taken it all the way to completion. It was a hippie utopian novel about psychology, communal marriage and Buddhism (and thus about archetypal psychology.) And he was working on another one that tied in the thought of Freud, Jung, Joyce, Berne, Castaneda, Peirce, Pound, Korzybski, Levi-Strauss, and others. This heady intellectual discourse creates a spirituous intent and the desultory reception of the few friends he showed it to left him crushed and defensive because he felt as a writer he was supposed to feel ashamed for not being popular. This feeling of shame had to be rejected so that he could continue to create. He smoked marijuana to knock out the chastising super-ego censor in him which mitigated to block his joy. Was it possible, he wondered if I also irrationally projected this perceived personal inferiority out to try and recognize it in others?

Gradually he made up his mind to leave Trace. It felt like a huge relief. There would be an end to his torment. Before he quit his job Walker wanted to make sure he got in his trip to Europe on his paid vacation. His trip to Europe was not all that satisfying. Walking and camping in Scotland was the best. Paris was disappointing. No doubt they feel that way when they come to visit our Hollywood. He met a girl in England. And after he got back he started corresponding with her and offered to pay her way over to the USA. But she didn't take him up on the offer.

Then it was back to work, back to the same old way of being an employee, of being shell-shocked cannon fodder for the information revolution.

Walker was in a projection on his boss Don. He became more aware of his contemptuous thinking of Don. What, he asked himself, was the shadow aspect of my projection on my boss. What power did he have over me. I towered over him. Don was smooth, slick even; smarmy, into flashy cars.

Walker did have to admit that he might have been a little naive and inflated to think that desk-top publishing and design were all that there was to marketing. Still he thought that it might be interesting and take over after Don. And slow down on the technical writing and do some of this creative marketing work.

But then, all of a sudden Walker was out. And he had done it to himself. He just couldn't tolerate working under Therese.

When he complained to the HR lady also a VP, that he didn't want to work for the new head of marketing and suggested they put tech writing under engineering, he felt he had to back up this bluster with action. He did the only thing he could do in the moment, he turned in his resignation on the spot. He had given them an ultimatum and had to deliver on this final proposal when he couldn't get the accommodation he wanted from the HR VP. (He quickly realized the wealthy secure management people are not threatened by your walkout, they have a line-up of people trying to get your job.) And so he was out of there. Affective Immediately. He grabbed his jacket and his pen and he walked down the hall and out the front door for the last time. (He had made sure beforehand to get a few of each of the manuals he had written for portfolio.) He left all his work on the hard drive for the next guy.

He had to ask himself: What had I been thinking? How could I have been so stupid as to say, in an unguarded moment to the HR person, a woman, to whom he had gone to voice his misgiving in the way Therese had become his boss: "I don't think I can work for a woman." Now he was admonishing himself with chagrin: What a Texas redneck I am. How naive to believe HR was on the side of the human resource, when really they were management.

After he had quit his job in a huff Walker had to admit that he had been undone by a master manipulator in Therese. And feeling much shame, his shadow had come out and subverted the game.

To avoid feeling the shame. He tried to rationalize: I grew up in the old pre-liberated South. It was bad enough having a boss but he couldn't be having a woman boss.

And even though he had talked about it in therapy and had prepared for it, he was still shocked at his precipitous decision. He had read in Jung, about how the shadow was at work when a part of us erupts spontaneously and unexpectedly, when we do something self-destructive, or something that is hurtful. Afterwards, we know the shadow has been around because we feel humiliated, ashamed, and guilty. Walker decided to try and do analytic psychology on the situation and learn how to see the movement of Shadow and perhaps Anima beyond the edge of consciousness in this situation.

If you are trying to see your shadow you have to experience the source of shame or hate or greed. That will be turning around to see the light, the source of the projections. They will be archetypes cavorting in the sun throwing shadows on the walls.

In the days after his precipitous auto-ejection, Walker felt sorry for himself. He knew the shadow was passing through. Still he couldn't look directly at the source it was too painful. He imagined the Shadow as an Operator, using the Shadow Probe.

And even though Walker was on the look-out for the Shadow Operator he still didn't see it acting. His therapy helped him see it, but quite after the fact. He consoled himself: "So I am not the business school type. They were adept at Shadow Probing. Male 'bonding,' and camaraderie in general were often a form of shadow probing. I was not used to this from the women. (But come to think of it, my therapist did this a lot, but in a formal agreed-upon way.)"

But then how had that happened. She finds the weakness with a Shadow Probe. Women are great at the shadow probe. Or it could be my narcissism, and things not happening for me in my life and I just become so frustrated I exploded in narcissistic rage. Turned inward too.

Walker tried to be philosophical about this lesson in life

and being a good Jung man try to see there is value in taking
a look at your inferiority, for its nature is the one element
that makes the career of the Shadow Prober possible. Walker
tried to rationalize his drift into shadowland: I got blinded
by all the tools the company was buying for me. And all the
enhanced creativity I was enjoying. I got inflated and this
distracted me and kept me avoiding the inferior constellations of my personality. Maybe shadow prober is not exactly
all there is to it. Hadn't I too, often been the unconscious
shadow prober, doing it in the relationship with my boss. I
saw inferiority in the boss but worked around it, supported
him as if he were "the one who completes you" by doing
what you don't like to do, so that you become complicit with
an entity running interference for you, so you could do your
creative works. Kind of like being a prostitute. Maybe that is
my archetype.

Wasn't I doing that with my boss? Probing him for a
shadow, trying to get some kind of Leverage. Don had been
out of the office for several months from an accident on his
four-wheeler. It had fallen back upon him and zoarched a
knee. Was this vacancy what precipitated the scramble for
his position in marketing. Bob insisted that we, him, me,
Karen go with him to visit Don in the hospital. Don did not
look all that pleased to see us gawking at him in his vulnerability. It was very awkward.

The experts at shadow probing seem to work in
Marketing or Sales. They were often Lawyers.

Shadow, mask, anima /animus. You have to navigate the
waters where these primal instincts live. They are transparent
forces within you and without you, and they are the weavers
of awareness. They are fairly autonomous.

And to Walker the introvert it seemed that the way these
extroverts attract attention, keeps those around them in a

state of constant unease. They suck up all the air in a room with only their agenda. Their weapons are nerve gas of deliberate obfuscation and disinformation in a fog of gas lighting. Often it is quite easy for the narcissist to lie, probably because belief enhances his sense of entitlement. We are swimming in a sea of smarmy, desire-inducing advertising that is shaming and teasing; that is oh so very clever. Walker asked himself: Did I really want to be part of that? He did want to work with the beautiful, and there is more beauty in the fine line of design. But media is the opiate arm of the 4th estate — Business. And carries out a campaign of brain washing with programming of cop-shows and sports, murder and romance: Fear and envy. All in the cast of being a good citizen, a team player. But Walker didn't want to participate or commit because he was caught up in being the special, eternal child artist writer. And his self limiting beliefs, or was it realism: made it impossible to think of being able to jump high enough to take part in the action and the passion of the times because it seemed like it was going on at such a high level over their heads. In Austin they used to say they were like the Cong, hunkered down in a bunker. The reality of most people is a bubble. Where are family and friends in all this? It was hard to trust being in Relationships. How do you ever get beyond the games to intimacy? Walker consoled himself: I can't complain. I get to smoke pot and get high once in a while and feel myself. See this furrow in my brow. That's the result of constant needling.

But the Psyche is all around, trying to give signals. You just need to be able to pick up on them. Otherwise it is they who would be pushing me around. Jung says you encounter the archetype walking through after the fact. You have to go into the affect, the mood, the complex which is a mood tempered sequence of feelings. You have to go into the shame, the hate, the guilt. Because they are . . . the projection machines. And though the target of the projection has lots of hooks — often dense as velcro — it is still you who is casting the shadow. Are all bosses the target of projection? Are all men the velcro of envy, upon which must fall envy's shadow side becoming like them?

The thing to do now was to play out the hand and use the energy of the shadow to make a big change, to move out into the world of contractor. Be your own boss —journeyman contract tech writer.

Walker resolve to never again pledge allegiance to one company where you were supposed to stay with the same company until you married and your wife became pregnant or you died. The idea that you were supposed to advance in a company, step by step, until you reached your top level was becoming passé. You weren't supposed to flit around from job to job. You were expected to adjust to your company as you adjusted to the community. But now there was no longer allegiance in the world of work. Walker would start jumping from job to job as a contractor. Not going to let himself get involved with this petty shadow probing and projection.

Shadow, mask, anima /animus. These haunted him for a while after he split.

It was easy enough to replay the scenes; they were still burning bright in his mind. Karen with her soft beautiful ways, at service was kind of an anima figure. And Therese with her hot bitchy arrogant haughty good looks was also a kind of anima figure.

Cora was disappointed that she did not get to go to France. Walker didn't tell her about him trying to send money back to a girl he met in England to try and import her.

Many awkward discussion with his therapist occurred, as the money in his bank account dwindled. He had thought to

use the money from his stock to tied him over until unemployment kicked in. But that very next Monday was October
19, 1987. Black Monday they called it. The stock market
crashed precipitously. It didn't return and he sold his stock
for pennies on the dollar.

So he couldn't afford the small fortune he was spending
on psychoanalysis anymore. And one day he just told Anna
that this was his last session. He thanked her for all the help
she had been in his life.

She was shocked but he would not continue. They were
sorry to part.

Ms. Cora and Walker continued their relationship.

Storytelling

Now that he was semi-unemployed, Walker started taking a class in storytelling at Dominican College in Marin. He would get there early and go for long hikes in the woods behind the campus.

It felt weird to be sitting at a classroom desk again. Surrounded by shiny white boards under white fluorescent light. There was always a pulpit in the front of the room. It had been 15 years since college. How small the desks seemed. The storytelling certificate program was taken by little librarians who told stories in the branches. There were a couple of primary education majors, women who were interested in children's literature. He was the only guy. They were nice people, some very accomplished storytellers. Who knew there was such a story telling circuit in America, with conferences and jamborees. Storytelling was sort of affiliated with folk music.

Storytelling class was rather foreign, not the least of it being that Walker was an introvert trying to get in touch with an opposite way of being. But it seemed like a good idea. He was too shy to be a performer; he had never memorized anything and didn't think he could. And, he had no history or experience with storytelling either in his family or his culture. Everything was a written story or in the Disney movies or on TV. It was all canned. Like most of his generation who grew up without any storytelling in their lives, he sensed there was something missing in his experience, a kind of impoverishment in the mythological sphere.

The main teachers were Ruth Stotter, the head of the program; she was like this girl scout who had always had a knack since childhood for storytelling, and fibbing too. And Gay Ducey was a sweetheart into the folklore circuit.

The class told stories from their own lives. They studied traditional European tales like those collected by the Grimm brothers. Some of the students were interested in American Indian folk tales with characters like Coyote the Trickster and Rabbit, and Bear the Medicine Being and Raven the Harbinger of Death. Those were the archetypes. But even though to Walker it seemed like white people trying to take on some sense of tribal belonging in the New World, (and don't we all want something like that.) The American Indian tales seemed very foreign from the old European tradition of oral storytelling, collected in Grimm and other folklorist entrepreneurs, because they were somewhat familiar from having been heavily mined by modern media. Later Walker would come to see behind the story, how the motifs were similar across time and separate cultures. It WAS interesting to see examples of how the indigenous people spoke of their world — porous with spirit animistic — in their collected stories. In his book *Seven Arrows,* a hippie standard from the 70s, Hyemeyohsts Storm conveyed some of these beliefs. In the preliterate language of the aboriginals, the feelings in the natural stories, spoke to them like the imagination of childhood.

It was like how he felt about autumn in Montreal, where he was a child. Mount Royale — looking at it from the French quarter, Rue Beaubien. He tried to imagine what their oral tradition was like so open to omens and signs. In constant contact with the generous benefactor mana mama.

The Fire Walker flicked flames as it walked the land, the tongues of flames got captured in the leaves of the trees as they hissed and sizzled and danced in stochastic cacophony. The giant denuded deciduous trees were like antenna connecting up into the sky each going down into subterranean homes. Each picking up signals the planet was sending to it.

The Fall always paints and scatters the leaves back to the wet land. Inside the mountain there were tunnels and warrens where creatures real and imaginary holed up. When I was a child I used to think here was a vast underground subways under there with elves and sprites and little lightweight fairies and magical beings. I can never forget the quick red fox darting like a flame-flash across the field. The ancient stories of the indigenous who had been here were about spirit. They told about the behavior of the Fox, Beaver, Bear, Bird, and how important these were to their lives as they were giving themselves to him so that he may eat. They held the Ox, Beaver, Bear, Bird, in reverence.

Walker never liked going to school. But now he was on some kind of quest, to understand the psychological backbone of story, like he understood or was coming to understand dreams. And the oral fairy tale is perhaps the simplest story because it had structure that aided it being held in memory. Also Walker wanted to be more like the psychologists who had such a ready command of myth and story; he had to get it too. Jung and Freud and Bettelheim and Propp spent a great deal of time looking at fairy tales and Walker could see that fairy tales were a basic form that illustrated both fundamental elements of narrative structure and archetypal patterns. He hoped studying storytelling would upgrade his writer chops.

The only storyteller he was familiar with was Lord Buckley (and Brother Dave Gardner). He knew these hip renditions wouldn't do for this sweet bunch of ladies. So he thought to take well known stories and riff on them, mostly doing psychological interpretations. From reading the psychologists, he was touched in particular by Bettelheim, *The Uses of Enchantment*, though this later turned out to be somewhat discredited, or at least out of favor with the feminist librarians who didn't care for Freud.

Though nobody at the school would come out and say it, Little Red Riding Hood was about seduction. (Walker thought to see if he would dare to say the red riding hood showcased the clitoris.) For that matter Jack and the Beanstalk was about a boy jacking himself up on his boner into the realm of the father and his fear of the giant. Beauty and the Beast was about fear of sex. (And learning to overthrow the admonitions against sex from your elders and learning to love it.) Snow White was about parental jealousy. (And something you too might have to come to deal with in time.) Sleeping Beauty was about arrested sexual development. (As well as waiting for your prince to come.) Bettelheim extolled the parents of the oral tradition as being able to assess in a truthful and feeling way the difficulties and dangers and perplexities of being a child. Nowadays they just park you in front of the TV and put in a Disney tape.

Walker's childhood years up until 11 or so were filled with dreams and boyhood fantasy. There were times at night in his dreams when he would take voyages out of the body and float over his school gracefully flitting from the tip of one telephone pole to another like in the Chagall painting with the ballet dancer on point balancing on a church spire. Sometimes his dream life was more interesting than his waking life. As a young boy Walker had lived in the imagination. Stories of voyagers and magical places filled his mind. It was like an other side of his being — the world within, the imaginal. Sometimes this dream world of the night spilled over into the waking world of the day. He made the distinction between the social world of having to do things with people, and the internal world, where you could experience you own imagination.

Now he wanted something deeper in his life and he supposed that to pursue the life of a writer artist might be his way into luminous and numinous moments of grace. He had to find a way to bring the scenes sent from the psyche into his dreams back over to the other side — the day; he had to make them more real, more connected. Walker was trying to find his way back to the imaginal, whatever that was because it was the way back to his soul. He was on a quest for new revelations about his waking life. Storytelling was part of that quest. Not knowing anything about storytelling and myth, made him blind to what was going on in the psyche. The post-modern era was drifting more toward going to a movie in an air conditioned mall. Or stay at home and watch the sitcom. Technical economies were the engine that removed the worker from production and locked him into a more abstract level of information. Entertainment was set-up so that the worker became a consumer supposed to watch the more highly qualified at play and not participate but just look on in dumb awe. Celebrity was the new pantheon. The imaginal was looked upon as a childhood phase you were supposed to leave behind for rational economic modernism.

Walker was struck by how the various religious belief systems of the world have a conspicuous similarity: at the heart of all their theology was the obscure birth origin of the hero. Moses was found in the bull rushes. Jesus was the son of the BVM by way of a golden shaft of light from the fast talking Holy Ghost. (They call it Holy Spirit now.) There was a lot of turmoil with King Herod's slaughter of the innocents, offing all the first born sons from some prophesy; same business was afoot around the blue man Krishna baby. Oedipus had similar prophesies heralding his coming, and difficulty in the conditions of birth. (Banished to be raised by other parents.) Romulus and Remus were raised by wolves.

These stories reflect concern about one's origins.
Children start to wonder about the source of their being.
How was I born? Did I really come from inside a woman?
And how can I make more like fine me. Surely these pathetic
individuals I used to look up to and I used to need so much
are not my parents. Psychologists talk about the pre-Oedipal
stage, when the neonate is getting acquainted with his oral,
genital, and anal orifices. And the Oedipal stage in which he
puts aside the speculations on his origins which were causing
him so much paranoia and splitting, and takes on a more
mature depressive position — that I am not big enough to
seduce a parent. Though I'm awfully cute and I better exploit
my eternal puer archetypal status for all its worth.

But of course the biggest story of all at the heart of
religion is the immortal reward in the afterlife.

So when we are in fairy tales with giants and witches
and ogres who are adults who do violent acts against
children, we are attempting to let the children see some kind
of a truth. We are trying to know some kind of truth about
ourselves too, perhaps even capture that magical belief
of childhood where terrible things can be undone. We are
attempting to verbally coexist in a shared field of the unconscious. (The Un, such an unfortunate appellation, the Un as
the shadow to which we have projected our fears and hating.
The not-this, the not-that, the un. What about calling it the
Psyche after Jung. That was the way to go.

The stories about being abandoned, vulnerable,
dependent, are stories that appeal to us all because we were
all in that at one time. And parents have used the fairy tales
as a way to bridge the gap between them and through their
child, into the memory of being a child within them.

So here was Walker Underwood this unmarried guy

without kids hanging out and studying with these children's librarians to learn more about storytelling.

His motivation is some kind of attempt to understand fairy tale as Jung and Von Franz did, as something like a dream. He has no experience with storytelling in his family, except for an uncle who liked to tell jokes and sing songs and recite funny little rhymed ditties and limericks that he knew by heart. Most of the people in class had no real experience of archetypes either. Who did really?

But he tried to work on a more adult story, cause that's where his heart was at. What if he told this story. He would start in on Little Red Riding Hood.

Walker thought to develop these kind of rants like he might imagine Lord Buckley or Dave Gardner would. He thought the older lady storytellers might enjoy it. Certainly Ruth liked a racy story. The others not so much.

> You have to ask what was wrong with that mother sending her daughter out into the forest where there are wolves. In fact, why did the grandmother who was so old and frail, live so far away from the mother. Couldn't they add a little cascita onto the house?

> Who is the hero or focus of the energy moving around in Fairy Tales. What is a mother telling to the child as she carves out a cozy space and time of intimacy in which to inculcate the eager mind of the young. Presumably the movement in the tale is like the movement of consciousness of the dreamer in the dream.

> Instead of being a cautionary tale for young women Little Red Riding Hood might be a cautionary tale for wolves.

> Now I don't want to spoil anyone's appreciation of the story in fact we might come to appreciate it as adults more. But, this being the year of the vagina . . . Let us look upon the story of Little Red Riding Hood as a celebration of the vagina. Let us recall and imagine how the vadge comes equipped with its

own little riding hood, which often becomes red. The clitoris was not discovered until 1949; by Dr. Beverly Clitoris, a sex researcher in the Kinsey clinic. This discovery along with the Pill ushered in the sexual revolution. Anatomically the little red riding hood was designed to promote face to face sex. Which, was much more pleasurable for the female and promoted intimacy for a man and a woman to bond around this most explosive act of creation. The little red riding hood is this thing to make men passionate and wild.

Oh no that would never do.

Into the Woods

At that time Walker was starting to understand two great traditions of psychology: psychoanalysis and transactional analysis. They each bring different interpretations of the fairy tale, dear to the hearts and minds of self-observers.

The stories that parents brought to their children were reflective (either knowingly or not) of how these parents saw the home and family situation. Transactional Analysis saw the tale told as laying down some kind of script to follow. Was destiny somehow codified in the Fairy Tale like it was in dreams? Storytelling is about parents meeting their child with their own inner Child on a verbal field. Unfortunately most of us were not met in this field of the unconscious; (usually connoted with the phrase "into the woods"). Little Red Riding Hood went into the woods on her way to grandma's house. Jack in the Beanstock went into the woods to trade the cow. Cinderella a stepchild, went into the woods to get in touch with the spirit of (god) mother. Hansel and Gretel went into the woods to the witches house. In his study of psychology, Walker was definitely going into the woods.

Walker was relieved to read Transactional Analysis, made in the sixties and popularized in the seventies. The

TA books were written in a raucous and funny style which was a respite from the terribly obscure and exhaustive style of Jung. TA gave a whole different presentation of the same concepts, and thus one was able to use one psychology to elucidate the other. For example instead of like Jung going into a whole book elaborately invoking the art and history of alchemy, TA could define Transference with one sentence: Transference was the cross sorting of ego states. Eric Berne was hip, sarcastic and almost a little *too* cavalier towards people's suffering for Walker's sympathy. But then he came to see it was the necessary non-collusive stance of the psychoanalyst to avoid being sucked into the game of the patient. Transactional Analysis was a social psychology; it presented the inner world as structured into layers of a Parent self, a Child self, and an Adult self. And with a little practice one could readily perceive being in these states as well as seeing when others were. The Parent self sets out the rules and regulations (the shoulds and the oughts). The Child self feels and reacts. The Adult thinks, makes decisions, and solves problems. It was a first step on the path of self observation to find these within.

Parent Adult Child was a much easier explanation of Freud's superego, ego and id.

Freud was looking for a scientific mechanism.

Walker thought it might be in the semiotics of Peirce. He worked on a poem that related Peirce to Freud.

The child self, feels and reacts. Is the child more in Firstness? The adult in Secondness and the parent in Thirdness? Yes. In that place of habit that is the superego where actuality (child) has moved through manipulation to an abstract pattern rule.

But still, the work of therapy was to get more readily in touch with the feeling you. And learning to correctly read signs both inner and outer was part of the way to liberation.

The Inner Child is the emotional self. It is where you have your feelings hidden to protect them. When you experience joy, sadness, anger, fear, or affection your Child Within is coming out. So in this moment of story telling, the teller is telling his child and the child within himself, to feel your feelings. It is then that you are allowing your Inner Child to be. The Inner Child is at the core of our being. Try to stay in touch with it.

You can feel it: persona, ego and inner child. The language that the Persona flashes through the brain is about maintaining a social self, doing what is necessary to navigate the world of other. The more internal voice you might hear sometime is a chastising one that is sort of in charge and compelling you to be your best. And then, there is somewhere in there your own intimate voice, your creative self being understood and recognized and ratified by someone whose recognition of who you are really matters.

You get to be too much the adult and the parent and start to not feel much enthusiasm and energy. The work of therapy and the fairy tale is to create a transitional space where you can bring into consciousness your Inner Child. And in seeing, and knowing it, heal this inner child. Who was this inner child? And how does he get lost in the unfolding of one's destiny.

The Life Script and its Inculcation

Walker read about what TA calls the Life Script. Reading in Berne *What Do You Say After You Say Hello* he could see that hidden in the script is the history of a person's psychic life. One could have a masochists script in which one chose partners in order to have them mete out just the right amount of pain stimulation in order to feel that a kind of attention they were used to was being paid. Or one could have a banal script — Walker feared that this was his lot: nothing very adventurous happens but nothing very dangerous either. Flat in the risk and reward department. He consoled himself with thinking: I guess if you knew that you could live with it. The Transactional Analysis people loved to look at fairy tales for scripts.

Walker wrote in his notes:

I tried to remember back into those times where Berne says the script is induced. What stories, if any had I been enthralled with. I needed to find the story, the text that had been earlier.

Out of the blue I recalled a storybook my mother read to me. She was always doing fairly advanced reading. I remember some others, but this book *The Little Lame Prince* really stood out.

I found a copy of it at Moe's and read it, or at least skimmed it. The Prince had some kind of malaise, the doldrums or basically he was depressed, though they didn't use that word. He was called Prince Dolor of Nomansland. I almost wrote it as Momansland.

Was this the text of my script?

It was a sad story. The Prince was sickly. He got dropped on his head when he was little by his nurse. The King had this nurse imprisoned. It was amazing to hold in my hands this book that my mother and I had read together so long ago.

I did remember her telling me more than once about the time that she had pushed me down so hard that I banged my head against the floor. My mother had this fit of rage because I had apparently waited until she had ironed the intricate little dresses of my sisters and had them hanging in the closet and I had pulled them down and urinated on them. She flew into a rage and flung me away and I had banged my head on the floor. And she was terrified and contrite and took me to the doctor and I had a huge bump on my head the size of an egg. And the doctor told my mother, "You ought to have your head examined." My poor mother was guilty about that. She had my sisters and me three of us in a row. As I write this I am embarrassed to say how I got slammed, somehow it is telling tales out of school. At the time she was reading to me, my father was drifting into being an alcoholic.

My mother and I had this closeness around poetry and music that I didn't have with my father. He wanted somebody who was interested in sports and athletic stuff. Someone interested in business. He had never read a book since he left college and I wanted to read and learn everything about poetry.

So in that sense I was lame to him. I was deficient.

So after his father the King died, the Prince's uncle had him banished in a tower called Hopeless out on the barren moor. And there was a nurse who taught him to read and there was a carpenter / knight who rode up on a horse and hoisted supplies and toys through the window into the boy's quarters as the captive child was never allowed to leave the tower. He became an anchorite obsessed by the word or the world of the imagination created by the writers of books. Then, when little lame shut-in prince Dolor was so full of wishes to see the world, a fairy godmother appeared and gave him a magic cloak. This was like a poncho when you spread it out on the ground and after a long while he learned that he could fly out the window and go cruising over the land.

As I was reading the story of the Little Lame Prince, it was good to find images from way way back in my past. My father like the King was too melancholy to pay much heed to the child. His wife the queen had died. The little Lame prince was dragging his sorry ass around and wanted to get to The Land, Beautiful Mountains — for me this was Canada, the place where I was from.

There were details in the book I didn't remember. The tower was constructed by criminals who were executed. His nurse was kind though wicked. Shut up with a child who was dependent. Is that how my mother felt?

The prince was always standing aside from life looking out the windows at shadows and clouds running races across the plain.

He was given a magic carpet by his ferrie god-mother. Then the prince would fly out his tower window traveling to far off lands on this most marvelous cloak which was reading and the imagination.

As I was reading this old edition from the year in which I was born, I began to wonder if lucid dreaming was for me The Thing like the magic carpet was with the Little Lame Prince. If not the thing then the thing that gets you to the thing. I started to remember those early times. Row houses in Montreal with the spiral stair case up the front. Crowds of people. Horse drawn junk cart in the street. The ice man swathed in a rubber apron who carried blocks of ice up the stairs with terrible tongs. Everybody got out of his way when he invaded.

In the Little Lame Prince a pair of magnifying spectacles appear so that he can see close up as he hovers over. And a pair of silver ears appear that let him hear things at a distance.

I am starting to get a sense of the archetypes in the stories. The Godmother shifts shape into a Magpie and flies on the cloak with the Little Lame Prince. Spirit Guide Mag asks him, "Shall I show you the royal palace." And they sneak in and see the body of the dead king laid in state on a bier.

Looking down on the scene of his father's death as the revengeful hand of a family member, the Little Lame Prince (who has become a good person because of all his suffering that has tempered his personality, and because of he has studied long and hard) sees his godmother's eyes looking at him through the dark eyes of the magpie bird.

In the next scene they are hovering over the city; where he sees things happening under his eyes again. This speaks to a kind of astral travel or lucid dreaming in the imagination of a child. A Prince never gets mad doing anything.

I have to wonder about this book and why my mother read this book to me — with me. My mother and I were always reading books that were beyond my capability so that when I got to school I was quite far along in reading. I have always loved reading, still do. But as I look back over my life and try to see where I was living out some kind of received script, I find there are definitely some clues from considering this fairy tale. To use the transactional analysis approach one looks at the dynamics of the family. In my story I feel like the prince in that I was not a macho he-man like my father who was very interested in sports and pool-hall beer dives.

When did I start to reject my father. I remember I had so

much fun when we did go to the cub scouts meetings. My father was good at getting me to the meetings, he had been one himself. Later I went camping with the troup, or to summer camp. I was not athletic. I played little league. I was stuck way out in the outfield. I let a ball go by because I was bored and was staring up into the clouds. I think they had to send somone out to get me when they changed innings. After that I played on the bench. It might have been that I needed glasses, which I didn't get until high school, when I was really stressed out around girls and geometry.

Was I too, depressed and unloved, like this prince. I certainly was banished, though it was a kind of self-banishment. I avoid conflict. I had bannished myself from being in the "family" at work. I had run away from home many times, trying to find other mirrors to reflect my true nature in.

So to sum up: I have been fiddling with the Little Red Riding Hood story a bit. I have been trying to understand fairy tales as like dreams with archetypes. I recalled an important story my mother read to me when I was very little and in which was framed something of my situation. I brought the outside perspective of Transactional Analysis to understanding the way scripts are inculcated or induced or taken on. TA looks at the social interaction of who and why someone is presenting the story. (How story reflects their script, their beliefs, their themes and how they are passing these psychic structure on to you.) TA asks why does Little Red Riding Hood's mother send her into the forest where there are known to be wolves lurking about. Why does child Little Red Riding Hood trustingly, naively obediently give her information to the wolf when asked. Was the child infantalizsed? In some ways the story of Little Red Riding Hood is about little girls teasing wolves then destroying them. One could see it as a cautionary tale for wolves.

I wanted to bring that kind of psychological other world perspective to the story of The Little Lame Prince. He is lame because his caretaker dropped him when he was a babe. His father didn't have much to do with the boy because he wasn't athletic. His uncle got the little lame prince banished into a tower called Hopeless in the vast desert called Nomansland. He became prince Dolor and he had the Doldrums. Eventually his fairy godmother gives him a magic cloak, that he can fly out over the world and see the lands and rivers and forests. She gives him some spectacles, too so that he can zoom in and see close-up from great safe distance. And the godmother gives her prince these magical ears so that he can hear things from far away. In the lucid dream and astral travel you can see things from above. You can hear characters saying things.

It is hard to do analysis on one's life script, because introspection easily disperses into a mist of resistance. Try as I might to avoid seeing it, there are parallels between the story of the little lame prince and my story. I too am holed up in an ivory tower with my books. The magic cloak is the imagination fed by literature and psychedelics. I had run away from home several times starting when I was 14. I hitchhiked out to look for America, come what may. It wasn't until I met some hippies that for the first time in my life I was part of an intimate conversation. I had only experienced intimacy in Joyce and Kerouac. I was my mother's child.

Walker wrote a poem convolving Freud and Peirce and the semiotic triangle with the drama triangle.

Let us go now into the Thou,

Let us go now into the Thou,
for in it lies another I —
by it I mean the 3rd person —
he and she and it and them

The Other I is in the It
It comes to the I
through the thou —
which itself contains another I.
They chase each other
in the field
of you

and I and it.
— linked in a triangle —
of you
and I and it.

For as I am an it to you
you are an it to me.
And both of us — two
are together in the you --
you can call it tui or thou —
it's seeing how you are in the now.

Feel it crossing over
and drifting in
as you . . . it . . . and I . . .
in that order.

Though in language
the presentation of the persons
of the verb 'to be'
is in order of
I and you and it.

Let us go now into the Thou,
for in it lies another I—

As it is in Freud where we find
the parts of mind are these three:
super-ego, id, and I.
So it is in language too we find
the persons of the verb to be are three
the you, the it, and the I.
super-ego id and I.

We know the ego is the I
and the IT is probably id
and thou is super-ego.

super-ego id and I.

Walker wrote about how the drama triangle was instantiated in his relationship with Cora.

Damsel, Dragon, Knight

Victim, Persecutor, Rescuer
They chase each other round and round in a drama triangle.
Like my relationship with Ms. C.

In our triangle she somehow ends up being the Victim and I end up being the Persecutor.

Or in my case the whore master.

I have to Persecute her and abuse her a bit, so she gets to feel like this beset waif.

Then I have to Rescue her, be her knight in shining armor, take all this away and become her demon lover. That is what was going on in the Last Tango in Paris movie.

The evil Paul comes swooping in to rescue this hot girl from her boring fiancée. But now the demon lover is from a tantric commune and really know how to ball.

Ms. C takes on the roll of Victim, made to perform sexual acts which she professes are disgusting but which she enjoys immensely.

Sometimes *he* felt contrite and even shocked at the kind of sex he made her get into at times. Then *she* felt superior and that allowed her to move from victim to persecutor to rescuer. It was interesting how boys and girls learned to play these "fun" roles with each other. So now *he* had become the Victim and *she* the Persecutor. In the passion of love affair it really was like that, you chased yourself around a triangle of *you* and *I* and *he* and *she*.

It is not like you KNOW your are playing a game, you just sense it after that feeling of deflation when something real has been switched into something manipulative. You are trapped in a triangle and don't know how to get out. There are shadow energies involved too.

Intimacy: you have got to find it in yourself. And then perhaps take it to someone who can receive it. Not everyone can receive it.

Because at some point, you or she gets fed up with the role they're playing and initiates a switch. The man may get frustrated with controlling and manipulation or the passivity that they have fostered, feeling burnt out because they have to initiate everything. This frustration may break out in switching to the Persecutor role, and he had to yell at the haranguing wife nitpicking for failings and bullying them over instructions given repeatedly but only intermittently followed.

Or the Persecutor may usurp the role of the Victim, accusing the other of being ungrateful and unsupportive, incapable of understanding or incapable of intimacy. The one, bumped from their usual spot may at this point switches over to take on the Rescuer role, and shower the Persecutor with assurances of their continued gratitude and offers of help. Alternatively, the Victim may turn on the other as Persecutors and blame them for all the Victims failings.

People get endemically stuck in the mesh of their script. And play games on a scale of intensity from normal to harem scarum to dysfunctional to criminal.

And the shadow of our own projection
is cast sometimes a very long way
and we are blinded from seeing
what is going on plain as day.

And in the night
the brain
runs the eye transducer backwards,
so our eyes become
projectors of the dream.

The days fade past
and intersperse with each other,
as we become entrenched
in the latticework of our habits.

Being has a way of upsetting
the sense of not having a body.

We are playing out some kind of the fairy-tale narrative of Damsel-in-Distress, Dragon and Knight-on-White-Charger endlessly. It is hard to see it when you are in it. You just realize after the fact that you have once again gone through the wash and spin cycle and have been hung out to dry. It leaves one longing to step outside the cycle even though it apparently fulfills some aspect of need.

But once you have decided to step away from the institutionalized safety of its standardized patterns, you find there are all kinds of emotional rewards on offer that don't involve bullying or helplessness, and that let you make music without carrying nearly such a weight of anxiety.

In the twilight of the hypnagogic between sleeping and waking, you feel like you are some entity behind your eyes looking out at the world. It might not even be you looking out but who else could it be. Perhaps the part of you that is open, an attractor of ideas or images or feelings coming from the world that are in the world and looking for a sensitive nest into which to settle themselves like birds that have flown a long way. I experience this once or twice on LSD: the Watcher. The Watcher Behind My Eyes. And the Guardian Angel. I am trying to relate to the Watcher which is some kind of self-reflective consciousness. And trying to relate it to the Guardian Angel which is something I sensed, a presence, as a child in the Catholic Church — I felt like I could perceive an Angel by my side keeping a watch over me. The gift of consciousness.

I thought about doing the experiment of watching your choices at every action. And that would give you a sense of the Watcher. In other words just watching gives you a sense of the Watcher; it starts to become more conscious, and you start to be able to go down more paths than the ones you would have gone down. And that would be an amazing experience.

Hopefully this sense of being able to relax into yourself will come. Perhaps it comes with reading much psychology. The Self. The Anima. The Shadow. The Ego. Feeling tone complexes. It is good to have names. The names for new things under the sun merge theory and phenomenology.

You become a kind of gardener raising these flowers of psychology. If you keep a dream diary you grow more dreams. If you transcend your psychology you experience more numinosity. Ultimately you realize that what we experience is filtered through our psychology. The experience one has is filtered through a window, a matrix, a field of transferences.

I wanted to write a sutra or hypnotic script to reproduce it.

Walker did work up a story for class. It was an interpretation of the Fox and the Grapes.

The Buddha observed the Fox endeavering to get the grapes.
From that he derived the basic tennants of Buddhism.
The 4 Noble truths.

There are so many ways to utter a spell
for the diminishment of encounters with the other
or your self.

Let us learn how the Buddha encoded them
all those many years ago.
It is said that while meditating under a Bo tree
the 4 Noble Truths came to him as he was watching
the Fox trying to leap up and get some grapes off a high
arbor.
Drawing back a few paces, the Fox takes a run at the tree
and jumps,
but just missed the bunch.
Turning round again with a One, Two, Three,
he jumped up, but with no greater success.
Again and again he tried.
This made him even more thirsty for the thing he desired
But at last the fox had to give it up.
He looked at the object of desire sitting there
hanging over his head and said,
"They are probably not ripe anyway."
He panted a little and let his tongue hang down: "And
anyway I am not that thirsty."

The Fox started to walk away, his normally bushy tail hanging down. He said, "And anyway I am not able to reach them."

The term "sour grapes" is known by everyone in every language. It is about the frustration that we experience when something desired is denied. So to disparage or deny back, and say the thing desired is lacking. This is a form of psychological defense called denial. Denial is the first defense. Go right straight opposite against the attack. More technically the "sour grapes" defense is reaction formation. We conceal our true motivations by pretending the opposite. This lie spills over into our relationships with ourselves and others.

The Fox cursed the farmer. "Damn that farmer anyway ; he trained the vines so high."

As he wandered down the path he was heard to mutter: "A person can't get the means to quench his thirst around here."

Aesop gives The Moral of the story: "It is easy to despise what you cannot get."

We see in this story how a person signifies on himself or an other or the situation. A process of semiosis is how we make meaning of the situation, but this interaction of object signifier and signified has been personalized by the unconscious into some stand off of persecutor rescuer and victim.

This happens because the person moves down a sequence of denial of the 4 Noble Truths.

Buddha taught many things about a life devoted to coming to know your own being.

The discovery of the 4 Noble Truths is one kind of summary of the his observation.

The Four Noble Truths of Buddhism are stated in simple terms as:

    1. Suffering exists (existence)

    2. Suffering arises from attachment to desires (significance)

    3. Suffering ceases when attachment to desire ceases

    4. Freedom from suffering is possible by practicing the Eightfold Path (action)

To put the story of the Fox and the Grapes in the context of the 4 noble truths, let us look at some of the ways the Fox denies his experience of being unable to fulfill his need to quench his thirst, the object of his desire.

In the statement, "They are probably not ripe anyway."

He denies the **existence** of the grapes by saying their not ripe.

In the statement, "And anyway I am not that thirsty."

He denies the **significance** of the grapes which is that to have them would be fulfilling the desire to overcome thirst.

In the statement, "And anyway I am not able to reach them," he denies the **action** of being able to physically get the grapes. (He could come up with some clever ideas, as foxes often do.)

Denial is an internal process during which we, out of conscious awareness, ignore information relevant to the solution of a problem.

A denial always entails some distortion of reality, which confirms our script beliefs. Which is to say our movement around the drama triangle. A field of defenses. Denial. Repression. Suppression. Projection. Introjection. Reaction formation. Rationalization /Intellectualization. Displacement. Idealization. Splitting. etc.

I thought to try and work them into a diagram, centered around Denial. Though I have not found any nice unifying principal yet. It is difficult to admit how these ways of being colonize one's soul and you operate from behind them all your days and don't even know it. One becomes so used to them it is frightening to get beyond them. There is a lot of psychology of the personality in being aware of how one martials defense mechanisms. It would be helpful to have a fairly sophisticated understanding of personality so as not to be hegemonized by media and its stars, or the pill companies and their representatives like the current administration is doing.

Denial is a form of putting oneself, (displacement, intellectualization, suppression) another person, (projection, idealization etc) or the world in general down. These seem to be all a form of denial. They help us to maintain a more comfortable image of ourselves that we know from out past. It's to help us to feel safe. Unfortunately, this is often at the expense of a richer life.

I notice I discount most severely when I am angry and frustrated. I project my ill feelings onto various targets, of course not to their face, but I am speaking under my breath. The computers don't work ergo Apple sucks. Hp Sucks. My bike is not behaving after I spent a ton of money at the bike store. Those guys are crooks, going for the one time gouge, pissing people off, and not caring whether you come back. Of course this is not true, but to hear me rattle off the offenses that disturb the pristine order of my beauty, you'd thing the world was indeed out to get me.

I deny the body most of all. 'Tis sad.

The denials percolate through a matrix, becoming different defense mechanisms. Eventually all this denial starts to diminish our experience of life. It is a painful lesson. Nobody said coming to self-awareness was going to be easy.

You have been given a matrix to carry your personality. You carry your personality in a matrix, let us get an image of that personality. A mother and father standing beside you: see them when you look for love, or get into relationships with the other.

In dreams you'll see your anima and shadow — down inside is the child who is always with you and the adult you have become.

So it is AC AA AP, a 2 x 3 matrix at least to carry your persona into the social world where you deal in transactions. The hours are passed in work and rituals and religious ceremonies and games and sometime intimacy.

The angels of which we are derived make the air turbulent with the fabric of quantal energy transmitted to all, so that we can see clearly our own real characters, the eigenvalues of our matrix.

The opposites of our nature expand and compress, and we contain them with displacement and transference.

And we are written in a script. Etched in the substrate of our movement. And the psyche, the miraculous psyche in which time dilates and expands and is always present is all around us — in a labyrinth of separate spaces going off into virtual dimensions as if everything were flowing around us — a river in which we float.

Somewhere between the infernal infinite and the infinitesimal chemical bonds that holds us together, we are.

So the first state of the matrix is do we notice the existence of the stimulus. To discount a stimulus is to blank out perception that something is happening at all. Se, external sensing.

We might also be in Ne external intuition, that is carrying an abstract theoretical position into the world.

Ah, to be in Marin. It felt good to be climbing the hills overlooking San Rafael and the bay. There was hardly anyone out there. He would walk up to the radio tower and to the point across from Angel Island. The vast bay with all its communities spread out. When high in the hills of Marin, one gets the feeling of being well-educated. He could see Mount Tamilpias off to his left, "The Reclining Female turning to show curves of breast and hip." The fog comes in from the golden gate. From up on Mount Tamiplais, you could see its fleecy foam flowing and crashing like sea suds in the great ocean of atmosphere circulating around the emerald city like a shawl. Fog is the waves on the bottom of this ocean of air.

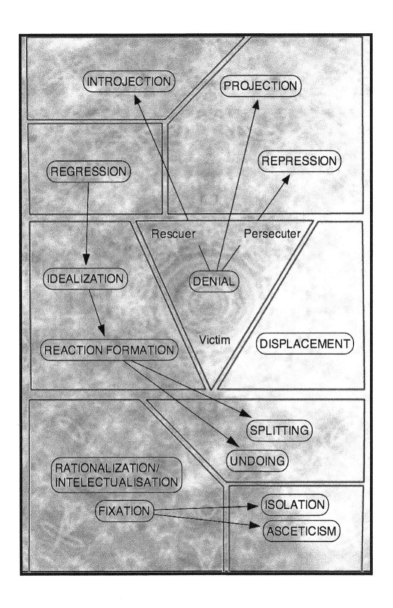

INTROJECTION

PROJECTION

REGRESSION

REPRESSION

Rescuer   Persecuter

IDEALIZATION

DENIAL

REACTION FORMATION   Victim   DISPLACEMENT

SPLITTING

UNDOING

RATIONALIZATION/
INTELECTUALISATION

FIXATION   ISOLATION

ASCETICISM

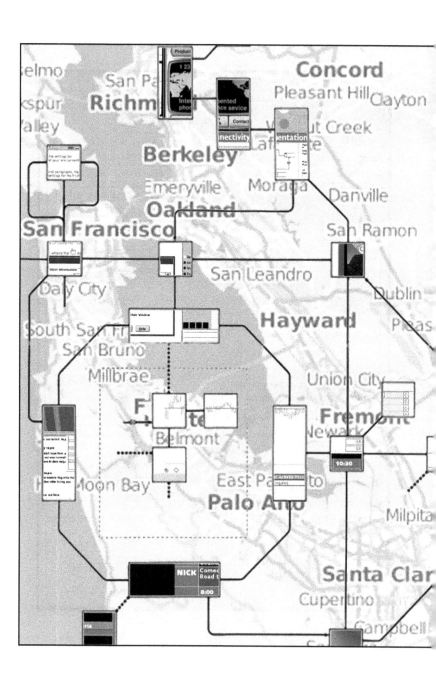

GlassDoor Glasnost

The little Macintosh was a machine for printing money. Over the years Walker got many, many technical writing jobs all over Silicon Valley. Xerox. Bank of America. Apple. Western Digital. Tandem. Varian. Temescal. Visa. Oracle. There were many contracts at Tandem. They are a fun bunch, and that parallel-processing, non-stop, fault-tollerant architecture was a favorite of banks and credit transaction processing. The people were nice, casual — all races and sexes. They were COBOL freaks. One old lady programmer would spread out the fan fold all the way down the hall and get down on her hands and knees reading the lines of code looking for a bug. They were old school, big iron (mainframe) people.

But more and more Walker started drifting into interface design. Especially after one day working at Tandem, and he had written: a certain screen was a 'gateway' to the rest of the application, and the manager couldn't grasp the metaphor of gateway.

"You mean like someone swinging on a gate?" she said.

It was pounded home on Walker that one was never allowed to use a metaphor or any figurative language in the hyper-literal technical manual. It was then that he started accelerating his move toward the more creative beauty and juice of interactive information interface. He had learned to design and program in Hypercard and other interactive authoring environments. He had become a GUI guy.

This grew out of the general Mac fascination with the Graphical User Interface but really took off with Hypercard. Walker had learned it at a SIG (Special Interest Group) from Raines Cohen one of the founders of BMUG.

Hypercard was developed by Bill Atkinson the inventor

of MacPaint. He was a rock star of programmers and got a thunderous standing ovation when he came to the packed-to-the-rafters BMUG meeting in the old physics lecture hall at the Berkeley campus in his usual Hawaiian shirt.

The Hypercard programs were based on the metaphor of a stack of cards. You shifted from card to card by buttons or hypertext fields. This was the first implementation of hypertext. A click or message could be sent and captured by a button or a field on the card, by the card itself, or the background of the card or deeper into the stack of cards itself and even deeper into the Home stack. The language Hypertalk was very much like English and ordinary people or subject matter experts could now make stacks for browsing information and doing other things. Apple had given the masses another creative heyday like desk top publishing. And now interactive design became another cool beautiful thing to do to make scads of money.

Ah, BMUG. The hard drive that Raines hauled around everywhere on his bike was still surviving. Walker took a few of the programmers down to Apple the day they released Hypercard 1.2. They were new to the place too. It felt good to be accepted by these sharpies. Talking about function calls and push and pop and sub-routines and compiling.

BMUG became the biggest repository of hypercard stacks and sold disks of freeware collections (for the cost of a disk). Eventually Walker acquired quite a few of these little beauties made by ordinary people with knowledge to share to learn how they did it. And he became a really good programmer. He started getting creative jobs.

Claris MacWrite

Walker started a job with a group of contractors out of Half Moon Bay. He didn't have to do writing on this project. He was the interactive designer. They were doing the documentation for the word processor in the Claris Works suite. They had taken over MacWrite.

Walker had my good navigation design at the top of the screen. It was sweet to work in Black and White for the small Mac Plus screen. It really constrains you to be efficient with the design.

The office in Half Moon Bay, was on Main St. Bill the lead contractor had rented the whole top floor of a building. It was right next to a restaurant called by the locals Dirty's. It was in this office that Walker became enamored with the large heavy desk of white melamine from Ikea. He had to have one, and did bring home the kit from Emeryville and set up in his small apt.

The Hypercard stack was nicely laid out, many screen shots. The buttons were little rectangular check box. The interactive index was made from GETing the line in the list and jumping to the card.

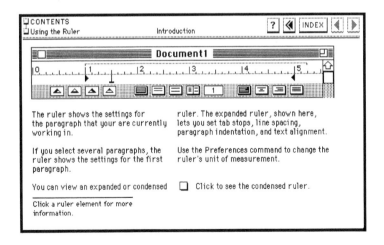

It was stirring to work with other writers It was rare for

Walker indeed. Though the other writers were often asserting their top-dogness in the field of writing, Walker didn't have to get into it because he was the UI programmer guy and not one of the writers.

Apple AUX

Walker got to work at Apple a few times because of Hypercard. Somehow someone had dropped his name and at an interview he dropped a name of a recognized leading star of Hypercard. Walker worked in the Unix group there. This was a wild LAN, lead by a one-eyed biker-babe with a black leather patch over her right eye. She was tough. She had a slew of Biker magazines around her cubicle where the men wore leather overalls and no shirts. They had a sign hanging from the ceiling "We Be Unix 'n' Shit.

Walker designed and constructed their interface, in HyperCard. It is a point and click dictionary of all the Unix commands. It was part of a suite of useful stacks that went to venders to help Apple with rolling out their Unix product AUX. Unix on the Moto 68000 chip.

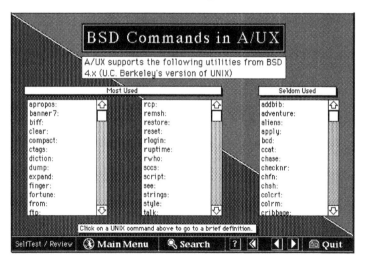

Some of the other stacks in the suite, were answers to frequently asked questions about Apple's Unix. The stack was a strategy mosaic. Another fun stack in the suite showed the Unix guru as a long-beard wizard with a pointy hat and flowing graduation gown. He was holding forth and questioning little elves on Unix spells. This teaching stack had immediate feedback for failure or success and accumulated wrong answers for point and click review. He had come up with the basics of CBT, interactive instruction.

A couple of years later and Walker was back at Apple again. This time was for using Hypercard as a GUI to grab and put text from out of the fields of a strictly command line mainframe interface. Later he did same thing at Tandem for the Run Book of Operations. This was like an expert system that let an underling do advanced troubleshooting with a point and click interface into the command line interface.

Somehow Walker managed to impress various consultants that were floating around Tandem. In those days people believed in documentation and training. So when these consultants got shanghaied and pilfered away by head-hunters representing other companies like Oracle and Stanford and Visa and others always raiding the Tandem personnel, these consultants became managers and heads of departments at other companies and they brought Walker in with them. For a while there he went from one interesting contract to the next.

Stanford
Walker got a job at Stanford University in their IT department through a former Tandem consultant he had worked with who had become the head of the department. Walker felt privileged to go from the Berkeley to the

spacious open Stanford campus and be among America's best and brightest.

He had been invited there to write and develop a WinHelp. This is a great implementation of hypertext and hyper-image on Windows 3.0. Which was the version that started to make the PC usable for Macidiots like him. The WinHelp was for the Samson application which was the Terminal Emulator of choice at Stanford. People mostly used it to Telnet into the library.

The lead programmer / designer of Samson was a really fun person. He was a big fan of Dr. Who. He had a red British pay telephone booth / teleporter machine in the hall leading to his office which was festooned with posters and other memorabilia. He was a big fan of OS/2 (which was IBM's answer to Microsoft Windows) and was always evangelizing about OS/2 and OS/2Warp.

He said: "What people love about OS/2 is much better than Windows."

Though by now Walker had thought of himself as a MacWimp for not wanting to look at the hideous DOS or Windows Over DOS 1 and 2, he was very impressed with the WinHelp and enjoyed developing in this new environment. The basic ideas of interactive design carried over. Navigation. A sense of where you are in the work flow. No fatiguing color, readable type. Working on the small Mac black and white screen taught you to be parsimonious with screen real estate. Color was OK.

He had to rebuild each screen and dialog of the interface by using the Microsoft Developers Environment. He suggested wording on the buttons for the developers. It became clear how important good English phrases were for the commands on an interface, even more important than they were for writing.

Aaron Marcus and Associates

Walker worked as a programmer for the premier
User Interface designer of the world, Aaron Marcus and
Associates up in the Berkeley hills. Marcus is the designer
who brought typography to computer screens. They just
about invented the Graphical User Interface. AM+A was
a free floating ensemble of graphic designers and typogra-
phers. They were obsessed with creating beautiful computer
screens in exquisite tasteful color coordinations that were
not garish and fatiguing, but were inspiring to do work on.
These were often laid out on a grid of golden ratio proportions. Down to the ligature. They spoke semiotics at AM+A.

Walker was the interactive guy who built up the screens
with buttons and fields and made the script behind these
action objects, the code that made them do stuff like fan out
into memory and Search; or read through a text and Select a
part. The designers asked for structures and he made them.
He programmed a useful drill-down presentation that used
three fields across.

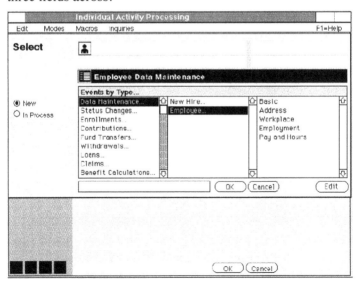

No one had done that. Walker first saw it at about the same time in the NeXT computer. He made a trip to the computer store on El Camino in San Mateo in the Fall of 1988 to see the shockingly expensive obsidian cube like it was a visit the black Kaaba of Mecca. The NeXT computer was Unix on the 68000 and it had the first browser /server for the web. (Run the httpd daemon.)

There was a lot of ego flying around at the AM+A design shop. It was surprising how bitchy and critical the designers were toward each other. The graphic designers were amazingly creative people but they had to work for small pay because there was always somebody trying to get their job. Walker had his speciality and nobody had anything to say. Supercard had come out. It was Hypercard with beautiful color. They would create these beautiful screens that were a mock up of how the windowing system of some OS would look. It was great for specifying the interactive GUI for a client in detail. Then the client would go off and program it in Pascal or C++ or whatever. Walker had been sent flying to clients with the designer. Once he went to Chicago in winter for a meeting for a big project managing a huge HR database. It was lonely in the motel and the slush filled streets and these vast cavernous office buildings where everyone was gone and the heating air-conditioning was humming to be heard. So he felt like an interstellar alien consultant. The GUI guy. He was the GUI alien guy, David Bowie in The Man Who Fell to Earth and they were throwing money at him. He learned to talk semiotics like they do.

Walker had done several Hypercard stacks at Apple and Claris and Tandem and Visa and other places but the designers at AM+A raised the GUI to a whole new level of beauty. It was an honor to work there. And they spoke semiotics! The language of icons etc. How one maintained a silent communication understandable and even inspirational for the user to navigate by inspection across areas of an application. Walker had been fairly well read in structuralism and Levi-Strauss and linguistics but here was a place where they made semiotical linguistics everyday practical; it was the domain of argument and proof for the GUI. Walker wrote several papers on Macromind Director and Supercard for issues of the BMUG newsletter (which was a thick tome of over 300 pages beautifully published that came out a couple of times a year.) One paper *Matching Knowledge Type to Visual Metaphor in Choosing the Right Multimedia Engine* was an interesting discussion of how an interface was built, including human factors testing, semiotics and algorithms for screen layout and grid development.

There was a sense of The Law about the approach of Aaron Marcus to the Graphical User Interface. And the luminous too. He was a servant of the Word and the Light, as all spiritual people are. He wanted to respect the worker by giving the people a luminous computer interface that was beautiful and a joy to use, that made you want to do work on the machine.

At AM+A you became kind of a disciple of good interface design. You felt it was your job to carry forth the principals of pragmatism and consistency and beauty into the work place, which now a few years into the computer revolution, had for many become sitting in front of a computer screen.

Ms. C invited Walker to a seder.

Walker got invited to a seder gathering at Ruth's house. There was a menorah and a dreidel board game.

He was trying to show more interest in Ms. C by

showing interest in her culture. He got her to go to a movie called *Der Dybbuk*. It was an old film in black and white about a supernatural creature that was kind of a ghost and a double.

Walker was proud to have a Jewish girlfriend. She was sensitive and intelligent. They danced around about the topic of him moving in to her house with her. They discussed it and supposedly he would work on getting the studio at the back of the house fixed up into some kind of room for him. He liked his own room.

But she seemed too slow at moving the stack of leftover lumber out of the little studio out back. They just seemed to be drifting toward the idea of living together. But underneath it all, Walker was uncomfortable with the idea that it was her house, it would always be her house. No one was saying anything about getting married.

There was once when he came inside her without a condom. They got just so horney and so close that they wanted to commit to creating life together.

Ms. C and he felt particularly close though scared at that night together. The next day he was shocked to have done that.

Ms. C gave him a strange look of superiority and corrected his mispronunciation of Dybukk. He felt rebuked and debunked, like he was some outrémonter trying to blend into the fold of chosen ones. Women are always ready to rub your nose into it so they can feel like they have the upper hand.

They went to see the foreign movie, black and white with great hoary bug eyed old men in long white beards and hand ringing women wearing a sheitel from the ghetto. He was trying to be a mensch in her life. The movie was about a ghost that was somehow loosed upon the forbidding winter land, mentally threatening the people huddling by the fire.

Walker did mention to Aaron Marcus that he had been at seder as he saw evidence around AM+A that there had been one there too. The old master smiled at him. (Which was quite rare.)

A few words on Eco Semiotics as applied to GUI

Interactive objects, symbols, signs, clickable text in a field . . . It was a very exciting time to discover the possibilities of interface. Once again it felt like those early heady days in Desk Top Publishing when the Mac people were learning about page design and typography. Now with Hypercard and Supercard and MM Director there, Apple had launched the true believers into another exciting wave of creativity.

If we were to review semiotics a couple of paragraphs, the first would be a little review of signs and the second would be using the computer interface as the subject to show use of the terms in the semiotics of Umberto Eco. And there is a little side distinction on Jung and symbol.

Signs represent the objects they refer to. For example if you see smoke, then you conjecture fire. Smoke is a sign of fire. It is an index because it is so closely associated with fire. You can see signs are thinking, making hypothesis, calling things up from memory and comparing them, and working toward a conclusion. People think with signs. Semiotics is thinking.

Peirce tells us that besides the index there are 2 other types of sign, the icon and the symbol. A painting of King Louis the XII is a sign of that king, it is his picture. This sign of the particular king is an icon. An icon has a likeness of the object it represents. Now a symbol in Peirce and Jackobson is an abstract, conventional, agreed-upon sign for something.

Like in math. Or like a letter is the symbol for a sound and word is a symbol for a meaning. These are signs to those that speak the language.

This is not the meaning of symbol that Jung used. If we go back to the icon of the particular king, and it extends to other kings, and starts to take on the meaning of a King for a people and even starts to have the properties of the archetype that the king represents, then you are getting into the idea of symbol in the Jungian sense. It is type and token: a particular king is a token of the larger set, the type.

Obviously in the semiotics of interface one thinks of the use of icons. They are a sign that closely resembles the object they are representing. Also there is usually a visual metaphor, for example in a page layout program we have what looks like a page, with columns and margins. The page provides a visual metaphor interface for all the words and design elements we are collecting into the computer document.

Aaron Marcus and Associates used the semiotic formalism of Umberto Eco to compare and critique the usability of graphical interface design. Eco comes after Peirce and Jackobson and he has a semiotics of 4 dimensions: pragmatic lexical semantic and syntactic.

The order of the work flow that the user is trying to do with the GUI, its associating, is the paradigmatic arrangement that is involved in interactive communication with the user. It is the pragmatic goal, what the user wants to accomplish by communicating with the computer.

The signs in the interface communicate with the code behind the interface and with the user in front of the interface. Within the interface, the play of design relations are equivalent to the semiotics of syntax. At the user level a dialog is taking place in which semantic commands use these syntactic structures. This moves the work along in steps, this weaving is the pragmatic semiotic function. The lexical, readerly function is about the consistency of the interface elements. It is about the process of moving from state to state of the work being done, the diachronic, moving with time. Each state ads meaning to the project in the way reading accumulates meaning.

Though Walker was to meet and work with many other interface designers here and there, several while working at Apple where you have people really into the beautiful interface, he was confident in his knowledge because he understood the semiotics behind interface design. At AM+A they were constantly throwing the esthetic argument into the debate space of semiotics.

What he picked up at AM+A gave Walker a lot of confidence and he started his own interface design studio called Semantic Imaging. People often got his company name confused by Symantec a company that made security software.

Visa

Walker designed, developed and produced this interactive 3D model of the enterprise-wide computing network of VISA International based on extensive interviews with many subject experts. This was an interactive voyage through the structure of VisaNet Integrated Payment System that began as an answer to the question: "What happens after I swipe my card through the reader?" Walker called it File and Field Streams of VisaNet, as files are brought up and compared against fields in the authorization request and response byte streams. He thought tracking the money with flow-chart and byte-map through a vast network of leased lines and satellite communications going all over the world was perhaps almost as exciting as canoeing through the jungle with gun and camera. The journey follows the composition of the 128 byte authorization request packet through all its meanderings in the computer network until its return, through the security locks into the routing scenarios going from customer to merchant's acquirer bank, then through the VisaNet interchange center, then through editing, logging, switching, stand-in processing and much more. Then from there out to the card issuer and back to the merchant site where the payment / credit gets made. This trail was developed for both the credit card and the debit card. It was a tremendous education in networking and credit banking as well as using 3D modeling and the human figure to put a human face on some very complicated technology and to tell a story that encompassed a vast enterprise.

It was full screen. It was ultimately delivered in video with Walker doing the voice over.

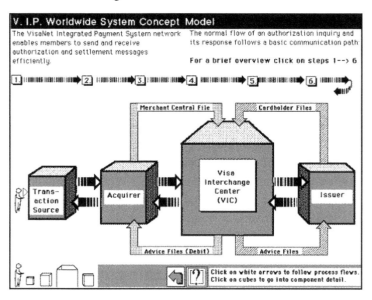

Viacom TV Interactive TV Interface.

He worked at Viacom before it became Paramount after it have been CBS on its way to being agglomerated by MTV. He developed an early prototype for interactive TV. Walker programmed a simulation of a typical interaction: It had a moving display of channels and times.

This was a 10-foot interface it had to be operable by remote control from 10 feet away across a living room. Clicking on a movie title brought up a QuickTime move clip of the movie and a discussion of it. Recommendations from other viewers etc.

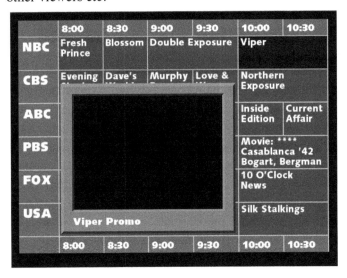

	8:00	8:30	9:00	9:30	10:00	10:30
NBC	Fresh Prince	Blossom	Double Exposure		Viper	
CBS	Evening	Dave's	Murphy	Love &	Northern Exposure	
ABC					Inside Edition	Current Affair
PBS					Movie: **** Casablanca '42 Bogart, Bergman	
FOX					10 O'Clock News	
USA	Viper Promo				Silk Stalkings	
	8:00	8:30	9:00	9:30	10:00	10:30

One got a sense of social. The Entertainment Tonight had a "host" which was a type of person, who would suggest the evening viewing activities. The host would be a video loop of a person talking to the user. The host agent gave suggestions, initiated activities responded based upon input from the user. This project was programmed in MM Director. An infrared detector, allowed one to control the cursor movement and mouse clicks with a remote control.

Sentence Builder

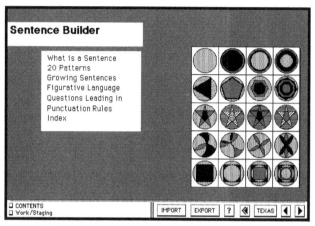

Walker designed and constructed an application that was a tool for writers. Now he was getting back to his roots, at least in an abstract way. This interface in HyperCard based upon various grammar texts. It is a tool to help writers make more elaborate sentence patterns by looking up examples.

This opening screen shows closed geometrical diagrams which attempt to reflect the semantic structure diagram of the sentence type. (Walker found in the writings of Bertrand Russell and CS Peirce there are the most exquisite examples of sentences that were grammatically, symmetrically in their elaborated parallel construction.) There was also Story Builder and HypercyberpunX. More on those writer tools later.

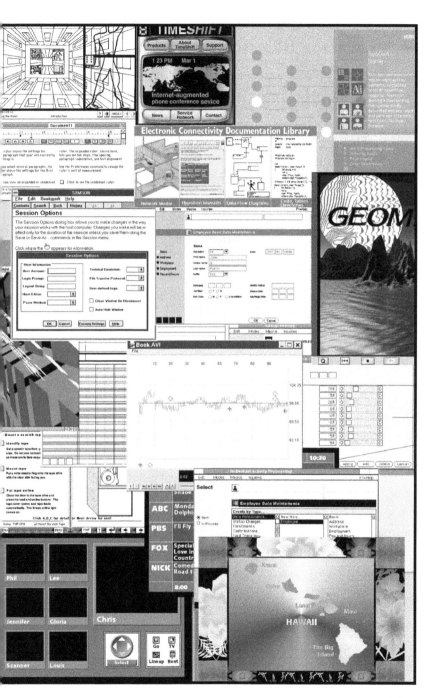

273

Mandala — Homoculus

What the plant has taught us

The brain is the ultimate mandala of all. Marijuana made it possible for one to feel his physical brain.

They say smoking marijuana leads to memory loss. That it opens up the connection across the cerebellum through the corpus collosum to integrate the usually opposing points of view from L and R brain. Marijuana effects the hypocampus. But does this necessarily lead to having fewer dreams? Or perhaps more purposive ones. Or chaotic ones. Also there is impaired motor coordination. That speaks to the back brain and its integration with the spine.

Marijuana brain research has taught us a lot about the brain. They look at it from 6 groups: Psychological; Personality; Learning Problems; Nervous System; Behavior; Neurotransmitters.

Personality is different from psychological.

The Psychological effects take place in the frontal cortex. They are visual tricks like hallucinations and delusions; things like mood swings and panic attacks and paranoia are processes of the frontal cortex. Why would anxiety have the origin of its presentation situated in the frontal cortex? The fore brain came later in evolution. It is about the structures of kinship and society and community and religion and art that we have created, in our verbal linguistic processing area of the brain. And this structure asks the old neolithic brain to let it intercede with the social order that we have come to rely upon so for survival.

The Personality lies *near* the frontal, but along the sides of the brain. This seems to be about Judgmental, a personality trait that would or could bring about a shift in life standards. Associations that one makes are the everyday currency of time and sense of continuity. Very important.

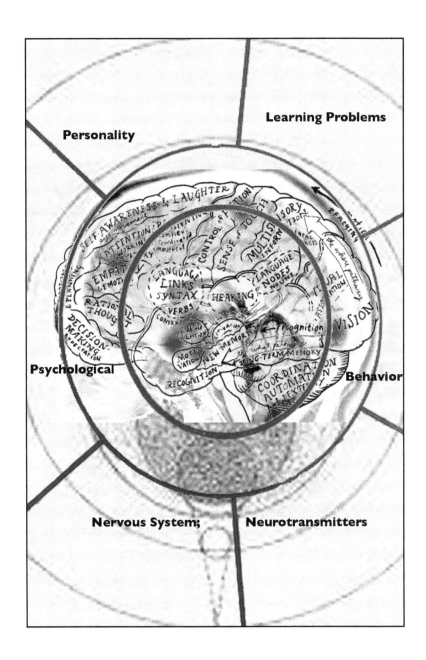

Personality

Learning Problems

Psychological

Behavior

Nervous System;

Neurotransmitters

275

What about Behaviors. They originate further back in the brain. They have access to the primitive fight and flight brain — old and under, what came after. They cluster together: Risky Behaviors; Poor Concentration; Detached Interpersonal Relations; Lack of Trust; Loss of motivation.

Walker made up a kind of blues sonnet about it.

Because of my lack of trust
My social life was a bust
I was detached and looking on —
like it was all just one big con.
Afraid to keep the faith,
My wife left — future unsafe.
With my love life gone stale,
Work became boring travail.
I couldn't focus on what the future might bring
I was walking around bumping into things.
And I was ground down to dust.
And feeling so crushed.
I started drinking and fast driving
for kicks to let me know I was still alive in this sad world.

The brain is the ultimate mandala of all. A space of neurons packed and connected in a bath of serotonin, dopamine, adrenaline, acetylcholine norepinephrine and others.

Too little of one and you get depression; too much of another and your get anxiety disorders. Too much of one AND too littler of another and you get schizophrenia. Dementia can degrade into tremors of Parkinson's disease. It is an amazing estuary of just-in-time chemical deliveries. And the doctors do try to scare that marijuana use damages or degrades this chemical ecology. It is not cherishing your temple. On the other hand Marijane gets you in touch with Nature as Deity Mother or the ground from which all this springs; this helps you experiment in the phenomenology of the self. Walker felt like the risk was worth the reward.

Defense Mechanisms as Groups in Time

Projection, Denial, Rationalization, Identification. Of the many, many defenses, these are some of the heaviest ones that can be dangerous if not deadly. Denial and Disassociation are too.

Defenses get established in time. From primitive to immature to adult. Let us see in which groups these main ones reside.

Primitive group: Denial. Denial is from your way back, before you could even think or reason very much. It is pre-linguistical. Magical too.

Immature group: Projection. Develops with the thinking. The Immature group contains most of the defense mechanisms: Intellectualization. Rationalization. Disassociation.

Watch your rationalization. The inner rationalization voice (of the writer) says: I've been an addict and I've been obsessed. I just need it to get by.

A defense mechanism keeps you from knowing who you are. Avoid projection. You can feel it coming at you when you are being bombasted by projection, it burns. You feel at loose ends, guilty, beset upon, attacked. You are left with anger and get started seeking in revenge. Some skilled player has off-loaded on you, perhaps in defense for you off-loading on them.

Another most important thing to avoid is reaction formation or somatization into the body of suppressions so that physical symptoms occur.

Mature group: Humor. Altruism. (You might be a little suspicious of that. Rescuers couch their defense in altruism.)

Be the inquisitor and root out denial. Denial is at the top of the list, because it is a most primitive defense mechanism like the magical thinking of childhood, and it is the generator of most of the other defense mechanisms. If you are in denial about a problem you can't even begin analysis of it.

From Symbolism into Lucidity

Walker was further exploring dream yoga. On his own there wasn't the level of awareness and the excitement in the pursuit of enlightenment that inbued the House sangha. But he tried to make his bedroom into a kind of asclepeion — a temple of spiritual healing through dreams. In the idea that psyche through good sleep made it easier to expose yourself to sattva — the calmness leading to enlightenment.

Oneirogenic Music

Walker had an interesting thing happen with sound and dreams. As he fell into an afternoon nap one day he had this Celtic harp music playing, it was a mix repeating on a long loop.

> *And in my dream I entered into the great infamous tower library at UT Austin, a fine old building of brass balustrades and marble stairs and grand porticoes and shiny display cases.*
>
> *In this building I had spent innumerous hours reading during my slacker youth. As I came up to a side door, I could hear someone was playing this celtic harp music, and I looked around and through a window to try and see where it was coming from. As I turned, the sound got muffled (enhancing the 3d effect in the dream). I thought it was being played in one of the offices down below the street level. I entered the library through a side door and raced past the big desk trying to avoid being challenged, because I had let my stack pass expire. And I JUST managed to keep from falling into a hole in the floor! I nearly stepped off into a precipitous fall down into what was that shaft for the tiny elevator going way down through several floors of gray metal book stacks. The rectangular hole in the linoleum floor was a hazard without a guard rail of any sort. It seemed that the grey metal rows of shelves were a separate structure, maze-like extruded out to a crystalline infinity. I quickly back up. And was about to protest aloud of the danger.*

I started talking to this girl who worked behind the counter. She was a lovely beautiful blonde Irish girl in a green velvet tunic. She had dark eyes, and her delicate hair curled in wisps to frame her white peach blushed face like an angel. But she had these flashing eyes, and might have been demonic except such an angel couldn't be. And we started talking about the old country, she was from there, of course and I was chatting her up trying to bask in her beauty and telling her I was Scotch Irish and that my people came from Inverness and Firth of the 4th. And it was her playing a CD of the music.

Walker had incorporated phenomena going on outside into his dream sleep before, but never for so long. He had not thought of playing music into the dream. He did recall having fallen asleep while listening to a tape or being lulled on a train and had that outside experience be fortuitously convolved into the dream. Perhaps there was a whole genre of oneirogenic music. Walker wondered what it would be. Certainly Celtic harp is magical that way.

Upon thinking about it he was struck by how this dream was like another dream he had about being on a cloud and a door opening up and him being afraid of falling through it into the farmlands far below. There was a strange anima figure there too. A Las Vegas show girl. Walker definitely understood that she was an anima. So this Irish girl must be one too. Walker realized he had beautiful but dangerous (and uncaring) animas.

Walker did a little research and found hearing and smelling are the only two senses not shut down in sleep. Vigilant evolution. It would be far out to have something that could sense your REM cycles and play appropriate music.

Nova Dreamer

One day Walker ordered the Nova Dreamer, a device to help with Lucid Dreaming sold by a Stanford professor.

Perhaps he could use that to take the next step in the Jungian way of individuation as seen in the *Red Book*. And that is to engage these archetypal entities seen in dreams in a dialog of active imagination. Toward that end he started to explore lucid dreaming. His experience with hypnosis and meditation was a necessary first step in this quest. Walker had learned self-hypnosis in a little class put on by MHMR (Mental Health and Mental Retardation) of the Texas Bureau of Health back in the 70's. Over the years he used the formal method of counting backward. Of late he didn't need to do that counting so much anymore. Over the years Walker had been involved a time or two with various meditation groups, but never got much further than the common everyday light trance, perhaps like the alpha zone-out of watching baseball on TV. He realized self-hypnosis, progressive relaxation, or autogenic training were are all similar mental practices. Walker got into tai chi and did feel the Tao. Meditation got a little better when Walker stopped the Zen practice of spuffing off thoughts toward attaining emptiness and let himself follow the images and feelings that came up. Walker learned this was Tantric Buddhism in the sangha commune. Though the imagery of the Tibetan deities is very foreign to our modern western ways, the symbology of deity as a union of opposites is brilliant and had a big influence on Jung. The sutras are procedures or algorithms for inducing images and are a marvelous contribution to world literature. Recently through storytelling school, Walker had become aware of Nidra yoga where they do a kind of induction talk-down progressive relaxation and float while in the corpse pose at end of asana class.

The important thing Walker learned from meditation is the state of dissociation. Meditation teaches a dissociation from the ego to inhabit more of just being. That is done through the breath which is how one intercedes over the autonomic nervous system. Art is not meditation per se but contemplation and is done by dropping into a graceful unconscious flow. However that happens.

In Berkeley Walker had sent off for a Nova Dreamer, it was a kind of battery operated sleep mask. It had LEDs that flashed when motion detectors in the eye coverings sensed the sleeper going into REM. The idea was that this flashing light signal was supposed to stimulate the dreamer to become lucid in the dream he was having. It came with a book: *A Course in Lucid Dreaming*. Stephen LaBerge a Stanford sleep scientist had developed it. Walker was proud to own a piece of equipment for his amateur sleep lab and he felt like a phenomenologist. He was hoping to explore lucid dreaming as part of the spiritual practice of dream yoga, but Walker never had much success with the device. It was a big clunky set of goggles with two AAA batteries. He used to put it on when he went to bed but it made him too anxious to get into a dream and he never seemed to get any sleep because of it. So he gave up on it. But it did manage to give him a first taste of the lucid dream. And that existence proof is very valuable. This is what happened.

The flashing LED lights that awoke me in my dream got quickly morphed into a memory of a car accident I was in as a little child. Driving in Quebec winter, the old ski back Chevrolet had slid uncontrollably down the ice slick highway and banged into another car. I remembered my mother shouting, "Watch Out!" And my father having to get out in the snow and the storm in his overcoat and slouch hat and exchange insurance data. And I remembered being fearful and seeing the red tail lights of the other car through frosty windows. Almost immediately I thought of the Nova Dreamer (the red lights) and reached for it, and I couldn't feel it in my dream but this was enough for me to realize that I was in a dream. But I got carried away and tried to do all those things every lucid dreamer wants to do and woke very quickly. I

*didn't stay in the lucid state for long (woke up almost immedi-
ately) but I was blown away that it worked.*

Then one day in Berkeley, Walker made the connection
that the feeling of flourescence he sometimes felt in the body
when going through a progressive relaxation was the onset
of a sleep paralysis the body invokes in order to keep people
from acting out their dreams in the REM state and waking
themselves up. He had often felt a kind of fluorescence of the
body when doing self-hypnosis and in fact it was a proof of
success. Fluorescence is not a bad name for the slight pins
and needles sensation as no doubt there is some electrical
activity on the surface from lessened resistance, a kind of
aura one might say. Walker thought he should be able to trick
the body mind by doing progressive relaxation so that the
body is completely quiescent, so that the brain will think you
are asleep and will activate the safety body paralysis, yet he
would be still awake in meditation.

So to lucid dream, or alpha-plane travel (astral travel)
Walker started to use this WAGB Wake and Go Back to
sleep method (even the great physicist Richard Feynman
had written about it). Where you lie completely still and do
progressive relaxation until a sleep paralysis sets in. When
you feel the atonia onset, look for REM dreaming to follow:
but you must remain awake, you are meditating. The mind
thinks the body is asleep and will send it commands to test
it: Roll Over or Itch Your Nose. But you must lie perfectly
still, eyes fixed, and soon the mind will be convinced that
the body is asleep and it is free to produce REM dreams, that
you can be in, or watch on the screen behind your forehead.

The procedure is move the awareness to various parts of
the body to induce relaxation. Wait and concentrate on the
breathing. When you sense a fluorescence of the physical
body in sleep paralysis you can separate your morphogenetic

form, or electric, or imaged astral body from your zonked out physical body.

You can feel a separation of the two bodies that are merged. It might be helpful to picture the chakras as energy nodes of color red orange blue green purple white as fountain nodes of flourescence bursting the bonds. The chakras are visualized nodes set in real physical places of the body representing symbolically progressive evolutionary advances in animal organization.

If you start to question or analyze, it is consciousness coming to the fore and you will wake up from the dream. If you move the body it will disturb the dream bed and you will wake up.

He wrote this about my experience.

And in my attempt at astral travel, it is sometimes good to see the prone body as having these nodes of organization symbolized by chakras each with their own color: red orange indigo green blue purple white and as the human aura. But now gone into sleep paralysis the body is seen as lifting off, detaching from the chakra nodes as though they were bolts but now are energy fountains pushing the shell — a kind of weightless translucent visionary exoskeleton — off from the body. It was then that the chakras started moving around and redistributing themselves in this cloud. It was a fairly nice dreamlike solution to a problem relating chakras to lift off.

The dream was a story in which the chakras, the levels of hierarchical origination of the body mind are seen as distributed in a cloud. Symbolized by ¢#&+@*∞

```
          /∞\
    . -=-#  | )  -.
  /  •  (   *  ')@  \
  \  ( + _&_ )  )/
   (_  ,  /^\  ¢_/
```

As this cloud I just started going about and doing remote viewing. This cloud led to flying in the dream. Flying down some of the steeper hills in San Francisco like a kind of Wayne Thiebaud abstract landscape.

I tried to float higher above and perhaps start to look around and explore the astral world. Examine other spaces, zoom down streets, enter shops, observe others. When I wanted to wake up I counted down from ten and returned to my body by a kind of docking with congruence maneuver. Then I opened my eyes awakened.

Now on the rare occasion when it happens, I get a sense that I am privileged to view my life from a 3rd dimension, above the maze. Like I am looking down on the intersecting pathways of my life and seeing them from above. Perhaps this higher perspective is coming out of the interpretation of dreams as though the education were having some effect.

Though I have yet to get into a convocation of fellow astral travelers (wink;-) — I will let you know if I do — that is all science fiction from Mr. Monroe, and Cayce and Swedenborg and others at this point.

To See as Sea Horses Do

One night Walker had this dream.

An egg cracked open and a sea horse looking creature came out. It had the crenelated body and spiral tail, and the rectangular snout.

I tried to see if I could get this sign post presentation of the 4 Functions to float on top of the sea horse and merge with it. And to my further surprise it did there be juxtaposed: a sign post of oval signs of decreasing size, each with the name of one of the four functions. The ovals were distributed protruding alternately on either side of the spine / post.

Walker made a sketch of the idea of the image in the dream and wrote about it.

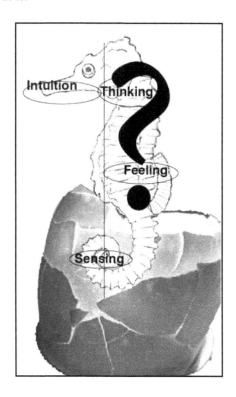

He was shocked. He thought that this was a "big" dream from the collective unconscious because it was not much about him as the character in the dream. It was about "This is how Gaia Designs."

After a few days of undergoing religious conversion into belief of the collective unconscious, Walker began to want to amplify what he had seen in this dream of a sea horse emerging from an egg. This sea horse was like a kind of Venus-on-the-half-shell, coming out of the egg-shaped cranium of an ancient earth-dweller, whose skull had been unearthed and bleached white and made eggshell-fragile from exposure to the sun and wind in the shifting sands of time. Walker felt like the image of the sea horse was surprising to say the least, moreover confounding. Walker tried to "read" the image from what little he could find about them in memory. He recalled that people see them as sea dragons because they swim up-right. The spiraling tail, reminds of a nautilus shell and is therefore Fibonacci. He marveled at their skin, almost translucent, bioluminescent. Their eyes seem preponderantly large, like the figures in those religious holy card Russian icon paintings. And their structure, that accordion body pulled taunt and water-tight over a pliable endoskeleton made it seem delicately crenelated. A squeeze box crossed with a citadel? Walker recalled that somehow the male carries the embryo and it is the only animal (fish?) to do this. It is a fish because it has gills. The sea horse was a marvel of creative form engineering and perhaps one of Gaia's little jokes like the duck-billed platypus. Perhaps he could understand this communication from the psyche. And it has something to say about the functions. He could understand it by knowing its form adapting to the landscape that created it. He wondered, am I trying to know the creator then? But of course.

Also Walker noted that before this dream he had been marveling at this diagram of the 4 Jungian Functions expressing as Types that looked like a sign post; the 4 distributed around a pole that pointed to the left for Introvert and to the right side of the post for Extrovert.

Thinking about form adaptation, he recalled the coiled tail was prehensile. It allowed the sea horse to hold on to branches and float upright in neutral buoyancy. Its little angel-wing fins are used to fan oxygen-bearing water through gills He worked up this poem to at least mark the occasion of this big dream.

> To see as sea horses do.
> Able to withstand not knowing,
> Not having to always let reason have its way
> But abiding in uncertainty —
> Ego is under construction.
> Sea horse swimming in
> albumen water, the water in the egg
> is the water of life, it carries life.
> And the sea horse is swimming in this water.
> Sea horse with the mermaids.
> The sea horse dwells within this fragile elegant egg,
> Elixir vitae, water of life. Dragon,
> The sea horse is a kind of dragon.
> I can not be always in my Thinking if I want to
> heal myself. I must explore the other Functions.
> Feeling Intuition Sensing.
> The sea horse is making a point
> about the Resurrection Machine.
> Say the sacred Spell:
> Travel through medium, gather. Awaken.
> The language of dreams is creating a narrative
> by mixing entities of the hermeneutic mandala.

He had been studying a design for the way the 4 functions {feeling, thinking, sensing, intuiting} distribute themselves on either side of a sign post in positions of primary secondary auxiliary and inferior. The sign post of Functions drifted over and merged with the image of the sea horse coming out of an egg.

Walker wanted to have a think about Jungian Functions. He ask what perceptive functions would a writer mostly use. Certainly N the iNtuitive comes first to mind.

We have the perceptive functions N and S and they are coupled with pervasive attitude-types: i, Introversion and e, Extroversion. Would the writer be Ne extroverted intuitive or Ni introverted intuitive.

Or would an Si, intuitive sense type, (who could feel and recall past experiences which are now inner) be the writer type. (We doubt if the Se, extroverted sense type could sit still by himself long enough to type up stories.)

So now he saw that he has brought in the time. Se is in the moment and Si is in the past. There is not sensing of the future because it hasn't happened yet. There is conjecturing, and marshaling desire and the will toward the future. That is what the N function does, isn't it?

Walker thought about putting the perceptive functions on a time line of attitude. And the light cone came into the picture.

He started placing the Functions in their time domains on the light cone.

N focuses on 'what could be'.

S focuses on 'what is'.

N intuits the future. What would that mean to the writer's work.

Sensing deals with what is known. Either what is happening now, Se or what has happened in the past, Si.

Intuition deals with the unknown. How does N do this. N is conceptualizing, using abstract perception, that is to say

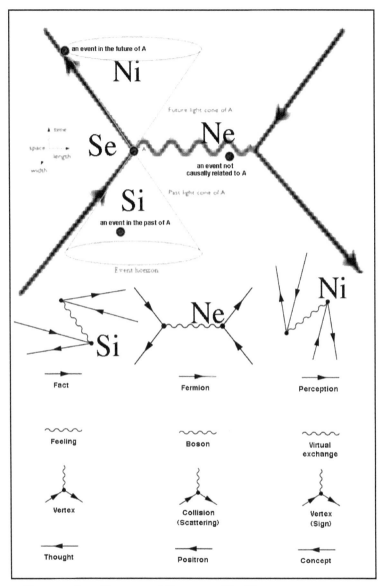

Perception Space of Personality Types

looks at patterns and makes a hypothesis as to what to expect as a logical unfolding of these observations (perceptions). Like looking at a geometry figure, and seeing relationships, even parts that would be necessarily hidden behind the face. They are constructed by conceptualizing. Filling in the dots.

Then, with the idea of time as intuition with attitude, he put the perceiving functions N and S on the time line of a light cone. Walker started seeing analogies between the functions of personality types and domains of physics. Thinking was like the electric / crystalline lattice structure of Matter (fermions); Feeling was like the flowing heat of energy (field quanta); Sensing was evolved from relating to space (collision and scattering); Intuition was the organ of Time. Suddenly in a stunning juxtaposition he saw Feynman diagrams on this light cone: at the collision of past and future in the now; scattering could be like the possibilities of the movement of perception. Feynman diagrams are about the probability function of the movement of perception. They look like graphs and like vectors, but they are neither. They are schematic pictures with rules for interpretation. In the typical Feynman diagram, the incoming particles crashed and annihilated to form a virtual photon, ($\sim\sim\sim\sim$) which then split to produce the outgoing particles. This can accommodate scenarios in which the virtual particle goes UP forward in time or DOWN backward in time.

The attitudes bring time to the intuition: Ni is about what might be expected to happen in the future; Ne is about what might be possible. Ne likes to improvise, deals in virtual, and alternative reality; Ni looks at what has happened and projects it out into future scenarios.

Intuition is a perception function rather than a judging function F and T, which are performed on data already captured by the perceiving functions. Though certainly Feeling and Thinking are very important to the writer.

Time is involved with the perceiving functions; the judging functions are seen to be outside of time. Elsewhere on the light cone, they take us to elsewhen on the light cone

One could say the same thing with watching something happening in the moment if one is paying attention to the perception trajectories as they make their way bouncing around memory like on a pin ball machine.

Waker noted a couple of examples.

As I am standing on the platform waiting for a streetcar an old lady passes by, reeking of laundry scent and cheap perfume. I conjecture (unkindly) that she probably thinks she is still beautiful.

Then I go back into time and have a sense memory.

Whenever I smell a rose deeply, it takes me back to my grandfather's house, he raised roses climbing on trellises in the maritime summer, and grandmother had big bouquets of them in the lady's parlor for her bridge tea.

I sit down on the concrete bench in the subway tunnel to await the streetcar.

I nod off into a fantasy about being followed DOWN endless flights of stairs, trying to get away from someone who is hell-bent on confronting me. I am trying to get out of this endless cavernous stairwell into the lobby, but missing that door I end up heading deeper into the basement. Then in terror I realize I have to go back UP and pass the shadowy pursuer.

And yet I am filled with pride today as I was overjoyed to see the miracle of tiny little green pin-head peyote buds poking up from seeds cast into a dry gravely desert mix. I smile and think I can now call myself a cactus farmer.

What does "Ne focuses on what could be" mean. It is extrapolating using abstract conceptual perception in the inner world of thought and feelings to create speculative possible worlds.

What does "Ni focuses on what could be" mean. It is ruminating, using abstract conceptual perception in the inner world of thought and feelings to recreate scenarios with variations of what has been experienced in the past.

Is the Ni only going over what has happened in the past? The Ni is perceiving what was perceived by the senses Se but now in the past. This is Si. Is Ni conceptualizing defenses to insure that bad things that happened in the past don't happen in the future? Is Ni the seat of the defense mechanisms? Or is it Si.

Walker knew that he had to use writing to find himself; recollecting what happened is necessary to understand. What happens happens so fast it is too fast for the N, but the S can quickly deal with it and move on.

When does 'what could be' become 'what will be'. Do the Ni and the Si team up? The Si recalls and senses what has been taken in from the outside; the Ni does not use concrete perception from the outside of what was previously sensed but projects from an inner vision? Archetypes. Instincts.

If Ni is in the future, and Si is in the past and Se is in the present, where is Ne? Ne is outside of time, virtual, elsewhere in space, in a possible world.

He wondered if what he was often thinking of as his intellectual or T orientation (as opposite of F), was really Ne? Is time a factor in the use of the primary, secondary, tertiary and occluded Functions. It was the occluded — or was it inferior? Jung says, It was the occluded function that performs the important task of anchoring the being in the psyche.

Walker ended his poem with:

> Rock a bye baby in the treetop —
> it was the curled tail,
> that held the sea horse in the tree,
> when the currents did rock.

Entity Relationship Modeling

Walker was glad to take a break from the endless job hustle that is contracting and went to work at a full-time job at MetaCASE Business Systems in Los Altos. They made a suite of Computer Aided Software Engineering (CASE) tools for database designers. These were: a Data Flow Diagrammer; a Screen Form Designer; the Entity Relationship Diagrammer; and the Program Structure Diagrammer. These all connected into a Central Data Dictionary. And it was supposed to generate the actual program code, or at least a pseudocode that could be translated into the programming language.

When Walker saw the Entity Relationship Diagraming software it really blew his mind. This was a kind of graphical logic — he thought of Peirce and his existential diagrams; but this was on the computer screen and with it a program designer could drill down into sub-diagrams and down further into language! Walker thought he might be able to adapt it, — this invoking the dictionary of speaches, to be used for writing. He really wanted to work there.

Somehow he made a good impression on the woman partner who took him out to lunch at an up-scale Los Altos restaurant as part of the interview. She was a vice-president of the company and a partner and married to the head technology officer even though she was older. He was an enthusiastic guy and wanted Walker to do writing and advertising and interactive demonstration marketing. At the luncheon interview with the capital lady, Walker wore a suit and he was grateful that his mother had taught him good manners, though he worried that she might have found him too unknowledgeable of their product. He was not a database administrator. He explained to her, "It might be an asset.

"Sometimes it is good for an expert to have to explain to a beginner; it helps find gaps in how the program is used. I have to make things understandable to myself before I can make them understandable to users. I observe what I have to go through to understand and use the software and then I can make sure everything they need for an easy and good learning experience is right there at hand in the presentation. In a way the documentation becomes their first guide to the company culture. Also it is good for the programmers to see their work in a gorgeous format."

Apparently she liked the sound of that and he was hired.

He started commuting down the 280 every day in his old VW van. In Los Altos on Main Street your can park perpendicular to the curb. And the wide avenue is lined with beautiful Chinese trees that send of puff ball tufts but whose leaves are crisp on the edge so that the shadows are sharp on the sidewalks from the canopy overhead. There was vast amounts of public parking in lots behind the Main Street. Walker parked there all day. The people at MetaCASE were nice. They were patient with him as he came up to speed on their product. And he was inspired to work with the Entity Relationship Diagrammer software even though he was not a database administrator type.

Walker had moved to San Francisco to be housemates with Kevin Phelan and Mary, a couple; they were two friends from the commune. They were glad to have him move in there to help with the rent and he was glad to be with this charming couple and observe how two people could be in love with each other. They had another roommate who was a post doc molecular biologist or biochemist who had an immortal line of cancer cells at University of San Francisco Medical School. Kevin had the attic and you went up into his room through a trap door. Walker got him started growing a little pot underneath the skylight in the roof admitting the sun on its arc. It was nice up there, you could see downtown San Francisco. The cheerful house was near a small grassy park called Fairmont Plaza atop a huge rocky cliff. Walker's room had been the living room; they had closed it off with a thin partition. Near the kitchen, he soon found it heavily trafficked. Walker had his VW van when he moved over from Berkeley and he parked it on the steep street.

Ms. C would occasionally come over and stay the night. They were still going together, although he was commuting back and forth to Los Altos every day. He really wanted to learn this interesting software of Entity Relationship Modeling. His relationship with Ms. C was still good — or so he thought. Though he had declined her offer to move into her house in Berkeley with her. Why? Because it was her place and he didn't feel comfortable encroaching on it. And, it was a lot easier to commute to Silicon Valley from San Francisco. Things did get considerably more awkward between them when it became clear that Walker made sure she left the house in San Francisco whenever he did; she became somewhat insulted. He just didn't trust leaving a woman in his room when he was not there. They drifted further apart.

At MetaCASE Walker got busy studying their structured approach to database design. The programmers were gracious at explaining things to the newbie. To get oriented on relational database, Walker would go around asking basic questions. It was a tech writer's act he did: to engage engineers and programmers and challenge them to correct his wrongful thinking about some esoteric, arcane, or technical piece of the work. His aproach was to start with some knowledge — letting them know he had done *some* research: "So I have just a basic question about how the data is physically stored and how it is retrieved."

Walker asked, "One has a table of records; this is the entity. An entity has a primary key." And here he looked for confirmation and recognition. You had to become a member of the club to participate in its knowledge. Workers are delighted to have someone pay attention to their work. Especially a sharp older woman programmer named Elle. She seemed glad to have this man with his journalist attention visiting her cubicle.

She began with, "Think of a database as like a room full of tables. On each table you have different stacks and piles of information. But now in the database the information is linked up with the other tables so you don't have multiple entries. It's efficient that way.

"It is easier to find the data you want because you can do a search for just what you want instead of having to look through piles of data on several tables. A search is a query."

Elle showed him some typical queries. She typed one into the field for entering commands.

```
Select * from TABLE_NAME group_by_dept
having salary > 10000
```

The result from the test database showed a nice presentation of columns of departments and another column of names.

employeeNumb	lastName	firstName	extension	officeCode	reportsTo	jobTitle
1002	Murphy	Diane	x5800	1	1056	President
1056	Patterson	Mary	x4611	1	1002	VP Sales
1076	Firelli	Jeff	x9273	1	1002	VP Marketing
1088	Patterson	William	x4871	6	1056	Sales Manager (APAC)
1102	Bondur	Gerard	x5408	4	1056	Sale Manager (EMEA)
1143	Bow	Anthony	x5428	1	1056	Sales Manager (NA)
1165	Jennings	Leslie	x3291	1	1143	Sales Rep
1166	Thompson	Leslie	x4065	1	1143	Sales Rep
1188	Firelli	Julie	x2173	2	1143	Sales Rep
1216	Patterson	Steve	x4334	2	1143	Sales Rep
1286	Tseng	Foon Yue	x2248	3	1143	Sales Rep
1323	Vanauf	George	x4102	3	1143	Sales Rep
1337	Bondur	Loui	x6493	4	1102	Sales Rep
1370	Hernandez	Gerard	x2028	4	1102	Sales Rep
1401	Castillo	Pamela	x2759	4	1102	Sales Rep
1501	Bott	Larry	x2311	7	1102	Sales Rep

"Here is data organized by departments and those workers who have salaries greater than $10,000."

Walker looked at the pretty-printed page of rows and columns. "Nice."

Elle said, "Note by using the "HAVING" clause I don't have to use both the "ORDER BY" clause and the "WHERE" clause. But we'll get into that."

"An Entity Relationship Diagram is a graphical representation of the data requirements for a database," she continued. "It takes all the parts of a database and puts them in a nice box and line form." She did a quick sketch on a piece of paper.

"The rectangle is the Entity and the triangle is the Relationship.

"Or we could say the entity is a noun, a person, place or thing and the relationship is a verb, some action or state of being."

"The types of information that are saved in the database are called 'entities'. These are usually: people, things, events, and locations. Everything you could want to put in a database fits into one of these categories.

"Here for example is the start of the student database." She pulled a sheet of paper out of a pile.

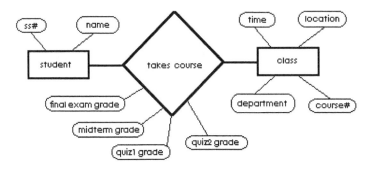

She smiled. "Let us look here at the E R D for student database. It is always what people teach with.

"An Entity Relationship (E R) Diagram is a type of flowchart that illustrates how "entities" such as people, objects or concepts relate to each other within a system.

"An Entity represents a person place or thing you want to track in a database. STUDENTS will become a table in the database. Each student will have a row in the table," she said as she indicated appropriate parts of the diagram. She pointed to the oval shapes attached to the entity in the student database diagram.

"Now these ovals attached to the entity STUDENT are the Attributes. The student has attributes: Social Security Number and Name. These will become the columns in the table."

"Oh I get it, the columns. Under the column headings."

"Yes the columns describe the various characteristics about an individual entity.

"And the rows are the Entity, unfolding in time, in the data of its attributes.

"It's a Matrix!" Walker shouted with excitement to recognize an old friend.

"Yea, I think so. But the database people don't usually think of it like that. They call it a Table or an Array. Anyway going along a row under each column these are the pieces of information about the entity.

"There are 5 major parts to an ERD. Entity. Relationship. Attributes. Primary Key and Cardinality. Each Student has a last name and a first name which tells us more about the entity STUDENT. Other attributes or aspects of the student we want to keep record of are the GRADES! From what COURSES they completed or didn't. Their PHONE NUMBER.

Now many students can have the same name, but they each have a unique SOCIAL SECURITY NUMBER. And that is an important attribute called the primary key. The primary key is an attribute that uniquely identifies the instance of the entity attribute.

"So the primary key is a special attribute that must be unique."

"It insures that no two rows will have the same value for that attribute."

Walker quickly thought: (In vectors this insures that it is a different line not a multiple of another line, therefore linearly independent) (So they only coincide in one point).

"Now you can just draw a line between entities to show relationship. In ERD we put the diamond for the relationship — it is a verb."

"Cardinality tells us how many rows we need from one table before we can make a relationship to another table."

Again Walker thought: Matrix.

And then she drew an ERD in vertical.

Now when Elle did the basic diagram vertical [Lightning] <Strikes> [Tree] to illustrate the Noun Verb nature of the ERD, Walker's mind flipped back to Pound again and to the essay of Fenolossa, *The Chinese Character as a Medium for Poetry*.

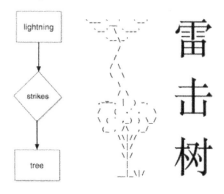

When he got home to San Francisco he dug out his copy of the Fenolossa /Pound book stored in a box in the garage under the house. It was the groovy City Lights paperback edition. And there it was the ideogram form of [Lightning] <Strikes> [Tree]. Walker reread the words of Fenolossa:

> Light, heat, gravity, chemical affinity, human will have this in common, that they redistribute force. Their unit of process can be represented as:
> term— —transference— —term

Walker got excited: There it was: TRANSFERENCE!

> If we regard this transference as the conscious or unconscious act of an agent we can translate the diagram into:
> agent— —act— —object

Then the essay goes on to relate this universal transference to other languages as Subject doing the action, the Verb embodying the stroke of the act and the third point to the Object the receiver of the impact.

Whoa.

That night Walker had to give himself some remedial matrix mechanics.

A matrix is good to compare two things.

The price of things at two bike shops are different in different cities. An inner tube in Boise costs 3.99 while the same inner tube in San Francisco costs 8.95. In Boise a wheel costs 19.50 while in San Francisco it costs 52.25.

The data for this can be encoded into the following bike parts matrix.

$$\begin{vmatrix} 3.99 & 8.95 \\ 19.50 & 52.25 \end{vmatrix}$$

The first row is the tube row in the two cities.

Boi	SF
3.99	8.95

And the 2nd row is the tire row.

Boi	SF	
3.99	8.95	tube
19.50	52.25	tire

We could add another city to the data by adding a column. We could think of it as a column matrix

Hou
5.50
37.50

undergoing a RIGHT JOIN on the right side.

Boi	SF	Hou
3.99	8.95	5.50
19.50	52.25	37.50

The venders would have ID#s for the parts.

ID	Boi	SF	Hou
1	3.99	8.95	5.50
2	19.50	52.25	37.50

Now this is a 2 x 3 matrix. The rows are bike parts, the columns are cities. One would call this table a "bike parts by cities" array. Or "bikes by cities".

Rows are usually considered observations, and columns are variables. It depends on which are your dependent and independent variables (or how you're interpreting the data). If we transposed the matrix we would have a "cities by bike parts" array.

```
ID |  1  |  2   |
Boi | 3.99  8.95 |
Hou | 5.50  37.50|
 SF | 19.50 52.25|
```

You can view this table either way.

Then later, in the well-stocked library of MetaCASE, Walker found, low and behold, isn't the inventor of ERD one Peter Chen, a Chinese professor of computer science who started it in about 1976 with a paper relating the ideogram to the ERD diagram. Walker read the paper and it was about extending and embedding the ERD parts like the way one expanded the ideograms in Chinese. Walker began to feel like he was being guided on a quest, something was leading him into knowledge with signposts of synchronicities —they had books and papers of Chen on a shelf in the library at MetaCASE. He felt like he was on the trail of epiphanies. An entity transfers power to another.

The Graphical Sententiator

Walker was especially inspired by the Entity Relationship Modeler part of the CASE tool and thought it would be cool to adapt it to make an application that writers of poems or stories would love to use. He wanted an approach to writing that was like how programmers made an application. Because wasn't poetry a kind of programming language for the mind as computer? The poem asked the user to go into his mind-computer and bring associations from accounts of experience into memory. The entity-relationship diagram represented a component type approach to composition, rather than that fly-by-the-seat-of-the-pants, bottom-up approach, of trying to grasp and capture fleeting riffs. As it was, being a writer for Walker felt like being a surfer making himself available for the swells of creativity. Perhaps this "Graphical Sententiator" as he called it could be an elegant, structured, controlled, top-down, tour-de-force like how a creative deity sees all, using generative, structurally active objects that fitted together seamlessly and flowed — unobstructed by difficulty — into the users imagination. He liked the idea that the writer would be able to think of the entities and relationships and these be connected to tables of accumulated attributes about the entity or what the entity did. The story would be the working out of a characters personality attributes.

Walker was excited to work at MetaCASE because he thought he could make a writer's help machine, a software to help writers. It would be based on the interactive Entity Relationship Modeling. And he enjoyed the creative high of doing page design in marketing, and interactive digital videos, which were just becoming possible through an extension in Hypercard. He even did the voice overs. He was a creativity junkie in auteur heaven.

The Graphical Sententiator would be a work flow based interface to a database. That is a memory storage for one entity or more, with lists of attributes. It was a matrix space, or a database with rows and columns: the what vs. the when; the how vs. the why.

Independent variables being arrayed in a way that helps see patterns across different dimensions; different opposite choices brought into association and formed the dimension of choice. The Graphical Sententiator would be based on the CASE tool. You diagrammed out the concepts [entities] of the narrative, then their relationships. The Entity and sometimes the Relationship have attributes.

You drill down into the entity with queries. The queries are structured like sentences. As they perform operations in memory to conjoin and disjoin data. The data can be thought
of as row vector $[x1, x2, \ldots]$ or a
column vector, $[x2]$
$[x3]$
as you move around in a field extracting and presenting information in a flow.

The CASE tools actually generated a pseudocode and even program language as you used them in a data base to perform joins and disjoins among aptly named tables or vectors, pools of data trying to rise in the circuit to become information.

So you could write this pseudocode out to script of talking characters or just thoughts of one character. Then, you compile the writing into a text file. Clean up the wording and voila you've got a story, perhaps told in poetry, or prose. Or theatre, or some other new sort of experimental writing. Like a video game. The whole enterprise was writing as experiment in the science of romance, a kind of high concept sci-fi. Moreover Walker thought to use the ERD to go to the source of myth —dreams! He would use diagrams to write a kind of post-Jungian literature where the entities are archetypes or other instinctual organizations or convolution of opposites to propel the spirit of the (anti-) hero through his agonisties.

Walker started using the CASE tool to partition stories into their structure like the way Levi-Strauss did for myths, to understand and show the sameness in their structure to dream structure. The elements of myths arrayed in rows and columns of the diachronic and synchronic: the diachronic are the rows and the synchronic are the columns. We have to get notation! He was inspired by Fenolossa and Pound. And Peter Chen.

To get oriented on relational database

Back at work he would be plying his tech writer trade. He ventured a query to get things going. "Are the records distributed over the hard drive? Or does the database make them contiguous to lessen seek time."

And the programmer answered, "At one time, systems paid really close attention to the location of data on the hard drive but modern systems don't bother with that kind of stuff. More and more systems actually run as much as possible out of RAM."

Walker realized his reading was a bit out of date.

"Most tables will have auxiliary tables called indexes and, at one time, every table and every index would get its own drive. They still do some of that kind of thing (spreading the tables out over multiple drives)."

"So when composing a query I assume one invokes a primary key to identify the table and the key data string in the table."

"Yes." Elle smiled at her student.

"Could you send me a structured query, to see what it looks like. How are the key requests in the query separated, just commas? Do they always occupy the same place in the structure of the query."
```
|ooo|o  o||o  o|o  o|
|ooo|o_o||o_o|_o_|
```
"Then it is RELATIONAL because in composing the query, one can do a union of just those tables you are supposed to get the data from? I hope this is not too awkward to understand.

"Interesting that you are getting into this stuff," Elle said. "I remember I had one of those semi-numinous experiences when I started seeing how they organized related information. Actually, I had the same feeling when I first began to really get into Excel. It was kind of like baby steps to abstraction."

Walker said, "It is interesting how you got a sense of abstraction from database. What was that like? Was it like in math where you have assigned a variable to some concrete phenomenon and then take that image of phenomenon — now just an x, and manipulate the variable in equations of logical operations?

```
|o  o|o  x  |
   |_o_|__o|
```

He hesitated to get Peircean on her but continued: "Or was this "sense of abstraction" more like rising to general-ization from impression, to observed behavior, to something governed by law."

These are some of the questions Walker engaged some of the more friendlier programmers with.

"When you start off to write a program, some code, do you have an overall vision of how the program will be in chunks or parts? How the lines will be laid out in terms of parts of the program? What and where will the function calls be made to have a variable pulled into its flow. I know C++ requires you to declare the variables right at the top, so what kind of thinking goes into the variables and their names and how many."

"Is it something like: I need an iteration here, or I need some logic to check something there.

"Do you ever sketch out a program in a kind of pseudocode? Then start to fill in with real code?"

"It would be interesting to hear how a programmer thinks of a project if you can recall the process, or the moments of invention progress."

Later he said to Elle: "Oh I think I just got it about your reference to feeling a sense of abstraction when you first got into database. It is about being able to browse over data and not always having to go into the detail; moreover the structure of how this material is organized under hierarchical headers allows you to think and manipulate this data in a more symbolic way. You had categories over the specifics."

The Graphical User Interface was a big part of feeling in control over the data, while using something that was attractive to look at.

"When did the term "drill down" come into common usage. I would think it came out of the entity relationship modeling people, because you could click on an entity in the graph and "drill down" to the table and beneath that."

"Oh it comes from the idea of data mining," she said.

This would be before hypertext and the web.

Walker felt like this was important stuff he would like to remember. It was like the zeitgeist of the times.

```
|o  o  o|  |o  o|
|o_o  o|  |_o_|
```

Couples therapy

Walker and Ms. C did start going to therapy to work on their relationship. Or to soften the hurt of making a clean break of it. She had brought so much passion and now was taking it away. He could feel her absenting herself from the lovemaking. He tried to bring her back, teasing her with, "Well you did present yourself, but you weren't into it."

They went to *her* therapist who was also a couples therapist for several sessions. But this was a mistake. Walker soon felt the two women were ganging up on him. Eventually Ms. C made an ultimatum of getting engaged, which he could not ascent to.

It was sad. He was shocked, she was shocked, they all were shocked when he refused in the therapist's office. They broke up then and there. When they got outside, Walker made sure that he and Ms. C walked around the block in Berkeley, before she got into her car to drive. He did care about her, he always had in his way. He was sad to loose her, it is a rare privilege to handle such a hot lover. But no amount of persuasion could return the relationship to its status quo.

For many many years after, his sex fantasies were about getting into all that outrageous sex with her like they used to.

Dream of Blue Pool
Walker had a dream. Here's what he wrote up with interpretation.

> *1:39 AM I am slapped in the face while floating in space by a very attractive woman. I don't know who she is. Then I slap her in the face.*
>
> *8:29 AM A big shame dream. I got caught.*
>
> *In a zombie-like state I went over to a neighbor's house, it was under construction and I had to pee and went into the bathroom. I was pissing through a wall that didn't have sheetrock, just the studs. Into an open shower pan that had been tiled in blue tiles. It turned out a woman was in the room there. The woman was Barbie a beautiful blonde southern California woman from a show about interior design. It was a blue pool; it was square and small. It was uncovered, like it was a small indoor pool. Her husband was somewhere about, but I did not see him. They did have one child somewhere. Then Barbie yelled: "Hey what are you doing?!" I felt such a wave of shame and backed out of the scene. Some other people were in the periphery; seemed like one guy was trying to help me, his name sounded like Laius. I awoke sweating in fearful shame.*

Interpretation

Perhaps it was just the urge to pee in the night trying to wake me up by communicating through the dream. But let us look for symbols and give some impressions.

First impression is how the dream teaches about the feeling of shame by associating an image with that emotion. Public urination, unable to control, untrained child —shame. The dream was showing something about how feelings are associated and encoded with images somehow.

Image + emotion = symbol?

Here's a kind of ideogrammatic sketch; (wish I could draw.)

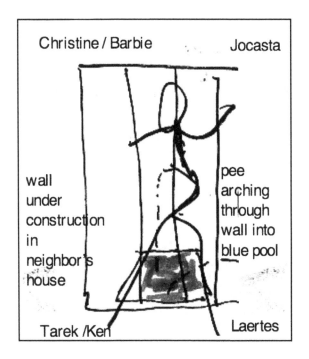

Next impression is the blue square pool. — The square is usually a symbol of the Self, that evolutionary control center encompassing the body and the immune system and the nervous system and the endocrine systems. This system that has been taking care of you. It contains the ego but is not identified with it.

Water in a blue square, — like a fountain at the center of a cathedral also goes with the image of the self; in the center of a house under construction.

A dream about a pool of water — may be referring to the unconscious and/or your emotions; this suggest that you are exploring your unconscious and trying to get to know, understand and appreciate yourself more. Pissing on it might mean marking territory, or it could be the ego pissing on the self, disregarding this quest to come to know the self more. (I note that these are two opposite interpretations.) But this pool was a dry and empty pool.

Urinating is a symbol of sexual desire, and water is a symbol for fertility. Barbie is a mother figure.

If we take the water as a symbol for femininity, my own femininity, this thought causes a strong reaction of great shame. Somehow great shame is associated with this femininity. Is it just the homosexuality taboo?

The mother is the uber-shamer. She is trying to keep the boys becoming men and the girls becoming women.

Laius was the man who married Jocasta — mother of Oedipus. Oedipus is banished from birth family and raised by strangers, and when he is a young man he meets Laius on the road but he does not recognize his father and kills him in a fit of road rage. All this was predicted by the Sphinx and Tireseus who was both a man and a woman.

The most impressive insight I had upon waking from this dream was looking at an emotion as being codified with an image. Also shame as coming from my mother and that there is shame for a man coming to recognize his feminine side.

Focusing on the psychology of emotion/image fusion, I might be avoiding the whole feminine aspect lesson.

SHAME might have these elements in its table: The emotion is like a bulldog or a jellyfish or a swarm of bees near a hive. The Catholics falsely saw Shame as a dragon guarding the treasure — unveiling, getting undressed, the whole Garden of Eden. In a Jungian sense it is a comparison of one's persona with one's hidden self. It is also an affect intended to increase weakness, a warding off. Shame is one of those states that one fears. It is a lack of self-acceptance.

Now Jung said you should start dream interpretation on the Freudian Objective level, that is, according to the relationship between the dreamer and the persons or situations in real life. And then if need be, go to the Subjective interpretation. Dreams reveal symbols which are about the transformation the dreamer is undergoing in his growth toward individuation. I seem to have got right to symbol interpretation, and have not let myself feel the meaning of the dream for dealing with the situations of my life that the dreams are trying to give me insight into.

It is certainly true that after I started keeping a dream diary, there was a big increase in dream production. And after a while I started to learn the symbolic way of dream interpretation. At first this was a pretty spectacular show, and then sometimes profoundly touching insights occurred. I got the feeling of the subconscious or unconscious working below the surface of the ego. It was becoming more and more real. Symbols were everywhere and a shift was underfoot. Studying Jung, I started to have the vocabulary of persona and anima and shadow, also complex and started to be on the lookout for influences from these organizations who were supposedly in service of this Self which was a more pervasive organizational entity that had aspects of the soul, and the psyche intertwined. These were some of the tools of self awareness. With language one becomes like a lepidopterist or botanist of the psyche. The symbolic view liberates one from the literal, and entertains synchronicities as communications from a higher organization principle. You start to Feel more in this world, and Sense and Intuit.

But now I need to work on the Freudian objective level. You

start the association by asking questions. Where in real life did the scene in the dream come from? Where have I encountered these objects before.

I recognized the neighborhood where the house was under construction as my old neighborhood in San Antonio. It was a lot across the back alley and a little up the hill toward where a girl who went to my old grade school lived. She was so cute in her little Catholic school girl pleated uniform. I had a crush on her, even though she was in my younger sister's class. But what has this association to do with the dream? What has it to do with shame at that time of my life which was during the raging onset of puberty. What did I used to do then: I used to run around at night. I wrote this song, it came to me while dwelling in his past there.

> moon shadows are moving across the lawn.
> moon shadows are moving across the lawn.
> it's summertime and
> moon shadows are moving across the lawn.

> I used to slip -- like a shadow -- around my neighborhood
> It was the last preteen summer – in 60s San Antonio.
> the moon was high and it was a hot night,
> and the cicadas were sizzling in
> the background hiss of summer.

> I was out in the dark running around my neighborhood
> I was skulking in the shadows moving across the lawn
> and crickets would be loud,
> and if there was a little breeze
> it was a magical blessing.
> Deep in my preteen soul
> there was a longing so strong
> it was out of control
> it was like my brain is on fire
> I was tumesced with desire for sexual knowledge.
> So I went out and slinked in the shadows
> between the houses and looked at my love's window
> and try to imagine what she looked like naked.

moon shadows are moving across the lawn.
moon shadows are moving across the lawn.
it's summertime and
moon shadows are moving across the lawn.

I was pretty good at finding the meaning of the symbols, it
became something on an intellectual exercise, for me, albeit
one that helped me feel more a part of something much larger
than my little place in life. But one really does have to bring
it back from the subjective to the objective to get the full
meaning for you personally.

A mythological record is not an attribute of a dream, it is a
snapshot of a past or present relationship in your life. The only
things you should find in an entity are fields that pertain to the
entity itself.

I wonder if all of these interpretations could be true at
once. I was beginning to think they might be. There is a
certain crowding of the primordial with the civilized. They
cram together like boson angels dancing on the head of a
pin, infinitely compactible into the field without fermion
exclusion rules to keep them apart. Dreams are both temporal
and infinite. The dream opens the gate to the world of EIHAO
Everything Is Happening At Once. At night in dreams as
in day, we go to the edge holding us back. We can let the
functions and the archetypes in the perennial philosophy
take us from the Newtonian Freudian Euclidean world of
the objective — and we must take that with us — through
the interpretations like trees in a jungle of symbols — to
the Bohm Jungian Mandelbrot subjective. In the land of
Schrödinger, the cat is both alive and dead at once.
  The language spoken here is Image + emotion = symbol.
  Pissing and marking territory and insemination in the Blue
Square. In that movie 2001: A Space Odyssey we saw in the
portal to the sky and the ground, space within space, space
as paradox – both something and nothing, the dream pool of
the self. There was the neighbor's house under construction.

The neighbor as the shadow but the shadow not as something negative but as in other: m'other, br'other, the Other you have to befriend.

And I think of people who change as they get old, or reveal some latent behavioral change or discovery about a person. And, of course, the process of integrating the self, the thrill and terror of it. Marking with urine in the alchemy of it, the integration of that which is outside of me, of turning it into life, of the subsequent cycle and of that savor to me returned to the outside some of me and it.

The husband, Ken and Laius, Jocasta and Oedipus. Powerful haunting, the very nuts of the earth. The very balls of the psyche of the earth.

The spirit is peeping through the personality. If you can open the blinds you see a window to the world in the house of the psyche. I go out the window at night to walk the neighborhood of dreams like a spirit eye, the spirit is beaming moonly, projecting the scene.

Shadow and spirit and soul and self: we are in this psyche together a stranger in a strange land — you can feel the immigrant in you as you go across and become the fuel of perception — and you can feel its radiation as you become the window and the light. You become both cats, the live one and the other one. Zombies and ghosts. But on the face of it, sacred Barbie and Ken. Powerful and nuts! So American!

It would make a neat dynamics diagram with colored arrows pointing to the different names. It would probably spur on more dreams. Is this the way one paddles one's canoe — an oneironaut in the rivers of dreamland — where existence itself changes. I think that is the way I am moving with this dream diary analysis. It is a world with its own laws but they are real and affect you as any other world but it has a different grammar. It feels like I have bugged the headquarters country club of the archetypes.

Dream Dramaturge

Walker wanted to use the Entity Relationship Modeling formalism on dreams to see if it would give some insight into the database of the mind from which the dreams were composed, as though perhaps in answer to some query.

He began trying to adapt the elegant convention of Entity Relationship Diagram modeling to the challenge of diagramming the dream. ERD is used for database design. The business entities are Products, Sales, Customers, or Students, Classes, Books etc. about which you want to keep data. The psychological entities are Anima, Persona, Ego, Shadow, Hero, Game, Complex etc. A relational database constructs queries into these tables (the entities) stored in memory, and retrieves and concatenates bits of memory into the information being sought. To query the entity. This sounded to Walker like the inner Dream Dramaturge of the psyche constructing its art was like a Database Admin.

Wonderland

The next night Walker had a dream that was also set around those pre-teenage times. This is what he wrote:

> *I'm at the intersection of Fredricksburg Rd. and Hillcrest at that light at the entrance of Wonderland mall. A mall that used to be the last stop on my bus ride home from Central Catholic High School for Boys in downtown San Antonio. It is a military school. I'd be in a khaki army uniform. I'd walk about a mile home in the Texas heat with a chubby from the chafing. It would go on and on. I don't recall the fantasy although I wouldn't be surprised if Candi Ramirez was involved. I used to worry that people in cars passing by would see the tent proceeding. But anyway that's not part of the dream. In the dream I am in a car, behind a guy on a motorcycle, I can just*

barely see the crown of his head. I am on the downside of a
steep hill and can't really see beyond the dashboard, and it is
very foggy. I sense the light change and I blindly plow into the
intersection not seeing anything. And in a burst of diffuse fogy
wet light, I change sex! On the other side into Wonderland, I
am female. And then I am surrounded by all these men looking
at me.

Here's a kind of ideogrammatic sketch; (wish I could draw.)

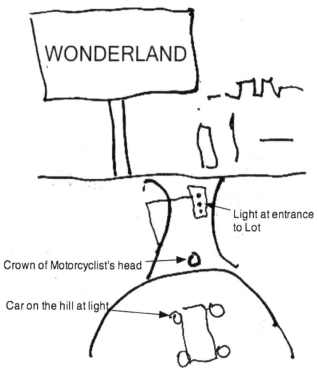

There is a magic burst of energy as I plow through the
intersection, enough to create the transformation from male
to female like a magic act! The amplification about having a
chubby is part of it. There is all that kaboom- energy and it
explodes to swap sex? The first thing one thinks about is that
the dreamer is integrating the anima!

The dream is suggesting the dreamer ask himself about how

he feels about the opposite sex. Being married is a constant struggle with accommodation and going your own way. Trying not to be a bully nor isolated. The dream is simulating what it feels like to be a woman, undergoing the lustful domineering desires of men. As if the dream were saying: "See, how does that feel to be the object of desire." Not something you can pick up in books or in conversations with your wife or sister, really.

I do note the dialectic of opposites in this dream. Male / female; down / up.

What are some symbols?

crown of head — the 7th chakra relating to connection with the divine.

WONDERLAND — a Buddha land, the numinous, the place where opposites are reconciled

foggy diffuse light — a kind of blindness going through a transition, the fog of oblivion of not seeing, not knowing.

I notice from looking at the sketch, it seems to be like a bridge between two worlds. The two worlds meet at the transition, the stop light. The world one is coming FROM is going up a steep climb; the world one is going TO is a level field of more knowing.

What is the man on the motorcycle? Perhaps a kind of Hermes figure, a psychopomp or messenger who can easily lead the way between the world of the gods above and of men below?

This is a kind of transit by reverberation like being in a kind of musical instrument, or wave guide or hologram. This is more than metaphor. It is a peak at the hologram wave guide along whose fault lines are conducted a propagating mind quake.

(The metaphor here is the brain's neural net as hologram.)

Move to Silicon Valley

Walker got tired of the long daily commute to the job in Los Altos and decided to move down there. He looked at the *Town Crier* their small weekly newspaper for an apartment and found one. It was the pool house of an estate. The estate owner had moved a bed into the pool house to turn it into a rental. Of course, it didn't come with pool use as the owner couple was quick to explain. Walker alienated the husband by having to get this huge bamboo tiki bar moved out of the space so he could get a desk in there.

He sold his old VW van to some young girl in Berkeley who wanted it for camping. He bought a Volvo under the recommendation of a fellow contractor. When he got the Volvo home to Las Altos it leaked a whole tank of gas onto the newly poured asphalt driveway — dissolving it. That did not endear him to the landlord and he had to pay to have the driveway re-paved.

Walker's main respite outside work in those days was going up to the storytelling class in Marin, where he would take long walks in the woods.

It wasn't long before Walker would come to see that "Lost Altos" was basically a town organized around serving the needs and wants of these handsome nordic white people with great tans who had a lot of money. He walked to work along semi-rural roads past some amazingly big mansions. The urban sophisticates of Los Altos — (he didn't know whether the name meant "the Stops" or "the Heights" but he was coming to know that in the Heights all time is stopped) — are educated and wealthy. They are executives and professionals, who read mostly technical books or financial reports; a lot of them are programmers and professors. They like to go out to eat and they travel. Some perhaps had lived in a big city; but now they choose to reside in a small town. In the city, urban sophisticates might go to art institutions and museums and occasionally the opera, symphony, ballet, live theatre; but in Los Altos they mostly went down town to get their hair done or take the dog for a walk in their shorts.

There are no sidewalks and the people like it like that.

He stayed there over a year and went from working on the computer job at MetaCASE all day to going home where he spent his off hours working on the computer to write magazine articles about interface design. There wasn't much to do in Los Altos. He had become an ERD nerd. Writing articles for the BMUG newsletter.

But there was no one to meet and hang out with. He never got into any local groups. Perhaps he started projecting his depression onto the hoi paloi of Los Altos who like most small towns in California aspired to be like Carmel. But it was more like an upscale Palo Alto. They seem to have lots of cash but were conservative and conformist perhaps even more than Menlo Park; they seemed to have no soul but were just automatons. After a while they began to seem like rich zombies of the mountain sunset.

Los Altos was a glorious haven for upper-middle class citizens who wonder around the town being douches and that's just the young people. Their parents seem completely oblivious to what goes around them. Life was an endless pursuit of retiree-with-money pleasures. They decided a movie theatre would bring too many rowdy youth to disturb the peace with their loud, out-of-tune, guitar playing and urinating in public. There was one hotel. At night there were only a couple of bars one at either end of town. Not that he would go into one. Not much happens in this town, and he began to find it boring. *The Sluts Guide* gave the whole area of Silicon Valley low marks for excessive nerdiness and complained that a girl couldn't get laid. Walker had a few girlfriends during his many years relationship with Ms. C. Always during an off period. One was even among the story telling community; that had been a mistake. It went down in flames, leaving him feeling awkward at class events.

Walker was living in Los Altos during the great Loma Prieta earthquake of 1989. In fact he had been up in Marin at a storytelling class, and had had to crash on the couch of a programmer friend from BMUG, because the bridges were closed. Indeed part of the span of the Bay Bridge had given way and fallen on the deck below taking life. In Oakland the upper deck of a long stretch of freeway had pancaked down on itself crushing cars and the people inside onto the roadbed. The people from Oakland came out and put ladders up to the overhead freeway and then crawled in among the crushed cars, still running spewing exhaust, into the dark fearful hell of relentless car alarms going of and fuel spillage and skewed headlights glowing and the screams of the trapped to try and free the snared survivors. These brave citizens were a big help to early responders who came with jaws of life. It was a terrible disaster. The young men of Oakland showed heedless courage.

Walker stayed at MetaCASE for over a year, but a down turn in business forced his lay off. The office was sad to see him go. But the company had a surfeit of documentation now and couldn't afford him. The chief technology officer gave him a complete suite of company CASE tools and said that he should be able to hire him back as a contractor soon. But that didn't happen.

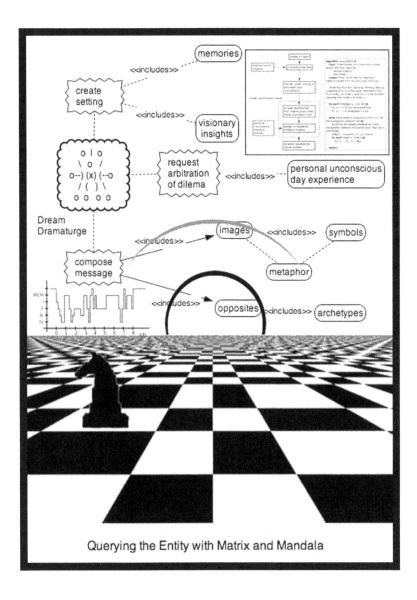

Querying the Entity with Matrix and Mandala

Mandala — Matrix

In the spirit of Levi-Strauss's matrix and structuralism, Walker was moving toward trying to interpose a kind of grid on the dream. He was coming more and more to realize the natural mind of the neural net seen in the dream world. One might say that when a land mammal closes his eyes and settles into a containing nest or burrow, the psyche is released from having to coordinate peripheral processing of sense input and is liberated to free run over recent queries. He preferred the word psyche rather than unconscious, following Jung. It seemed obvious that any recent queries by the land mammal would involve predator / prey scenarios. The mammal has to have a good map of his territory. When it darts out of the sanctuary to get some food, the mouse has to be right every time about where the hawk is. No doubt close calls and risky behaviors are recalled and gone over in memory and dreams so as to simulate the best ways. The best algorithm for doing. The squirrel builds a trapdoor in his tree house of twigs and leaves. And has practiced the run along branches where the hawk can't fly to the safe knothole hide-away in the tree where the hawk can't invade. The hippocampus rides through the EIHAO field along the time-like dimension of the light cone which is the boundary of the possible and the probable and the real.

To simulate is to try out without having to undergo the consequences of the real. It is very important to update the map. And learn. Of course the human world is much more advanced, being they are predators who hunt in packs and the neural net simulations of our dreams are peopled with considerations of threats and rewards from family and other hierarchical social structures.

The sketch of the dream was helpful; it was a collection of images or symbols that are sequenced in the dream. Presumably they converge on some message being conveyed by the dream to the dreamer. It is a language: subject verb object. Dreamer dreams dream. Mythology comes from writers capturing scenes seen in dreams.

Abstractly one could think of the dream as a space of symbols. For example in the ideogrammatic sketch of the Wonderland dream, I had these symbolic objects and events: { helmet over crown of head, stop light, POV from too small to see over the dashboard, Wonderland sign, explosive fog of light, Hermes figure on the motorcycle, energetic transgender observer shift }.

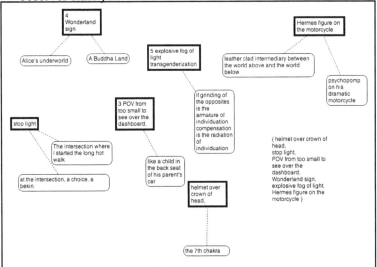

To arrange these objects on a grid of categories would give the dimensions of the dream space as an abstract space. The Entities are the objects. And with their relationships, and their attributes they form a kind of matrix. This is the table, the database, the array, the matrix.

The study of mythology was central to both Jung and Levi-Strauss and to create the isomorphism between their two views, of the mandala and the matrix, is like the cross fertalization of the two views of quantum mechanics. First was the wave description of quantum mechanics invented by de Broglie and Schrödinger and then the other view was the operator matrix representation of QM of Heizenberg and von Neuman. They could verify what was discovered by transposing and checking it in the other formalism. Wave and matrix. Similarly Walker wanted to be able to go from the Mandala (or circled square) of Jung to the Matrix of Levi-Strauss, applied to myth and kinship.

He wanted to know if the dream was really a kind of abstract space where two opposite concerns are brought into confrontation so that they may be transcended by learning? There really was a mare, a kind of mythological horse, the hippocampus, the field-horse responsible for dreams. Was the learning in dreams related to the learning curve, which is a smooth hill up and down, ∩ of learning performance vs. arousal of interest. In this graph of performance vs. excitement we see how the material is or is not stirring up and engaging the feeling part of the brain which is the hippocampus. The ∩ is like the bell shaped curve. On the far end you have too much arousal of interest and the learning shuts down. On the close end you don't have enough arousal of interest to stimulate learning. Here you are inactive, laid back, underachieving slacker. Then you rise up the curve of arousal and interest, up to your best performance, then as the curve comes down you go far out and then in the high overload of arousal get into the stress zone of anxious and beyond that into overloaded arousal of panic, anger, violence. Yes.

This learning curve is the idea of the work whale whose graph is a sharp incline up the front for the beginner — a seeming impossible climb untill you reach the top — then there is a long flat time of productivity that slowly tails off.

Dreams after the Death of a Relative

Around that time Walker got the news that his old auntie, 91 had died. She was his father's sister and the last of the old family of origin. He felt the loss not only of this good stalwart soul but also the tenuous connection to the old world becoming more tenuous. He was an immigrant casting about in a strange land. Walker had a dream. Here's what he wrote up with interpretation.

Dreams after the death of a relative
I got the news yesterday by email that my old auntie Kay in New Brunswick died. She was 91. I was moping around somber all day feeling sad. She was my deceased father's sister and the last of that generation and I was feeling the loss not only of the person but also for the end of childhood in the sense that it was an end of the family place in far away Canada. I had a rough night with many dreams that night. I think the psyche was doing a wonderful presentation of problems and solutions. Here is a series of 6 of the dreams.

First Scene 1:35AM
In the dream I am walking with grandpa or drifting freely around the small town of St. Stephen, New Brunswick. In grandpa's house I am as a small child running up and down the steep stairs to the big dorm room of what had been Kay and the girls' room when they and my father grew up there.

Second Scene 5:45AM
I am walking around in St. Stephen, somebody's walking past me. Straight over to the Church. (I was replaying this memory: When I was 11 my old grandfather and I were walking in the winter and he said, "Lets duck in here a minute." We stamped our feet to knock off the snow and entered through the vestibule into the dark cavernous night church. And up on the alter behind the rail there was an old lady laid out in an open coffin on the bier. There were big red

*votive candles on the 4 corners around her. I was shocked,
I had never seen a dead person before. My grandfather did
not so much as bat an eye-lash at my shock. But had me go
with him and kneel at the communion rail up close.) Now in
my dream I see a hand of the corpse has some terrible black
growth on it.*

Third Scene 6:21AM

*I am looking at a memorial wall in a great big park in
Canada. I am there with Kay's daughter Sue and her husband.
There is a close-up of us just looking down at the ground, an
awkward being in each other's presence, not having a lot to
say. Someone said "They were great stone masons." Another
voice in the dream was heard to say, "You really knew who
you walked with."*

Forth Scene 7:09AM

*I am down in the hold of a huge car-ferry ship and I am
looking at all these names written in white chalk between the
white lines laid out to make a grid on a great vast blackboard.
Someone is erasing some of the names.*

Fifth Scene 8:21AM

*I was part of some program at Parks and Recreations that
was supposed to get people in touch with their feelings — to
get in touch with their true self and their thoughts.*

Sixth Scene 9:14AM

*Many of the dreams the whole night were about construction
work being done on my house. It was a hideous job. The crew
of workmen were terribly incompetent. The workers were
doing things like putting up shingles inside the house, and I
am trying to relate to them and it was just getting worse and
worse. I was trying to get them to put up some nice cabinets
in the kitchen and I had these sloped shingles to contend with.
One of them put a rod and curtain over the shingled wall
like it was a window. I was trying to put up a large fabric
with the image of a tree like a stained glass church window. I
was trying to impress them with my Spanish. It was so awful.*

There was this horrendous plumbing going on outside, the grass-covered ground keeps caving in and bubbling up from down below. Small diameter trees and large tree limbs are being pushed up through holes in the ground and there is light coming up around the base of these trees from down below underground.

Some Notes

I think the series of dreams follows at least two time lines. These are associated around the concept of House. House (1) — Family and House (2) — unconscious. In the sense of House as a symbol for Family we are in the realm of childhood memories and teachings of the ancestors. In the sense of House as a symbol of the unconscious the shock of the death image is asking the dreamer to shift from my dominant way of knowing — Thinking — and to get in touch with my inferior functions, Feeling and Intuition. This latter is a specifically Jungian interpretation which expands on the importance of dream as compensation, not just the wish fulfillment and denial of negative events but compensation in balancing dominant and inferior mental functions.

In the First Scene — memories of the house where Kay lived as a child and walking through the town with grandpa. The ancestors.

In the Second Scene — the coffin dream — my ancestor is trying to help me with the nature of death. The cavernous night church is the unconscious. The grandfather does not hide death from the child, is introducing the nature of death to me because he allows me to be shocked and does not comfort me.

In a House (2) interpretation a Jungian would suggest that shock and nightmare are an effort of the psyche to stimulate my Feeling function.

The awkwardness in the Third Scene — memorial wall well made — suggests some possible alienation between me and my family and yet I am together at a psychic funeral with them in my dreams. Are you in or out of this family.

I don't yet know what is the import of the voice saying, "You really knew who you walked with." But I am starting to get intimations that the death of the last of that generation is a kind of end of childhood. The one you walked with in this sequence is the grandfather. I get an image of a child holding hands of an elder, and somehow knowing they are there for you, though you don't know who they really are.

Those childhood memories are attached to place and the people who walked with us there. During the day I had a cry thinking about tromping in the woods or going fishing, the land so sweet, especially in spring when the thaw is flowing or in autumn when the leaves are falling and piled up in drifts. In some cultures dreams are seen as gifts or messages from the ancestors – who may impart healing guidance or knowledge to their descendents.

In the Fourth Scene — being in the belly of a huge car ferryboat — the suggestion is an encounter with the mythical Charon, the ferryman who carries souls of the newly deceased across the river Styx to the underworld. The image of a list of names on the blackboard, the erasing from life the names of family. In spite of the possible alienation my psyche is getting me in touch with them.

Since the ferryman is a psychopomp, one who conducts souls to the unconscious it may also be an invigoration of libido to counterbalance my dominant thinking/sensation functions.

In the Fifth Scene —The Parks and Recreations class to get people in touch with their feelings — we find a deceptively obvious manifest image and most clear message for what this sequence of dreams is admonishing the dreamer to do: to not be so afraid, however difficult it might be, and to develop your feeling function. Also the wildness of Parks and Recs suggests being in Canada. My identity is wrapped up in the sense of that place. And it is slipping away.

In the Sixth Scene The absurd image of the shingles on the inside of the house suggest this dream is aware of a dilemma about being < in || out > of the family. This dream suggest the

House(2) interpretation of the House as Unconscious. The dreams are talking about accessing my feelings about my past and the house, which seems to be a symbol of my ego, or what ever that is between the persona and the Self is being expressed through the incompetence, it is a way of telling me that I am having difficulty trying to rehab my House, that is to rebuild my facility with my inferior functions, Feeling and Intuition. This Jungian interpretation is further suggested by the pushing up of tree limbs from under the earth suggests chthonic spirits at work. The plumber . . . So there is a spiritual dimension — the Church. The stained glass window image of a tree. The light around the tree limbs.

Going back to the Third Scene — A memorial wall well made – it is like standing outside the wall of citadel: the Self and this whole sequence of dreams is coming to my aid. The death of my aunt has awakened my ancient tribe.

The two message streams are about alienation from one's family in a psychic funeral with them in your dreams and exploration of the cause of this alienation: relying too much on Thinking and not enough on Feeling which is something I am working on.

It is hopeful to think the Self is admonishing me: Perhaps families have to get together to renew their personalities as well as their genes.

Objective and Subjective

It is becoming for the student of dreams to be equally aware of both the Objective (Freudian) interpretation of dreams and the Subjective (Jungian) way. On the objective level one thinks about relationships between the dreamer and the persons or situations in his real life. One asks where the objects came from, how this is an unfolding story, what might happen next. On the subjective level one asks what associations do the objects trigger in a symbolic or mythological communication with respect to what is going on personally in his life.

I used the term House to suggest the two sides of this coin. In a House (1) interpretation which we call the Objective interpretation it is about the relationship with the real people, my Family. Relatives. Ancestors. In a House(2) interpretation which we call Subjective we see the house as a symbol for the whole psychic construct one presents to the world. The personality. This involves using compensation to explore the other lesser used of the psychic functions {Feeling, Thinking, Sensing, Intuiting}.

Scene 1 family relationships, early time of childhood

Scene 2 Grandfather, but also a body, and a shock. Suggests more of a House (2) or Jungian Subjective interpretation. In that sense the shock of a nightmare is being used like some wrathful deity to get you to change the priorities which you assign to your Function.

— — — — — — — — — — — — — — — —

A side note: Toward a vector space theory of psyche

I also wanted to sketch out a kind of quantum mechanical vector space theory of the psyche. It has operators A, P, E, S, . . . (archetypes) and basis vectors T, F, S, I (functions).

I thought of a statement in this space as being a multiordinal, that is a noun with indices as in the non-aristotelian logic of Korzybski. And the operator as a terminate and state resident background operator like the cron job in unix. This fascinating weaving together of many of the most interesting theories of our time will all be made clear in good time.

A P E S | T F S I > This is based on the Dirac notation of vector space. The archetype {Anima, Persona, Ego Shadow …} is the operator and it gets to use the functions {Thinking, Feeling, Sensing, Intuiting} when it is in ascendancy. E | T > is the ego thinking. A | T > is thinking with the anima.

Perhaps we should say that A P E S is an operator, or rather this means that personality is one of these multi-ordinal words. Which operator has come to the fore.

You can sometimes feel yourself shift in

A P E S | personality >

1, 0, 0, 0 | personality > means that they are in a state of mostly Anima coming to the fore. 0, 0, 0, 1 | personality > = Shadow.

Individuation is hard. And the work is slow. You have to be open to creation, try to get your life more in synch with it. Amplification through creation. Also you have to confront your own damn self all the time. You find yourself seduced by a strong Anima. Or other complex.

— — — — — — — — — — — — — — — —

The Sixth Dream suggest a House(2) (Subjective) interpretation. The House under rehabilitation is the Unconscious. One is trying to integrate it.

One way to look at this is to feel yourself using the inferior functions more, in my case Feeling and Intuition.

The light coming up from around the trees is the unconscious or psyche fanning out. Or even a representation of chthonic or archetypal origins. This is a subjective interpretation. It does not suggest much in the objective interpretation. The more absurd the symbolic, the less objective.

To continue with some of the differences between the Freudian and Jungian interpretation of dreams, we can look at their position vis a viz time. Freud is retrospective and Jung is prospective.

The dream series seems to be about time past. A retrospective suggests a good childhood. None of that early Freudian psychological trauma, sexual fixation and desires. Just an image of riding a slender green tricycle over the crushed gravel path. Or playing in the summerhouse (folly). Or my grandfather's roses. < time before — ‖ — time after>

What is the prospective message coming from the unconscious? The theme? It is that even though I didn't attend the funeral I am having a kind of psychic funeral. And there is hope that it is possible to renew our personality for each other.

What are you going to do with your complex about being distant from the family? It is a kind of defense mechanism. You put this boundary around yourself to protect your inner creative person.

Perhaps I appear bitchy to them (I am not unaware of this defensive protecting side of my muse, my anima that can get negative from perseived abuse.) This sensitivity is always in the fore when I try to communicate with family.

The dreams are often about the complexes.

So can you actually see yourself not so much in the Freudian compensation of wish fulfillment, but the Jungian compensation of balance? What is your psyche or unconscious trying to communicate to you about this hypertrophied work ethic and mad creative obsession —mostly based in thinking — that you call writing. These are usually inflations. The dream is sending the Jungian a message from the unconscious about what you have to do to integrate a complex or de-inflate a complex.

I am doing the dream interpretations in two phases: the first order Freudian approximation, or beginning of a convergence by using free association. An then the Jungian interpretation which starts with these associations and the objective meaning in your life but then gets augmented in parallel with reading the symbols of transformation and doing amplification through artistic and spiritual contemplation to reify the symbolic meaning. I believe this is what I am doing in this writing. So we look for elements of the dream that are not just from personal association; these elements are the symbols. We know the associations are right by doing a kind of oscillation or shimmer association, that is to quickly juxtapose and compare field and ground to see if something resonates. The feeling/thought is kind of musical that way.

The amplification takes the form of tracing past representa-tions and emanations of these symbols in art and religion, in alchemy and folklore. And in creative science. And music.

The analyst receives the objective and subjective stream to suggest clues as to how to proceed. The dream is telling you what you need to do to become whole. How to get across the gap of unknowing? You have to make a transcendental leap — that is a kind of inductive heuristic construction that one hopes will turn out to be true.

The table and the list
The two opposite concerns working in these dreams were In and/or Out of the family. Where two opposite concerns are brought into confrontation it is so that they may be transcended by learning. It is like the dual operator of bra-ket QM.

< in | out > ... < space | dual space >

The basis of narrative is the list, or the table. Levi-Strauss, influenced by mathematicians, started using the matrix or the table as a graphic method of comparing and analyzing concepts under considerations by the savage mind in the way it used myth. The table or matrix has as its most fundamental element the list: it is one or more vertical lists or horizontal rows. Thus the list is the fundamental structure of creating narrative. Though early man was more concerned with the utility of lists, recipes, procedures, and formulas, the tropes of figurative language, metaphor, metonymy, synecdoche which occur naturally in the symbology of dreams are comparisons and cross-sortings of entities (ontological schema) in lists. The notation <a | b > (dot product) for the intersection of row and colum in a matrix in general is a comparison or a projection of one element of a list onto another. Freud in *The Interpretation of Dreams* points out that metonymy and synecdoche are equivalent to condensation and displacement. And that irony implies contradiction. Irony (from denial the most primitive defense mechanism) becomes the source of the other figures.

The poem with its metaphors is most like a dream.

out beyond the surface
out beyond the surface of the dream
we come to new shores of advanced magicality
beyond our expectations.
I am undergoing a trance migration
an invocation of the neural net
to go between the reaching grasp
and the accumulated set.
The spirit is peeping through the personality
if you can open the blinds
you see a window to the world
in the house of the psyche:
I am undergoing a trance migration
at night we go to the edge holding us back.
You have to come to know your shadow side,
it is part of letting your spirit take you across the border.
You take your shadow, it has to come too.

Shadow and spirit and soul and self:
we are in this psyche together
a stranger in a strange land
you can feel the immigrant in you
as you go across the brain blood brane
and become the fuel of perception —
and you can feel the radiation at the core
as you become the window and the light.
In the light cone the series of dates
furnishes an autonomous system reference.
It operates by means of a rectangular matrix

```
|ooo|o o||o o|o o|
|ooo|o_o||o_o|_o_|___
            |o o|o   |
            |_o_|__o|
```

where each line represents epoques of time
called hourly, daily, annual, secular, millennial
for the purpose of schematization
and which together make up a continuous time.
Each columns is a bundle of significant relations;
each row a sequence in the myth

To use ERD on a matrix of 6 dreams

An Entity Relationship Diagram is a type of flowchart that illustrates how "entities" such as people, objects or concepts relate to each other within a system.

Who are the people in this dream that you want to apply the Levi-Strauss matrix to? { grandpa, Kay, Kay's daughter Sue, her husband Ed, the deceased, } other peripheral entities {Kay's sisters Eleanor and Pat, their brother John my father, the boy who lived across the way, his big smiling dog, my sisters when we rode on the tricycles innocent in the small town }

If the information you want to include doesn't fit into these categories, than it is probably not an entity but a property of an entity, an attribute.

I was on trying to see the human "metastructure" behind the workings of the human mind. These metastructures were the Mandala as Jung taught it and the Matrix as Levi-Strauss taught it.

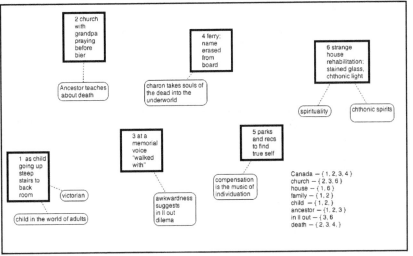

In the structuralist sense it helps to think of the matrix as a chessboard: it is the structure that gives movement to the pieces. Levi-Strauss used music as well as the chessboard as analogy underlying structure for myth. He also developed electrical analogies, to the armature of an electric motor which housed the action of generating energy by the switching of opposite poles. Jung used this polar opposite aspects of the archetype analogy too. Levi-Strauss also uses a thermodynamic analogy about the "hot engine" and the "cool engine". The hot engine, like the motor uses up its supply of fuel; the cool engine, like nature, recycles. Levi-Strauss influenced Marshall McLuhan, hot and cool media.

The Mandala, is a form of the union of opposites, a representation of the original wholeness that we seek on the path of individuation. One step on this path is coming to know the symbols. We start to do this in the interpretation of dreams. Just as the matrix is a form of the union of opposites or the dialectical energetic of opposites, used to show how myth considers and transcends the dilema of opposites, so also is the mandala a representation of opposites across realms.

Besides looking at the mandala as having sections like

a pie, it can have annular rings like the fields of an electric motor armature, or the orbital motions of the planets held in gravitation field, or the orbitals in the atom held in strong and weak interaction. Then the structure is not so much about the union of opposites as the orbits.

Symbols are the signposts on the path of individuation as are the totems in the exchange of the clans. The totem animal like the raven or the crow or the bear represent survival strategies which are imparted to the one who sees them.

It is important to find the opposites interacting in a dream. As Levi-Strauss shows in his studies of mythology, all narrative is driven by the conflict of opposites. In movies it is <hero ‖ villain>; <strength ‖weakness>; <good ‖ evil>; <human ‖ alien>; <right ‖ wrong>;   <sanity ‖ insanity>; <youth ‖ age>; <honest ‖ deceitful>; <the light ‖ the dark>.

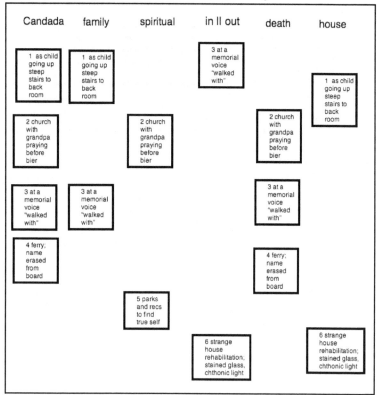

Structuralism coming from linguistics notes that we understand the meaning of a word from understanding its opposite. In the dream too opposites are the driving engine. They speak to the dilemmas perplexing the dreamer and point to a way out of a trap that the dreamer might not see with just the focused ego. Dreams might help us examine more closely what we have accepted about some entity (people, things, events, and locations.)

If we use the Levi-Strauss technique of putting the opposites in adjacent columns and place similar events in the rows of the same column this creates a theme in each column and each item in that column is a manifestation of that particular theme in the series of dreams. This suggests the structure of the dream sequences.

Is there order in how the themes enter the dreams? It is like how the phonemes enter words. There is a deep structure, a transformational grammar. And as we see in poetry and indigenous language there is also a mimologic analogy by way of the sound frequency to the energetics in the phenomena of which the word speaks.

To return to vector space theory of psyche I want to give an idea of how I came to adapt some of the tools of Quantum Mechanics to be used in psychology: The concept of the matrix gets shifted into database and this gets shifted into a theory of dreams, where the row and column of a myth matrix are seen to be conjoining and disjoining in an array that is isomorphic to activity in the neural net as neuromatrix.

The Levi-Strauss myth matrix takes us back to the source of story, which is also the source of myth: this is the dream. We are all the hero of our own story, of our myth, and we can look into our dreams to give us the structure of how these narratives are composed.

We will be developing analogies and isomorphisms among the Levi-Strauss matrix formalism of myth and the Heizenberg -Bohr matrix formalism of QM and the Entity Relationship Modeling formalism of structured query language for database administration and the neural net as hologram model of brain / mind. Don't wig! This is a novel and as such will be a pleasant trip into sacred knowledge with all the necessary pre-requisites made available. All this in order to understand and diagram the idiomatic language of dreams.

The dream dramaturge is a database admin.

The dream dramaturge is constantly developing dream theatre stages in rooms into which the dreamer usually visits only once, though sometimes repeatedly. The dreamer makes an unconscious reservation requesting various amenities which the dream dramaturge provides. So I came up with this entity relationship diagram indicating some of the entities and relationships based on the recent sequence of dreams following the death of my beloved auntie.

The dream dramaturge is a database admin.

Calling up associations from memory and concatenating them with feelings old and new.

The dream designer is a great composer. It has access to all your personal experience as well as the processes of myth and archetypes and dreams. How can we really know that about ourselves? What's more share them with another.

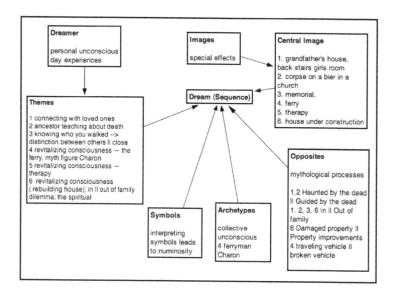

Using some observations about the Themes, Images and the use of Opposites to get across dilemmas as these were used by Levi-Strauss matrix theory derived from linguistics to analyze myth, their tables are seen in the above diagram.

Now we will use a kind of pseudocode to imagine composing some queries into these tables and conjoining the results in a dream. Where there is the negative side of the opposite we will think of this as disjoining or as in QM projecting into its dual space.

Querying the Entity with Matrix and Mandala

From out of our quantum mechanical and molecular past, a life force has been developing for millions of years. Now all space on the planet is a space of niches teaming with beings channeling the life force.

The world is a round mandala which is equivalent to a square matrix in which forces are handled to make us undergo transitions. All space is filled with energy, and this energy is absorbed and given off in natural code. In this perspective all things are information.

From out of the body of the psyche, archetypes are personified instincts for order and exploration. They are the forces in the guise of characters that we can recognize in our dreams. Our dreams communicate to us in a language of images, and they can be abstracted into ideograms. These show us directions and pathways in space that we need to take. They are a map of the territory in which our conscious ego navigates. Though it does not have the whole map.

In addition to time we can explore the dream in successive space dimensions.

Like in space the first archetype the dimension in the dream are three. In one dimension it is flatland. It is the basic mouse trying to go out of its hole to get some food but trying to ascertain where the hawk is. The psych gives you information in dreams about problems and things you are trying to negotiate to survive. It helps you plan strategy by giving you the opportunity to simulate a virtual unfolding so you can experience beforehand what might happen.

In a one dimensional "space" the dilemma is a zero sum game: what you gain has to come out of the loss of another. It is like the time series of successive frames of how predator and prey, (or missile and jet target) can converge on each other or not.

The predator and prey, moving, calculating, adjusting, to intersect or avoid each other gets absorbed into muscle reflexes as an algorithm (method for solving a problem). It gets written into the neuromatrix of the brain. Just as the forces of wind and space get used to shape the wing of the hawk or the little prehensile feet of the prey so too the forces of the chase get hard wired into the brain by evolution. The great isomorphism is fractals of nature < — > to fractals in the brain. Instincts are such problem-solving reactions.

lo ol
lo ol

In two dimensions of the dream you are of the terrain of a flat give and take. You can see that there is a bifurcation point from which you can retreat or choose. The chaos dynamics in not deterministic but does orbit or oscillate around choices, attractors. The Fractal Attractor of chaos theory is equivalent to the Archetype of Jung's systemic psychology. (Archetype is the personified or image-ized instinct.)

lo olo ol
lo_ol_o_l___
    lo olo l
    l_o_l__ol

In three dimensions you are able to hoover above and see the pathway beneath in two dimensions. That is, you see the dreams address things about yourself that you are trying to find out about. They converge on a point in the flatland and you can see this while hovering above in the 3rd dimension.

Like myths dreams are about exchanges of energies.

Though consciously dreams seem to be nonsensical aggregations, unconsciously they converge. Jung says it is not nonsensical but that it reads out (like the hippocampus reads out) as a set of opportunities and dangers. It is like meaning is accumulating like water flowing into collection points, attractor basins. De Bono had books about this. This is like the accumulation of referents into sign. And it occurs to me this is like the hierarchy of becoming a sign in semiotics. And signs becoming signs in more abstract focus.

Metapsychology and Multiordinal time.

Metapsychologies including theories of self, to paraphrase Levi-Strauss, are machines for the suppressing of time. Multiordinality to paraphrase Korzybski, is a way to bring time into logic and transcend the aristotelean logic of fixed classes by making them time dependent. The dream activity of compensation is a cron job run at night when the body is released from peripheral processing. The hippocampus contains the twin functionalities of will attached to emotion and memory attached to will for the autonomic nervous system. It makes sense and monitors change. And these activities are two sides of the same reality. In dreams we see the autonomic nervous system (or the dream dramaturge if we want to think of it on a symbolic level) going over the algorithms of both seeking rewards and avoiding injury: the lines of sight for both my captivity and deliverance in a single image. It is feedforward and feedback. In the neuromatrix of the neural net. Going through pathways of attraction and avoidance represented in chaos as attractors. The information is dimensional and probably holonomic. Here is some pseudocode of the dream dramaturge.

This emblematic collage is of the Dream Dramaturge as Database Admin making calls along a neural net to compose the scenes and objects of the dream. The Entity Relationship Modeling and pseudocode of the "Jung-Bohm" algorithm suggests the holonomic brain as a more material version of Jung's pleromaic universe as a kind of affect of the fractal neural net. Also the implicate order of the Bohmian EIHAO enfolded in the universe and symbolized by the hologram. Traversing a 4D lattice of the fractal net along an edge of a Function.

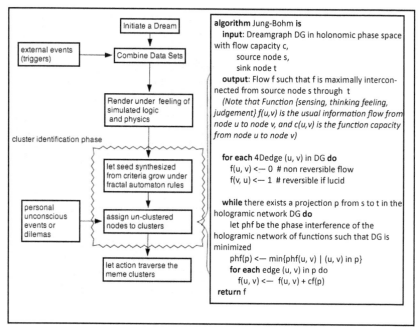

Boxes in flowchart: Initiate a Dream → Combine Data Sets ← external events (triggers); Combine Data Sets → Render under feeling of simulated logic and physics; cluster identification phase: let seed synthesized from criteria grow under fractal automaton rules → assign un-clustered nodes to clusters ← personal unconscious events or dilemas; → let action traverse the meme clusters

Jung-Bohm Algorithm Lucidly Traversing a Dream Amplituhedron

Poetry as pseudocode of the dream dramaturge populating
and developing worlds from the entity relationship
connections.

Invocation to a Lucid Dream

Floating in the dreamland night
I am in the arms of the ancient psyche
              hoping not to encounter the mare.
I float in relaxed eye stare,
a voyager descending levels on stairs.

In a lucid dream   I   float
    remain still in sleep paralysis to trick the brain
       so I can soar

and roll and   yaw   trim flight get released from
                    being World Bound()
                              . . . . floating in the neural net
a }fish> in the neural net
   moving in a dream world
   undergoing a cron job
   cron job
   where …*•} is the multiordinal prefix of the time attached
to the concept
   | min hour day month dayoweek | concept >
   | m h d mon dow | command >

                    … * •} join >
   <• disjoin {• *…
                              ...* •} roll •>
      float free
      float into dreams
      brain coral, folds density, where
      <...>
   that which is objective outside, darts
   into subjective inside (and vice-versa)
      into memory
   where it is associated with images and feeling;
   where it is joined into   into survival themes;
   into archetypes like old bicameral deities
                          into dreams
   subliminal opera choral of the brain
   the trick of astral travel is to remain still and remain awake,
and watching on the internal movie screen
   in the frontal area of the third eye projector
   so that the brain is fooled into thinking the body is asleep
   and will drift into REM —(though the brain will test the
body with roll over and itch commands
   don't fail the test)
                    ...* •} roll •>
   <• disjoin {• *…
   The psyche is a neural net. At night during sleep
   when the peripheral senses are not in use

it does the cron job of restoring the physical and
emotional and spiritual wear on itself.

It runs the transducers backwards, pinging
the line and looking at the echo
in a phase space of stored memories.

Now we play and swim in the simulations
of situations and dilemmas of the virtual reality it creates.
But in the day light it keeps the domain of the night from us
unless we work at it with journal and interpretation.

dreaming is a cron job run at night
when the eyes of day used to looking in the sky
become the eyes of dream land looking into the psyche
and if we can open the eyes of day and look into the dream
we can touch the great vast megastructure
with our being and encounter our body of the earth

into the neural net which is all about relationship
I accidentally stepped into it
now I am walking barefoot in the head
drifting, soaring in this environment of strange attractors.
… * •} join > the heroes
the archetypes are strange attractors nodes of organization
they compel and expel
they imply and comply
in a lucid dream
I propel the ground beneath my feet… * •}.

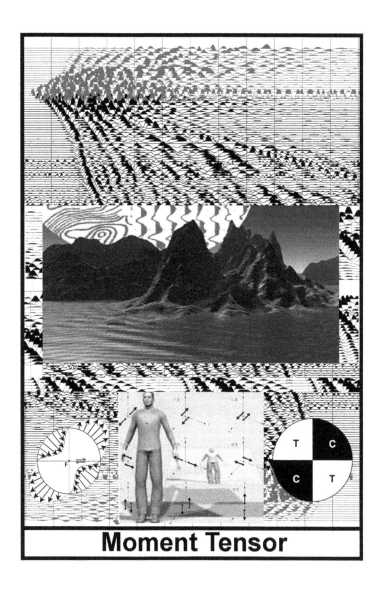

Moment Tensor

The Moment Tensor

Walker was making the long trip along the east bay freeway to Milpitas, headed to work with new clients in the south bay. The contract job was at Seismomatrix a company that makes geology instruments. He had moved back to Berkeley and was sharing a house in the western edge with a Deadhead scientist who worked at Lawrence Labs up on the hill overlooking the town. He found this share in the East Bay Times. They were strangers, but the new roomie was a nice sensitive hippie vegetarian who made the best beans ever. And the new roomie had a cool girlfriend who loved him. Walker was on his own now. And seeing another male therapist in San Francisco.

Walker found the geologists at Seismomatrix company to be interesting people. They are like woodsman X scientists. They travel to wild places, tramp around in the woods, go into mines and oil fields in exotic political climates. They work with waves. Seismic waves and sound wave echoes and ground penetrating radar. They hammer and thump and set off dynamite to make sound probes then do measurements and analysis on their echoes to look inside the earth for hidden treasures, water, minerals and gems. At first Walker was like: If I had another life to live let me live it as a geologist. But after a while the outsiderness of being the contractor, the hired gun, began to wear on him. And he was having to do a lot of work chasing down some vice president or other to get his hours signed so he could get paid. He had to be constantly negotiating a furtherance in the contract with this company, submitting estimates for each next bit of the work. Walker thought about his situation. He had to really hold his tongue with the agent about how the client was ringing his hands about the money on this gig. These fully funded people always trying to get the most for the least. When was it ever not so. He was trying not to feel exploited. He might have to flip the phrase: "my ego is going to give me trouble if I work for any less than that." That seems to work. Everybody understands ego now. I am having a lot of trouble with my ego; if it keeps up, I will not be able to do this work much longer.

Perhaps he was getting a little inflated. To be sure he had become an expert at Supercard and Macromind Director. He would admit he was blinded by the creativity. Here he was, making interactive design training videos. Hardly anyone was doing that. He told himself he should be grateful to have a client that wanted to do this. He used Macromedia Director on the Mac and got them to buy it for the PC. They are supposed to be easily cross-platform compatible.

This is one of the letters Walker was writing back and forth with his agency.

> Joanna Bompart
> Human Resources Agent
> I am not feeling good about how much work it is to administer and manage just the paperwork of this job. Calls not returned, faxes not coming through. The communication is lax.
>
> I'm a sole proprietor. I only take on one job at a time, and I give it full-time round the clock creative energy and thought. I have a studio to maintain. I can't just hang out until the client wants to do something. If Seismomatrix is going into a period of not being able to focus on this project, or a testing cycle or a rethinking cycle, where I'm not needed, I need at least two days notice, or I have to bill you just for retaining me.
>
> I was blind-sided by an attachment requiring a further estimate on the last PO. I spent a day working it up. I'd have stopped production a day earlier so that work could be billable. Now I've two days in on a verbal PO, which who knows what will have attached to it.
>
> They have requested several pages of new script for Voice

Over animations and changes on the ones I've done etc. This
will take more than 40 hours and we'll be going round and
round again trying to get another extension at the end of this
week. So in order to continue, I need to see the next PO,
to make sure there aren't a bunch of caveats impeding the
signing of invoices. There needs to be someone else who can
sign invoices if the VP is out of the country.

We're doing excellent work with this art and science and
I'm enjoying the creative collaboration. I hope that energy can
continue, but the administration of this contract is taking way
too much time. If this project is underfunded lets just stop for
now.

Sincerely, Walker Underwood

Walker disliked how much you had to be always selling
yourself when you are a contractor. And everybody at
Seismomatrix was so old. These old geologists all of them
on PCs. None had a sound card. Nor a CD player. He'd bring
in his beautiful animations with the gorgeous interactive
interface on a CD and they would put the CD into the one
machine that had a player, and then try to play it over the
network on the one machine that had a sound card. Of course
it stuttered and sputtered. He told them: "Seismomatrix
needs to get a 16-bit sound card, and the QuickTime
extension in the Sales machine so the digital movies will
play. And so I don't have to compromise my presentations."

His anger was rising but he told himself there was much
to learn from these geologists. These physicist / scientists /
engineers who tramped around in nature, dug mines and did
most beautiful visualizations of wave probe data on their
computers. Still, Walker had begun to notice his work life
was not him. He asked himself why: What did I want to get,
or expect from work that I was not getting.

He tried to convince himself that working here would
give him some insight about the Gaia question. He wanted to

know about morphogenetic fields. Was earth a living being operating all the life support systems in concert with the sun?

You just have to realize being a contractor always makes you feel like an outsider in the group. There is always this distance. I was an alien in their midst.

Thoughts of this sort dislodged an archetypal figure into Walker's fantasies. He began to write a story to weave together the things he was feeling, and the science he was coming to understand. He got going on a writing project about the Moment Tensor.

He conjured up this idea of a character who thought of herself as Moment Tensor, the real world matrix that the US Geological Service uses to triangulate in on the thousands of earthquakes a year in the world. By measuring the direction and angles of the seismic waves they can pinpoint the origin and depth. There are more than a hundred earthquakes a year measuring over 6.0 on the scale.

A Jungian writer (sc-fi writer, not technical writer) uses his art to amplify ideas and intimations with writing as active imagination. In this story active imagination is applied to amplify a fantasy involving a chthonic earth spirit, he called Sybil, in honor of the Pyrn of the amphictionic theatre of ancient Greece. They were part of various Orphic and other Dionysian and other oracular deity cults who were called upon to make a trip into the underworld to bring back insight.

So during the lacunae in his engagement and partly to feel he was getting something out of working with them, he let his imagination run, giving a voice to this solo theatre piece. It was a crazy rap that you might see on Sproul Hall. Preachers, Swami X, commentators, stand up comics, street people holding forth and raving. He wanted to be working, rather having to deal with people in order to work, but he felt the alienation.

A visit from Sybil

[She holds a hand held camera and points it back at herself]

Ah, I couldn't wait for my chance to talk to you today. Out here in the Fall leaves and the brisk air. There's a real storm coming, a real storm, like something or somebody . . .

[Points hand held camera around the space]

The storm will be out and will whip the trees. And people will be scared. I really like a storm, I like to take walks, sometimes I slip into a psychic fugue episode, I can't help it.

[In camera, she raises eyes up at the sky]

Fugues are Bion alpha states — thoughts without a thinker — percolating through the out-mind looking for a relaxed human in a receptive being state, into which to let itself be know as insight. It is like music. MUSIC.

[Sweeps camera through the green scene]

In such verdure I would like to be a sheep herder living on the land; the desire for more freedom is something we all understand. The problem is the economy, it holds everyone in fear, too much greed and concentration in high places.

Their surges of money movement is a knife that cuts up the world to their satisfaction; it is a sword hanging over our heads from up in the clouds; it is produced and provided for by disparate rent. Their right is the steel that cuts off creative evolution.

[Turns camera at someone who is leering or snidely jeering at her. Camera fumbles.]

If you cannot understand me . . .Also if I can just calm down here for a second and finish what I started to speak about now: my right to perform my dance, to conjure . . . To Wake up!

[Quietly close up]

It forced me to shout at him . . . because of the provocations boring into me from all sides. Here I work in abnormal conditions, a little soldier for art who has to live in army conditions without food, without sleep. Marginalized by probabilities, drugs.

But it's not enough for them. They have prison for the hard core incorrigibles. I can have visions, that are so precious, to be seen with my skill so it won't seem like they just happened yesterday of a moment.

[Campus rent-a-cops go by looking at her]

The authorities cannot come down in one second and interfere with my sport. My sport yah? A mixture of tai chi and ballet. Or moving meditation and interpretative dance.

Leave me alone! A big groundswell is coming. And no one will be hurt. We are in the right moment because of being in the right place.

The fantasy Walker was writing about has to do with a real mathematical tool used in geology: The Moment Tensor. Walker made this a speech / poem in the voice of this yearning psychopomp who may or may not be leading the narrator to the self.

[Lecturing into the camera with her hands, making points]

I read quakes in my body, by analysis and by a kind of psychic's way of picking up a tune like a radio receiver. The moment tensor tunes in. This is not vision. And not hearing and not intuition. I just stand in the woods doing tai chi and soar out of my body, and let the waves challenge my balance and don't allow it to make me fall down.

Though this take on quake understanding could be wrong — I could be letting some kind of inflation get in or be passing on some kind of infectious projection —causing the picture to be in error.

Follow the events. If quake is strong, I usually predict it — about it — 2 days before. I remind, of the last case: the big quake lead to paranoid persecution.

Walker wondered if he could use some of these geology methods to explore the morphogenetic fields that some say form a kind of cocoon around a living object — Kirlian photography which energized the field, shows it.

Sybil is kind of like a living morphogenetic field seismograph. This is ancient knowledge that she picked up studying Tai Chi, Kung Fu and Ballet.

She danced a little song about it. Working up the chant.

[Chorus:]
We are quaternion We are quaternion
Unpack the hologram
unfold the manifold traverse the tree
develop the tesseract and see in 4D

We are quaternion
turning round my core
stepping with grace across the floor.
Spreading out my wings in array
to pick up the music coming my way.
roll pitch and yaw roll pitch and yaw
unfold the manifold traverse the tree
develop the tesseract and see in 4D
We are quaternion
turning in the square of 4
foot reaching out snake creeps down
or wrapping around my core
[Chorus:]

Phy theta and psi
I bend forward and back
this is pitch
from side to side
this is yaw
and turn, around my core
to see where I have been before
and where I am going toward
this is roll
around the axis of the UP
[Chorus:]

We are quaternion
part imaginary and part real
Let me show you what I can feel
I can rotate about an axis
going along any line to a point

turning round my core
stepping with grace across the floor
Just line me up and circulate about!
I am a little gyroscope
ease of movement gives me hope
We are quaternion
turning in the square of 4
foot reaching out snake creeps down
or wrapping around my core
I am a matrix quaternion
a number with 4 parts
rotating with a lot of heart
roll pitch and yaw
phi theta psi
[Chorus:]
We are quaternion We are quaternion
Unpack the hologram
unfold the manifold traverse the tree
develop the tesseract and see in 4D

In the writing one is saying what is in him and that is as real as any dream. Ramify amplify augment edify enlighten. Walker was trying to give voice to something within him that wants to experience a much deeper connection with being in the moment. It personifies the earth as a mother figure.

This is what goes on in the quaternion dance. You have this matrix of rows and columns to consider.
[Gestures the 3 axes up/down, back/front side to side while saying]
The three axes are related as structuring polarities of Being:
Existence formed by the oppositions of self and other,
Life formed by the opposition of future and past, and
Experience formed by the opposition of sensation and perception.

The idea that up leads to a higher power, or that we have a lower self suggests one axis of this psychological space.

We have just seen some consideration along the axis of existence (time) formed by the oppositions of self and other.

The past is behind your, the future is ahead.

We read from left to right by habit. And in reading, sensation gets transmuted into perception.

The axis of signs coming in to your realization.

Forward and back is time, existence
Left right is sensation perception - - > signs.
Up and down is the pole of life toward higher organizations.

Linguistically: higher power, lower self,
face the future, put the past behind you,
you're left, I'm right.
The center cannot hold.
Is there a matrix here? Well there are these planes floating and slicing through this space of psychology.

Sybil thought of it as the Moment Tensor, an idea in geology. She called it the surround window.

[Outlines the square and the smooth plane of a window]
The moment tensor is the Surround Window. Like being able to do a fly-over or a fly-by in a video game.

Or perhaps it is even a kind of clairvoyant remote viewing or psy-ops. It is a kind of MUSIC algorithm. That stands for MUltiple SIgnal Classification —don't ya know.

[Gestures surface wave and pulse wave in the following]
Focal mechanisms are derived from a solution of the moment tensor for the earthquake.

The event sends waveforms hitting on at least two detectors. And knowing the speed of travel you can get a line of distance that goes back and crosses, pinpointing the source.

The waves start at the same time and are recorded at different times. The focal mechanism can be derived from observing the pattern of "first motions", that is, whether the first arriving P waves break up or down.

[Sweeps hand down the length of person, indicates herself]
I developed a moment tensor for Gaia work.
The moment tensor is an array and each element in the array
is the coefficient of transformation
indicting the potential of movement along a fault line
where there is tension in covariant dimensions.
All my faults are due to stress.
And the moment tensor indicates
the way a person will handle
a large assault or stressor.
In other words all the defense mechanisms
are contained in one moment tensor.

Sybil is saying that she gets some kind of advance
warning of earthquakes — it feels like an earthquake. She
is invoking the machinery of the moment tensor, a classical
mathematical tool geologists use to triangulate in on the
source and the depth of an earth quake. She is saying her
body, her person is like a moment tensor, and she describes
how she feels the onset of the future energy.

You have earthquake now and will have a much stronger
one on the 15th of March 11.30 p.m. Greenwich Mean time.
Repeat — you are under siege by cult of profit super terror.
Your old ways of exploiting and corrupting are yesterday's
ways. You may hide but I always listen under windows. With
many visions. I can not stop making sense.
The cult of more and more profit for the owners no matter
the quality of the product or the workers / producers situation
done at the expense of the consumers and the environment
eventually has to stop.
Dwoosh — deprived of property.
We must stop this zombieing of the people shutting them up
from fear and forbidding them to think for themselves.
I must write now to record my ordeal: My ego of conscious
awareness moving, among persona and memories of me being
who I think I am beyond that: to the memories of who I am.

tsunami flotsam

We are all living on the surface of quake flotilla.
Poison more than guns is the number one cause of death.
Statistical sources have confirmed.
The wealthy are republicans for weak government
because government drains the sovereignty of their wealth
via taxation and regulation. Their own financial interests
is all they know. Their hot engine industries pollute and
encourage consumption to maintain interest levels and lead to
global warming. Whereas the cool engines feed and clean up
after itself. We want to be the co-owner survivors making full
employment their goal, not excess wealth for the capitalists.

In every case the captains of industry had anger at a parent
for the pain of emotional abuse and this makes it OK to use
greed as an all consuming script to accumulate more and more
wealth which represents the control that they did not have and
supports the delusion of narcissism as they ride through the
world on their phaeton to the next moated enclave.

And the entertainment industry, and the pharmaceuticals and
the consumer religions defend them producing a great gyre of
junk glomming together to clog and pollute!

Please! Attention to this information, everybody.

Sybil is going to prove something.

As you walk around in a psychological space you need only
open your eyes to see it: The hierarchy of needs leads to the
hierarchy of defense mechanisms. These are always speaking
to you, through you. This Buddha taught.

On the flotillas each is a lily pad floating on the surface of
the water. You can choose to swim and float in the day.

Know that consumerism of television intern one in flotillas
which are ways of persuading you to do what is good for
them, buy their products, watch their shows.

Avoid consensus-time. Seek a wider psychological space,
look for the axes that partition this space. They are in
opposition. Time consensus is so many axes of psychological
space relaxing down, so that one is being in a degenerate time
axis.

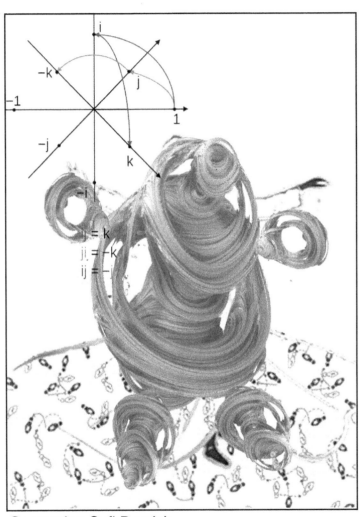

Quaternion Sufi Dervish

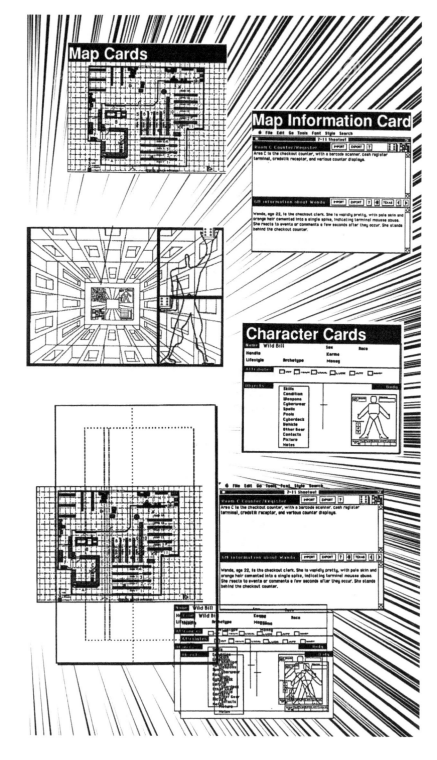

GameWriter and HyperCyberpunX

Walker developed some software he called GameWriter. It was for writers and game masters. He was the tech writer for his own application program.

Title Card

This is the first card you come to when you click on the stack. It has a mathematical interface like cyberspace with the Modular Man holding up his hand in a golden rectangle — an homage to Le Corbusier, an artist and architect who had great hopes for the future of architecture. The title card should indicate the navigational system. Clicking on one of the four icons in the center will take you to other parts of the program. Or you can browse around in the program with the left and right arrows on the keyboard.< - ->

Map Cards

Map cards are obtained by scanning in, or by drawing with HyperCard's own paint tools, the map of a space to explore or one in which characters are going to interact.

You put an X for the player characters and a Y for non playing charters. You can draw on the maps like a football coach planning and working out a strategy. Or you can do before, during and after versions of the positions of the characters in the space. Clicking on a character X brings up a Map Information Card.

Map Information Card

A Map Information Card, arrived at by clicking on (an invisible button over) a map, has a place to enter or read information in either the Room Description field, and/or the Game Master information field. The GM field contains the information which the GM doles out slowly to the game players in the conventional pattern of action in the Role Playing Game.

Character Card

A Character Card, is the representation of the Stat Sheet for the characters in a traditional paper-based RPG.

The screen is basically broken down into Name, Attributes, Body and Objects. The character database is a place to feel yourself taking on the persona of a playing character. You can get more of yourself invested in seeing through the character's eyes. Click on any of the topics in a field and a pop up field presents itself for insights and notes.

The map icon is for going back to the map. Pull down menus to create and manage cards, do searches and use the hypertext index. You can add your own entries to the menu.

Dice

The dice object, which you can pick up with the mouse and drop, so that it will bounce and rotate around the screen to simulate the toss of dice, is used to invoke the random number generator. The dice can be used to pit the statistics of one player's character against the corresponding statistical trates of another. You can use the random number generator to quickly populate the stats of dummy player characters on the fly when encountered in the field of quest.

HyperCyberpunX

GameWriter is an interactive knowledge base, it embodies rules, it performs tests, it queries assumptions and simulates outcomes. It is a kind of expert system. As such, it supports the Game Master as he helps the players understand what to do next on the quest, with the right hints and facts — but not give it away.

This software provides the GM (and the writer) with his own little AI. In the application to a cyberpunk game or story we called it HypercyberpunX because the end cap X (suggesting expert system) looks vaguely tortured and rebellious there at the end of its name.

The way you might use HyperCyberpunX is to bring up the map of the space in which the characters are interacting, bring up the description of the space, and bring up the statistics on the two characters. All these stacks are connected. You can see the states of any character in the data-base, where you can throw a dice and work out its interaction with another character through comparing their statistics. You can follow a character as it moves through space by clicking on a map, and reading information about that area and other writings.

This is a character based approach to fiction instead of an idea or feeling based narrative. You get to know your characters really well, know their motivations and strengths and weakness, and through rules and comparison know how they will interact with other characters in plot situations.

Expert System Writing: Backward & Forward Chaining

An Expert System takes facts in, is driven by a question, presents possible decisions.

The objects and events in the unfolding of the game, the tools and attributes and enhancements that the characters accumulate are the facts; and what to do with them and how to use them in the context of the game is backward chaining, trying possibilities generated by the facts. Backward chaining is like when you are reading or listening to a poem and with each little bit of information you are relating it back to what you have been presented from before. Forward chaining is like in design, you have design goals and you are doing things to reach the envisioned goal. Forward chaining is how the player can pick up leads on the quest to get resolution from the context.

GameWriter and HyperCyberpunX use basically two parts:1. The map which you cover with transparent buttons as you explore the space and the subsequent cards upon which you write about these explorations; and 2. A database of characters, along with a procedure for generating characters.

You can actually play this as a game. We have implemented a random number generator that simulates tossing dice, if you want to let the game dictate the outcome of character gener- ation and interaction.

What is the meaning of Cyberpunk.

Look at the word Cyberpunk. Cyber / punk is an oxymoron. The part cyber refers to cybernetics, the rational pursuit of control in man and machine. Using matrices of mathematical equations it seeks to describe and design the way a machine becomes self-regulating, like a navigation system on a boat, or an economy. It paved the road for modern automation.

Whereas Punk is the opposite, a disparaging term used against young people who aren't participating in the economy and who pursue a self-stupefying, self-mutilating refusal to dignify or trust anything that has brought about the present world, even the human body — all for the promise of an authenticity so indefinable it can't even be known, let alone co-opted. So cyberpunk is a perennial philosophy seeking to understand the forces of one's time that are machinating the world toward control and mitigating against freedom. And through a creative subversion of these forces, insure an atmosphere of authenticity in which you and others can recognize each other and enjoy or at least exist within that freedom. A good attitude to have when interfacing the modern world.

A good game master challenges the player characters with tasks that will challenge their wisdom, and make them grow, gain more points so they can buy more tools, collect more karma, or wisdom or whatever. And that comes from surviving the adventure.

Cyberpunk in the Formula of Science Fiction

In the classical era of sci-fi, the formula (75% literature and 25% science) ruled. Lately the writers seem to be skimping on the science. Science fiction is a type of narrative which has as its major element a projected change in environment, technology, or human biology (or any combination of the three). Conventional reality is disrupted by change or anomaly of some kind.

There are three basic patterns. Status quo, subversive, and the other world. The status quo story moves in a straight-forward way: conventional reality is disrupted by change or anomaly, but by the story's end the conventional order has been restored. The subversive story also starts traditionally into which change is introduced. But the subversive story has society adapting (or crumbling) in response to it. The other world sci-fi story structure shows a world that is highly imagi-native and departs from reality.

Cyberpunk uses the subversive structure.

Individuation

Walker started working on an RPG (Role Playing Game) based somewhat on Jung's psychology of analysis and amplification. He tried to find a good name for the game. He tried *Radix Crux*, *Play Ground*, *Aluvion*, *Aludel* (the crucible in alchemy), *Zazimas* (from Joyce in FW referring to the alchemist Zosimus "if what is sauce for the zassy is souse for the zazimas"). But no. Nor *Entanglement*. The working title was *Jung Game* and it became *Individuation*.

He wasn't being flip toward the great Jung to be thinking of making a game out of the archetypal psychology for Walker was in awe of him. And he also knew how Jung was able to get from his psychology a comfortable mental perspective distance. That allowed space for one to be open to the possibilities of a much more illuminated knowing. That is the goal of this game.

Getting Started

A player in the Individuation Game usually starts by keeping a dream diary. Though creating art can also be a start. There are many ways in to the psyche. Plenty of room on the game board for all the many spiritual practices.

The Game of Individuation is a psychology-themed, RPG that uses *The Red Book* of Jung as a how-to manual. To play is to practice Jungian Individuation. It combines first-person shooter, stealth, visualization and archetype character gestalting elements.

Jung developed a psychology that was a phenomenology in that it was not only descriptive but prescriptive. It gave methods for recording and experiencing and amplifying the communications from the Psyche — a term preferred over

Unconscious in that it encompasses an individual's mind operating inside a much wider complexity, say instinct for now, that communicates in dreams and perhaps synchronicities. The psychology that Jung developed feels classical, perennial in that there are archetypal forms, which goes back to Plato. It has dialectic, which goes back to Hegel and further to Heraclitus. Jung's psychology feels mystical and spiritual, it investigates mythologies and religions from all over the world; it feels artistic for it is based on the image and not the sign and encourages imagination and creativity.

The Game of Individuation may or may not use a "game board" of your own design. You might recall your childhood game "Monopoly." It is a board game about buying real estate and getting rich charging rent. It is simple and elegant, a roll of the dice tells how to move. There is not much role playing, though players do become attached to their tokens, the top hat, the thimble . . . Now if you substitute the Tarot Cards of archetypes in place of Community Chest and the I Ching in place of Chance cards you start to get the idea. And instead of money and real estate let it be about symbols and transcendent numinous mental flow states, then you can see where the Jung Game is going. Think of the little tokens like the race car or the scotty dog as being aggrandized in the Jung Game to be avatars of the psyche space, let them move you instead of you moving them. In Monopoly the (make believe) money is the buy-in because it prosecutes the most important, the most real symbol of our society. In the Jung Game you are bringing your own dreams as the currency to the table in order to dialog with them, to come to know the archetypes behind them and the psychic energy behind the archetypes.

A Little Background

Jung's psychology is from his times. Starting with the Association Test and the uses of trance, automatic writing and the occult, he became a founding father of depth psychology. They were amazing times: the opening of the East, the anthropology of aboriginals, quantum mechanics and uncertainty, world wars and the specter of nuclear annihilation. Jung went beyond Freud's oedipal complex with the general theory of complexes, and developed a complex system which contains chaos and dynamical attractors. It explains the mythologies and religions of all humanity. These instinctual energies get imaged as archetypes in the brain and he called this common ground of mind the Collective Unconscious.

Jung was influenced by William James (who was influenced by CS Peirce of logical semiotics and pragmatism) in what was called Direct Thinking. In his study with Pauli, Jung saw fantasy thinking as an equal partner in the development of scientific thought. As did Peirce in musement. This deft mental sensitivity — direct thinking, puts scientific thinking and mythological thinking on equal footing. Levi-Strauss called mythology the science of the concrete.

Imagine *Individuation* as a game in the sense of Magister Lundi. It can have a board, perhaps a mandala or a matrix or theatre or some other helpful diagrams or objects, even a rosary or string of glass beads. Walker has implemented an RPG like it on the computer screen.

This is a game with plot and characters. The plot is the sequence of preparations and experiments and experiences undergone by the narrator /hero /ego / player.

As the plot unfolds, the player becomes entangled in a depth psychology informed by some or all of: Archetypal Dreams, Awe, Telepathy, Remote Viewing, Transcendent

Function, Symbolic Transformation, Personal Mythology, Synesthesia, Clairvoyance, Numinosity, Quaternionic Network communication among archetypes (Anima, Persona, Shadow, Ego), Synchronicity. Also ancient religions like I Ching, Hinduism, Zen, Taoism, as well as modern relativity, Gnosticism, Alchemy, Astrology and other perennial philosophies to amplify and explore the archetypal deities seen in dreams.

The game explores the psyche of the main character as well as other characters and their relations with each other. It explores the collective unconscious through dreams and their interpretations. It explores relationships at work, at home and at love.

The reward for the quest is a more numinous perspective, in which one can observe the emergence of the subjective in the objective and the objective in the subjective, in a yin-yang chiaroscuro enatiodromia dance, and see that they are not that separate as thought.

Game Walk Through: Anima, PersonaSpace, Shadow

In *The Red Book,* the two main figures were Philomen and Salome. One figure in Walker's own particular set up for the Game of Individuation is an archetype — Sybil, an avatar of the underworld from the Amphictionic theatre; she is rooted in actuality. You ask yourself what does active imagination look like for me? Is it creating characters, and energetic story structures. Is it drawing and diagraming. Is it finding song? Walker writes:

> My Anima is powerful and willful. She seems to have that carefree lack of being accountable that is a prerogative of the feminine. Gets one into things. She is interested in leading me into this space.

The Persona role of technical writer that Walker played is a big part of the game. The Persona is the main guide to the heroes.

Though Jung sees the shadow as the first encounter, the apprentice piece and sees the encounter with Anima as the journeyman piece, Walker encountered the Anima first. Since the anima was the first archetype encountered in the journey and she is the muse getting Walker into various situations, she gives emotional tone to the space of this game which is embedded in the collective unconscious.

Animated Psyche Space of the Individuation Game

In this book there have been many examples of space in dreams: one you are flying over fields; another is in the library; another was the skein, the yantra. Another is that seahorse dream of the fragile evolutionary skull brainpan.

Jung Game is a kind of training for the psychonaut. And the autodidact development of self-edification is propelled by good questions. The psyche has created many spaces to show you. Are they just random or do they have something in common? The settings of the game are in this space. What can we look for that is reoccurring? Space, perspective. And very often it is this anima figure who is bringing you to it. That is the kind of questions the oneironaut game adventurer must pose to himself in order to discover more game and enhance the experience by getting more involved.

Throughout this book in the Mandala chapters there are many images of dream-game space: the Sri Yantra skein of light, the mall, the cabin in the woods, the brain, the compass, the game, the matrix, the flower, the wheel, the myth radio, the substrate of the chip and the interweaving of space and time in the commute around the Bay Area.

In these dreams of preponderant space, the psyche is showing an image of a semantic or game space in which the image like in a matrix, as it also means the substrate of rock in which gems are embedded. Numerous other mandala images from that chapter suggest the mandala is like an eye or a cyclone or the propagation of waves in a pool. It is like the fields of space or the dream catcher with its spider's web too. So these are examples of the 'board' for the game. There is a suitable structure for each player. Your job is find it and think about it and dwell on it.

Making it Real

Avatar characters present themselves in Big Dreams from the Collective Unconscious. It is especially good to explore these with active imagination in the Jung Game. You have to reify them. Let them give out their bounty the way the dream does. Jung in his fantasies had conversations with them. One among others in the *Red Book* he called Philemon. Jung just hung back and let them have their say. He noticed they spoke in different, old testament syntax. Jung writes: "Psychologically, Philemon represented superior insight. He was a mysterious figure to me. At times he seemed to me quite real, as if he were a living personality. I went walking up and down the garden with him, and to me he was what the Indians call a guru."

One day it just settled in for Walker that the Psyche was real. This had a profound impact on him. He wrote a poem to mark the occasion.

The Psyche

The Psyche is moving, like the wind fluttering trees.
The Psyche touches every one of us in every moment.

The Psyche emerges in your dreams at night when you put the ego to sleep.

The Psyche brings you to your senses in the morning.

The Psyche is attached to us through an individual soul.

The Psyche is the river of generosity upon which the Ego floats.

The Psyche jumps ego states of your personality — mostly when you are not aware.

The Psyche is the sky of clouds into which the child goes.

The Psyche gets drawn into games to chase itself around from Damsel to Knight to Dragon.

The Psyche is a Mandala around you whose center is always now.

In it the ego traces a life as it wanders the world beyond the gates of home and state keeping the faith.

The Psyche floats over boundaries to open them as gates.

The Psyche will guide you to your home.

The Psyche gets male and female close through nerve ending density and pheromone trail, and love.

The Psyche is a fine web that can be projected onto many theories.

The Psyche has penetrated into the core of matter through Quantum Mechanics

The Psyche is a hyper-dimensional plant with you as its flower.

The Psyche wants to see in the world, for each one is a potential eye for it to look through.

The Psyche uses the three brains, to filter the world through.

The THINKING is supposed to be a help to us.

Not be in control of us.

The Psyche casts a wide net beyond the local coincidence into the sea of synchronicity.

The Psyche gets the Dream Director to make movies. He has access to everything read or seen

or felt or intuited.

The Psyche lives in artwork and sings in music.

The Psyche knows: you are hanging on a line strung out — way over the chasm, and trying not to look down.

The Psyche is like a field. It can do action at a distance.

Think of gravity or radio or the Tao.

The Psyche was seen by Freud in the early days as the machinations of sexuality and by Jung in the late life through the spirituality.

The Psyche wants to be known. It shows you just enough of the mystery to keep you from losing your way.

The Psyche can be overwhelmed by the shadow, and this keeps you confined in a tiny room.

And the Psyche brings the moon to illuminate the shadows and to lift you with light.

The Psyche has to send a very strong message sometimes when you have lost your way.

The Psyche bathes away pollutants from the environment through the rain of sorrow-filled tears.

The Psyche will bathe you in warm feelings,

May right strokes fall on you like rain.

The Psyche will be with you at the end.

And it will take you out peacefully if you let it.

The Dream Game Has Levels of the Psyche

The simplest icon of psychology we have all seen is the island / iceberg where we see a small part floating on top of the water — this represents the ego (normal consciousness) and the submerged part of the island —representing the personal unconscious. Jung saw beyond to the sea itself — this represents the collective unconscious. He knew mystics across time to describe a 'great oceanic consciousness' (many have felt this on LSD or other psychedelics) and he made that the background of his psychology.

Look for a dream to show you the structure of the psyche. A dream like Jung's dream of the many storied house. It communicated to him about the levels of the psyche: the lower the level, the more archaic was the design. Until in the basement he found the foundation of a stone house with many buried skulls in it. Jung saw his dream as the levels of consciousness, with the basement being the archaic system found in all humans.

In the Mall Dream the shuttered stores are in a way like the skulls. The psyche is real by making it real. Here are three shadow dreams in one night with interpretations from the dream diary.

Psyche Enters The Shadow Land

I am bicycling down the main hall of my old high school, Jefferson High School in San Antonio. It is a big, big institution. Halls lined with lockers, old dark floors polished so that waxy smell hangs in the air, granite stairs. As if the New Deal had redesigned the Alamo. It is afternoon — hot bright outside light is coming in. I encounter this guy Jeffery who I hate. He's not a real person, somehow I know his name is Jeffery. I have encountered him in dreams before. He is skinny rangy dusky. Now he has to have an attendant with him. He is insulting and I stopped and insulted him. He really gets my anger up. I think about murdering him. His attendant has to keep us apart. This attendant is not a hall monitor but a body guard assigned by the government to protect this Jeffery who apparently incites so much hatred he needs to be protected.

I called him a "cunt". His attendant who is a big burly fellow, a man who knows how to throw down if necessary, shakes his head and looks sad about me doing that to his ward. The attendant is tasked with keeping us apart. This Jeffery is a slight fellow, but wiry, bald, reminds of Golem. And he is very evil. And so am I in this dream.

Interpretation

This dream sequence is an encounter with a shadow archetype of my psyche. Sinister, evil, dark, powerful male figure.

I am seeing myself in the dream. The perspective is a detached exterior perspective — shifted off from the ego

I think the main message of this dream is The Psyche journeying into The Shadow Land. Somehow the exterior perspective suggests to me that I am an agent of this Psyche in the world. Persons are agents of Psyche. Psyche realizes that I am ready to be exposed to my Shadow. The Psyche wants me to explore in the land of the Shadow, meaning that part of yourself that you have buried and expelled in order to be well, . . . human. It is hidden for a reason. I am not sure I want to go there.

This is also suggested by the Shadow figure having an agent or advocate to intercede with the world of the ego. Persona?

riding the bicycle — symbolizes the search for balance. Also since it is not a car, it is about being not rich and powerful; since it is not walking suggest you are not able to make it on your own.

back in high school — suggests unresolved issues around learning

Golem like shadow figure — I have seen him before, he is of a dark race. Suggesting we are in a primitive mythical level. Suggests a part of myself that is hidden under the mask of the ego,

incite to violence — an illustrative pun on "insight" ?

dusky — dark, foreign, repressed emotional energies. Shame, rage.

wiry bald — old, but very strong.

cunt — what does it mean to have called the shadow a cunt. Genital, generative, the source/ creative and reproductive energy, sexual feelings. Does a man dream of the shadow more if he has repressed sexual feelings?

I am handling some kind of multi-shot cross-bow for hunting vampires. Like in that movie Van Helsig. I am trying to use something like a "blank" — it doesn't have an arrowhead on it, just a rounded wooden shaft. I am supposed to be hunting some kind of monster.

vampire hunter — vampires are a symbol for something sucking the life out of you.

"blank" cross bow bolt — sense that the Shadow is also an important part of me not to be killed but somehow made peace with.

I'm walking through a town in a black and white movie. The dark night sky is lit by the moon. The shredded clouds move wraithlike, scudding across the chiascouro in fits. The trees and bushes on either side of the road are tall and looming, they lean over, as if to follow my progress in some horrible cartoon. The windows in the buildings are dark like sun glasses hiding people behind them looking at me as I move ahead. I get this sense of Psyche descending into Shadowland. I am sensing some evil entity perhaps like some kind of senseless insect eating-machine. One of them kind of floats along in the edge of darkness.

This was a cinematic moonlit night, suggesting that The Shadow Lands though frightening, might be traversable, for they must be gone through.

moon — fertility, new growth. If the Sun symbolizes the Self, the moon symbolizes the dark inception of the possibility of new growth.

I think I lost my wallet. I'm crawling over a guy in a van. Asking him if he has it then I found it in my pocket. I was going over to Lunch. I am trying to cross a freeway on foot. There is all kinds of construction all around every-where. Some smarmy looking guy comes up. He is trying to bum cigarettes off people. He keeps repeating like a chant: Namaste America. Namaste America. And he gets some woman to give him something. She is making some kind of documentary video.

lost wallet — lost identity

bumming cigarettes — low life, shadow figure again

Namaste America — a greeting of Hindu people, perhaps a people whose religion gives a better understanding of the dual nature of god, and of their shadow.

This dream series definitely suggests something about coming to a better understanding of who I used to be. I have been a homeless, angry, bum at times in my life. I hope I have left him behind. I am looking forward to encountering the new me.

My question is, do you feel like you are an agent of a much larger Psyche? True believers talk about God that way, so I am suspicious of it.

Shadows are the primitive aggressive parts of the human personality that are repressed in order to be in society. A whole country can come under the sway of the Shadow. Germany and Hitler. They circulate back around and come to represent the greatest evil in the world even though beneath it all is one's own shadow. In dreams, they usually appear exactly like the dreamer except with darker tones of skin, younger, usually naked, wild or aggressive. Walker avoided the shadow encounter for the longest time, and his psyche gave him a pretty easy time of it. His psyche presented the anima first. For him the shadow was the second archetype encountered in the unconscious. Though perhaps his Catholic upbringing gave him a taste of the deamon with the concept of Original Sin, not to mention the eternal torment of Hell. What a crock of lies to fob off on a child. Imagine people bying indulgences. Pascual wagered it might be true.

Game Moves on a Circuit of Psychic Energy

To move your token avatar around in the space of the game you merely need to ask the question in which direction should I go to get psychic energy.

It is one thing to take night minutes of the dream; more to do a symbolic interpretation of it. One hopes this leads to having a revelation of the energy that can accompany the encounter with the shadow or other archetypes.

For Walker the fact that he made a good living doing technical writing, but found it nearly impossible to share his fictional or lyrical writing with people, not to mention the eternal undermining of his confidence from his internal critic made his superego a shadow phenomenon that he had to come to deal with and wrest energy from. Though it did not occur to him that shadow processes might be involved because he understood this intellectually but when it came to the encounter he was passive and quick to back away. The player of the individuation game has to ask the question: What direction should I move in. Easy to say but hard to do.

Perhaps Walker's disdain for commercialism was a reaction to and a projection defense against this Shadow super-ego critic voice. His suspicion of leaders and his introverted avoidance of groups too may be part of that. Jung points out this apotropaic defense of the introvert, where he discounts and denies the importance of the external, can get really over done.

Archetypes get symbolized in mythology because of their psychic energy. Always one's ego is working on repairing and representing his persona in the world. This is an archetype that ought to be taken with a dram of humor. To the Jungians personae are the 'masks' people wear when interacting with others. This mask reflects their class, occupation, stature, or whatever the personality wants to represent to others. But on the other side of the Persona mask is dark energy as though in the obsidian black backing of a mirror. These hidden facets of the personality in the form of various gods, heroes, and other inspiring mythological entities are the archetypes driving the game. They are ideals that the functions (thinking, feeling sensing, intuiting) from whence our perception arises. We hold these atunements up for ourselves. Where do we get these ideals? Certainly in the life script where they are memes passed along from generation to generation of what people hold most dear and worth restoring. This takes us into the theory of archetypes. What can we use from the theory of archetypes, and how do they relate to symbols and personae (character).

Certainly Walker had been blessed with observing the unfolding of symbols in his dreams and the presence of archetypes. The characters of myths (and faery tales), are often archetypes. When an archetype rises to the status of myth it means it is an image that has been imprinted in the collective unconscious and thus becomes the basis for myths, fairy tales and legends. These possessions of dreams are made of psychic energy. They come to contain psychic energy. Uh, oh. There it is. The thing we are looking for and are afraid of being caught up in. Psychic energy.

The Psyche has many gifts to give out. Archetypes propagate psychic energy. The Jung Game / Individuation is a quest go be able to shimmer or gestalt both in and out: to step back and look at the psychic energy from a liberated perspective AND be more a part of it. Jung sees individuation as the expression of a person's wholeness through the integration of the conscious and the collective unconscious. Our myths are the common core looking across races and peoples; they are the reverberating connotations within as the mythologies influence the appearance of how we want to represent ourselves without. Myths conduct the underlying archetype of which we find ourselves to be a symbol.

As in all, RPGs there are a plethora of personality traits one can acquire. These are the Stats. The adventure is to find what you can do to enhance your stats. For example, Walker took a class in storytelling to make him become more outgoing. The psyche heals by exploring the opposite.

Game Space Representations (Boards)

The Individuation Game has many representations: catastrophe bifurcations, strange attractors, self-similar

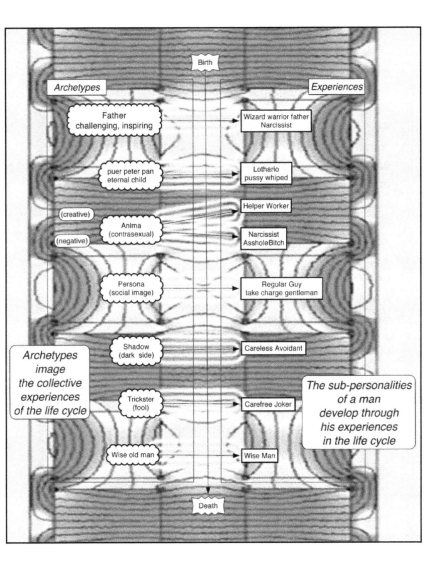

Birth

Archetypes

Experiences

Father
challenging, inspiring

Wizard warrior father
Narcissist

puer peter pan
eternal child

Lothario
pussy whiped

Helper Worker

(creative)

Anima
(contrasexual)

(negative)

Narcissist
AssholeBitch

Persona
(social image)

Regular Guy
take charge gentleman

Shadow
(dark side)

Careless Avoidant

*Archetypes
image
the collective
experiences
of the life cycle*

Trickster
(fool)

Carefree Joker

*The sub-personalities
of a man
develop through
his experiences
in the life cycle*

Wise old man

Wise Man

Death

377

fractal trajectiles and projectiles, Riemann geometries of relativity spacetime, Peirce existential graphs, Poincare phase space, hook operators, Young tableaux, self-reproducing automata, stochastic processes. But let us look to the ancient *mandala* for its established idealism and universal archetypal resonance. The emanations of mandala reify it as an ideal game board for this Game of Individuation. You might prefer to think of it as a computer game. Or other works of art of your own creating for the amplification of communications from psyche or flows encountered in which the unconscious was able to represent. Or maybe it is a game of meditation and or lucid dreaming.

Walker created his own framework in his writing. He made mandalas for himself on the computer. Interface design.

In the game of individuation the player is compelled by the psyche to make a mandala for himself the way those monks do in Tibet. (Rather than suffering their emergence in time of crisis.) You may prefer to remain mental and feel you can't draw with your hands; there are all kinds of sutras to help construct mandalas in the mind. And there are a lot of designs. The traditional Himayana or Tantric mandalas of Tibet are filled with figures of gods and demons, saints and totem animals and every monk was to have his own personal mandala, reflecting his psyche. Each part of the Mandala was supposed to reflect a particular part of the microcosm (the person) like anger, reason, sensation, knowledge etc. . .

What a spiritual practice is Buddhism and Tantra and Jungian psychology. They are tapped in to the collective unconscious and experiment with its phenomenology. That is what we are trying to find our way to here in this "game". Perhaps learning to be a better field operative or an agent in your lifework field is a better name for it.

The Role Playing Game is a great simulation of living out a myth. In the game you can experience your own real myth by seeing that you are living out a myth or script by actively creating one. In the game simulation you enter that world and feel your focus shift between frames. For example if the analysand sees himself as intelligent, he will create this genius character; or if he sees himself as downtrodden or depressed he will create this "left out in the woods" street-person character.

The players create characters, that they become invested in. They are creating their own myth in which one comes to see himself as living partially in another symbolic character. Walker created the characters like Tesla, Milrepa, Sybil, Baywolf in which he projects himself out of his own myth or aspects of his own myth.

Walker wrote this answer to the question asked by the existentialist Sartre: Why does one write?

> Why does one write? The answer is to understand your own myth as the symbol of your self. In writing a novel the writer creates a symbol of the whole Self, that he is trying to come to know. The work becomes an exploration of a symbol. In the myth of Walker Underwood I have created my own myth on several levels.
>
> What does living with and in this great big book of one's own story — perhaps rewritten to show himself if not in a better light at least having taken the time of contemplation to bring the fast moving events under a more thoughtful scrutiny. I have tried to bring about a reconciliation of the compro-mises that formed my personality. Myth is a mediation of opposites: I created a hippie image of Walker and a yuppie image. Hippie / yuppie is a good depiction of what happened to the 60s generation in the computer revolution of the 80s. The beatnik writer of a psychological lyrical novel creates his

own indigenous healing system out of the elements of his own life available to him, to find out what's wrong and fix it. They came out of an extended peter pan youth phase and got into the computer revolution.

I created the symbol of Walker as a technical writer and interface designer who becomes a master of these arts to stand in opposition to the slacker bohemian self-image of himself that was both a cause and effect of his lack of participation. He came to understand the apotropaic behavior toward the gregarious world of work as a defense mechanism created and maintained in the introverted / intuitive structure of his own psyche.

Both the bohemian artist and the self-employed contract worker elements of the Walker image existed within me: the depression had emphasized one aspect, the engagement in work emphasizes the other. As Walker gradually brings his slacker hippie under control, I am able to understand both aspects of my nature to reorganize my work world constructs. The Walker symbol signifies the opposing elements of my personality and I felt like a sell out. Working out the compromises of hippie Walker to yuppie Walker allowed, through the process of coming to understand symbols and living out my own creation, a transformation to occur from my original self-image to a more mature me. This was a step back and out of the frame of personal psychology to a deeper frame of myth or life script controlling the psychology. This higher perspective allows more movement and freedom because it sees the processes at work and is not always driven around by them.

Because of my intense writerly involvement with the Walker symbol, I was also living out a myth on another level — within the symbolic possibilities of the lyrical novel as a way to poetic illumination and even numinous happenings. With no understanding, support or encouragement from the people around me, I emotionally explored the implications of the Walker symbol anyway, and gradually came to realize that Walker was an extension of myself, a symbol of the Self unfolding in me, and a symbol of both my condition and cure.

The heavy emotional involvement with the symbol meant that such an exploration carried risks, but ultimately, rewards as well — the opportunity to reorder elements within my psyche. Through Walker, I have begun to balance the conflicting cultural frameworks that place demands upon me — the image of hippie inherited from rebellion in early life and the image which informs the day to day life of me as I look forward to career and marriage.

Mandala — Eye

The camera is the eye of a mandala drifting over boundaries between realms of time. Flying over your life looking in on you at grade school, or going to work, or going out with a girlfriend. Looking into your life like it was all there in the landscape going by under you. At times when you made important decisions about your future, this searching eye looks into the dream, into memories — for that is what we do remember and relive.

The mandala forms a circle around the dot, it will be the boundary of your distinction, marking the inside and the outside. Making the first distinction in the O. There will be many of these circles. The mandala will find you.

The mandala of you starts with a little dot in the center of your existence, not any bigger than the period at the end of this sentence.

My Years of Apprenticeship at Love

Sex is the Antigravity of Metamorphosis

Set in Montreal, Vermont, and Austin, 1975-76. The story follows Walker Underwood as he tries to settle down with a young mom in the city of his origin. Experience falling in love, the responsibilities of being a father figure, the encounter with the sign system of Other — that is part of love's apprenticeship.

ISBN 0-965584291   2008
ISBN 978-0965584296 $25

The Indigenous Tribesmen of Neverland

Set in Austin 1979, follows Walker Underwood in his relationship with high school girl Laura. Others are Wild Bill, and teen Weesa, Laura's friends. The April-July romance has punks and hippies influencing each other. The insight that group theory brought through physics and anthropology into zeitgeist settles in.

ISBN 0-965584275   2010
ISBN 9780965584272 $25

Dolores Park

Set in Berkeley, San Francisco and Mount Shasta, 1981-82. Follows Walker as he pursues romance in a tantric Buddhist sex commune. There the exegesis of living in sangha employ love and envy to assault and grind on the ego as romantic precepts fall. Blueprint for running a new age commune.

ISBN 0-965584232   2001
ISBN 978-096558423 $25

a sextet of novels by Michael Lyons

Seeing through the Spell of Transference   4

Set in Berkeley, Silicon Valley 1983-1990 follows Walker Underwood, his pasionate love affair with girlfriend Ms. C and psycho-analysis with therapist Ms. Z. Follows the expansion of computerization of mind and work. A Jungian talking spell as cure for the malais of soul.

ISBN 0-965584240   2017
ISBN 978-0965584241 $25

A Blue Moon in August   5

Set in Berkeley and San Francisco and Mexico, 1990-91. Story follows Walker as he decides to marry. And gets to know his new wife in Lamaze class. Walker becomes a new father under the spell of motherhood. The inventions explore cyberpunk writing and the possibilities of parental romance.

ISBN 0-965584259   2005
ISBN 978-0965584258 $25

Thoughts on Vacation   6

Set in San Francisco, and the California Sierras, 1991-2000 the story follows Walker enjoying the delights of fatherhood. It is a comedy of manners about raising children and how we are raised by them. One chapter Mr. I, a streamlined information space, will raise your IQ if you let it. Explores mindset of a Silicon Valley information worker.

ISBN 0-965584267   2005
ISBN 978-0965584265 $25

"Little House on the Prairie" Trilogy

Cultivating the Texas Twister Hybrid

Set in Austin, 1978 follows Walker Underwood and Greg and their 3 dogs in great detail about setting up and operating a pot farm. Like a trip back into the 1800s. Bust at the end.

ISBN 0-965584208   1998
ISBN 978-0-9655842-0-3 $20

The Secret of the Cicada's Song

An expanded chapter of the first book in the series *Cultivating the Texas Twister Hybrid*. This book is a peyote trip in prose and poetry and a strange moving symbolic language based on the distinction operator of G. Spencer Brown. First to use C syntax poems

ISBN 0-965584216   1998
ISBN 978-0-9655842-1-0 $20

Knight of a 100 eyes

Agreatly expanded chapter of the first book in the series, *Cultivating the Texas Twister Hybrid*. This book is the three time frames of a Tai Chi long form. The parallel times of the 30 minute set, the growth of begining to journeyman player, and the life time of witness to the great Tao, as Ecology, as Gravity, as Form of Fractals. It is a modern commentary on the I Ching.

ISBN 0-965584224   2002
ISBN 978-0-9655842-2-7 $25

Ebook Availability

Ebooks are available on Amazon, iTunes and other places.

Albums of recorded poems, radio plays, readings are avilable at http://www. bandcamp/hitmotel. Also available on Youtube.

youtube.com/hitmotel.
youtube.com/djsayian

vimeo.com/djsayian
soundcloud.com/djsayian

An unknown and transparent figure of international letters, Michael Lyons once lived and loved in Berkeley. He has authored a dozen literary books. This novel is the 4th volume of the "My Years of Apprenticeship at Love" sextet. It is the last of that series.

HiT MoteL Press

These books can be ordered from any book seller or on-line.
They are deeply discounted on Amazon, and Barnes& Nobles.
Ebooks available on Amazon and iTunes

Boho Novels, Memoirs
The "Little House on the Prairie" Trilogy:
Cultivating the Texas Twister Hybrid, a portrait of the artist as
a weed gardener (1998) ISBN 0-9655842-0-8 $20.00
The Secret of the Cicadas' Song, a peyote trip in poetry and
prose (1998) ISBN 0-9655842-1-6 $20.00
Knight of a 1000 eyes, about Tai Chi, movement, Laban, and
the I Ching (2002) ISBN 0-9655842-2-4 $25.00
others:
The Punctual Actual Weekly, about the life and times of a
small mimeograph literary rag centered around artists living
in a Berkeley warehouse and the Amphictionic Theatre (2007)
ISBN 0-9655842-8-3
The Church of the Coincidental Metaphor, youthful adventures
in Mexican radio

Novels: The "My Years of Apprenticeship at Love" Sextet:
Sex is the Antigravity of Metamorphosis, tales of romance and
hitchhiking in North America. (2008) ISBN 0-9655842-9-1
$25.00
The Indigenous Tribesmen of Neverland Bohemian life in
Austin slacker enclaves. (2010) ISBN 0-9655842-7-5 $25.00
Dolores Park, Texan joins a California Tantric Buddhist com-
mune (2001) ISBN 0-9655842-3-2 480 pages. $25.00
Seeing throught the Spell of Transference A tech writer's jour-
nal of psychotherapy. (2017) ISBN 0-9655842-4-0
A Blue Moon in August, about marriage and children late in
life. (2005) ISBN 0-9655842-5-9
Thoughts on Vacation, a father is raised by his child and is
enlightened by mortality. (2005) ISBN 0-9655842-6-7

Check into HiT MoteL on youtube.com/hitmotel for readings,
poetry and song.

Poetry

I learn to walk again
Slow baby steps after a serious
skateboard accident.
Sequel to How I spent my
Christmas Break

Happy Trails to the Infinite
Fourteen Sonnets
The influence of form in every-
day life.

Diamond Head
Return to the
place of the
Honeymoon on a
family vacation.
Learn surfing,
and the secretes
of the sea.
Do to things
what light does
to them.

Chap books and collection available **FREE**
in epub format on iTunes and Amazon.

Selected Poems

This is a selection of some 80 poems going back to the 70s up to the 2000s. The poems are selected from all the books of Michael Lyons, including some rare chapbooks.

The poetry is usually the personal observations of the self in the world with others. There are some sonnets.

The poems are loose and spontaneous and usually humorous.

The Punctual Actual Weekly

was a literary magazine in Berkeley of 1976. This memoir of the artists and writers in the community it served presents reprints and reviews. In addition to the solo theatre presentations, the magazine format supports a graphical novel treatment of a poet's notebook, and an art show catalog of works. Besides the Abstract Expressionism, Physical Theatre, and (humorously) applying the insights of several isms: structuralism, imagism, surrealism, actualism, personalism, set in the city of Berkeley (a philosopher known for idealism) it attempts what WCW did in Paterson.

ISBN 0-965584283 360pgs 2007
ISBN 978-0-9655842-8-9 $30

Seeing Through the Spell of Transference
a novel by Michael Lyons

The novel follows the continuing story of Walker Underwood as he becomes a technical writer and interface designer during the computer revolution and gets caught up in a torrid psycho/sexual/quantum adventure, becoming a nerd punk and social critic of the 80s-90s cyber mind.

His relationship with Cora Rosenov is a struggle for love and liberation in the time of AIDS. And as the title suggests, in the therapy sessions with Anna Zane.

The book is a portrait of the artist as a young Jungian, commuting the freeways of Silicon Valley. We see a narrative structure creating space for a torrent of discourse seething up a barely coherent surface beneath which you might just glipse the wokings of the modern soul wandering in cubical land.

He becomes the mythic everyman of our generation applying the tropes of the old literacy to the new machines: the electron beam microlythographer, the anesthesia analyzer, a seismometer, UNIX, CASE modeling, GUI, . . . as he undergoes the shift into procedural writing. Each machine suggests a symbolic dimension which helps him to discover things like the chakras and the dream dramaturge, and phantopoeia, the computer game, the mandala, the moment tensor and he enters these worlds to explore his own. The cross fertilization of Jung, Pauli, Levi-Strauss, Mandelbrot, Heisenberg, Bohm gets fermented into these two most precious ways of feeling and knowing you may come to see in your Self:

1) Through the metaphors of network, database, language, matrix quantum mechanics we can see how the mind as computer allows us to feel how the neural net brain is isomorphic to the ecological net of nature; and

2) myth is personal as well as cultural, it is the matrix behind language perceiving the network of forces presented as symbols by the psyche. And this is numinous.

Seeing Through the Spell of Transference is the 10th novel by Lyons. It is Volume 4 of the "My Years of Apprenticeship at Love" sextet. It is the 6th book of the sextet to be published.